desserts

desserts

250 recipes for every occasion

APPLE

A McRae Books Srl book

First published in the UK in 2008 by
Apple Press
7 Greenland Street
London NW1 0ND
United Kingdom
www.apple-press.com

ISBN 978-1-84543-268 3

This book was conceived, edited and designed by McRae Books Srl
Via del Salviatino, 1 – 50014 Fiesole, Italy
info@mcraebooks.com
www.mcraebooks.com

Publishers: Anne McRae, Marco Nardi
Project Director: Anne McRae
Art Director: Marco Nardi
Photography: Brent Parker Jones
Photographic Art Direction: Neil Hargreaves
Text: Rachel Lane, Carla Bardi, Ting Morris
Food Styling: Lee Blaylock, Neil Hargreaves
Layouts: Aurora Granta
Prepress: Filippo Delle Monache

Front cover photography copyright © Alan Benson

NOTE TO OUR READERS
Eating eggs or egg whites that are not completely cooked poses the possibility of salmonella food poisoning. The risk is greater for pregnant women, the elderly, the very young, and persons with impaired immune systems. If you are concerned about salmonella, you can use reconstituted powdered egg whites or pasteurised eggs.

Printed in China

CONTENTS

INTRODUCTION

Have you ever wished you could wave a magic wand at the end of a meal and produce the perfect apple pie, a luscious tray of chocolate cherry cupcakes, or a melt-in-your-mouth meringue cake? With *Desserts* in hand, you are well on your way to simple, elegant cooking. This book contains more than 200 recipes for every kind of dessert—from exquisite layer cakes and fabulous filled roulades to chewy oat cookies and crisp fritters you can dip in chocolate sauce.

Developed by an international team of food writers, the recipes are a mixture of time-tested classics and modern desserts, developed for contemporary budgets, taste buds, and schedules. Here you will find desserts galore to serve on any occasion. At your next dinner party impress your friends with the Black Forest Cake on page 74 or try the Chocolate Pots de Crème on page 179. For more informal gatherings, try the sticky Baklava on page 117 or the Apple Pie on page 91. On busy weekday nights you'll even find it easy to surprise your family with the Fruity Tiramisù

◁ **Hazelnut Cream Puffs with Chocolate Sauce (see page 115)**

on page 183 or the Pineapple Surprise on page 205. Throughout, you'll be inspired by the stunning photographs that offer serving and garnishing ideas.

Home cooks will particularly appreciate the feature panels that give instructions for special techniques. Want to know why your pie dough falls apart? How best to work with yeast successfully? The authors answer these and many other common cooking questions, letting you in on their personal tips and tricks to ensure every dish turns out perfectly every time.

A luscious dessert is a great way to end a meal and we believe that this collection of recipes will provide years of satisfaction and many happy endings!

 ## RECIPES FOR PEOPLE WITH SPECIAL HEALTH NEEDS

For those people who often have to skip dessert because of dietary restrictions, there is a selection of delicious recipes for them as well. Included are recipes for those with an allergy to dairy or eggs, for people who are dealing with gluten intolerance, and for anyone who is required to follow a low-fat diet. You can locate these recipes by looking for the little green icon that we've added to make finding them easy. To identify which specific dietary need applies, read the recipe's introduction. You may discover, too, that many of the fruit desserts also work for people with special health issues.

When you prepare food for anyone with food allergies and intolerances, be aware that traces of gluten, egg, and dairy can be found where you least expect them (for example, in chocolate and vanilla extract), so read labels carefully. In many countries, food manufacturers are required by law to list every ingredient used in their products. But to be perfectly sure, look online or inquire at health food stores for the names of reliable brands of gluten-, egg-, or dairy-free products.

Baklava (see page 117) ▷

COOKIES

Cookies are a great way to finish a family lunch or dinner. They can be prepared ahead of time and stored in airtight containers. We have included some classic recipes here, such as the Gingersnaps (see page 14) and the Oatmeal Raisin Cookies (see page 24).

◁ **Afghan Cookies (see page 14)**

Gingersnaps

These crisp cookies are better known outside of North America as ginger nuts. Serve them with coffee at the end of a meal; they are delicious dunked!

Makes: about 48 cookies · Prep: 20 min. · Cooking: 15–20 min. · Level 1

2	cups (300 g) all-purpose (plain) flour
2	teaspoons baking soda (bicarbonate of soda)
1	teaspoon ground cinnamon
1/4	teaspoon salt
1/8	teaspoon ground cloves
3/4	cup (200 g) unsalted butter, softened
1 1/4	cups (250 g) firmly packed light brown sugar
1/4	cup (60 ml) molasses
2	tablespoons finely grated peeled fresh ginger
1	large egg
	Granulated sugar, to sprinkle

1. Mix the flour, baking soda, cinnamon, salt, and cloves in a large bowl.

2. Beat the butter, brown sugar, molasses, and ginger in a large bowl with an electric mixer on medium speed until creamy. Add the egg and beat until combined. With the mixer on low speed, beat in the dry ingredients until just combined. Cover the bowl with plastic wrap (cling film) and refrigerate for 2 hours.

3. Preheat the oven to 350°F (180°C/gas 4). Line two cookie sheets with parchment paper.

4. Shape tablespoons of the dough into balls about the size of walnuts. Place on the prepared cookie sheets, spacing 2 inches (5 cm) apart.

5. Bake for 15–20 minutes, rotating the sheets halfway through for even baking, until golden brown. Let cool on the cookie sheets for 5 minutes. Transfer to racks and let cool completely.

🌿 Afghan Cookies

Despite their name, these cookies are actually a New Zealand classic. They have no obvious connection with Afghanistan so no one knows where their name comes from. These cookies are egg-free.

Makes: about 25 cookies · Prep: 15 min. · Cooking: 20 min. · Level 1

COOKIES

3/4	cup (180 g) salted butter, softened
1/2	cup (100 g) sugar
1 1/3	cups (175 g) all-purpose (plain) flour
1/4	cup (30 g) unsweetened cocoa powder
2	cups cornflakes
1/3	cup (40 g) shredded (desiccated) coconut
1/4	cup (30 g) walnuts, coarsely chopped

CHOCOLATE FROSTING

1	cup (150 g) confectioners' (icing) sugar
2	tablespoons unsweetened cocoa powder
1/2	teaspoon vanilla extract (essence)
2	tablespoons boiling water

1. Preheat the oven to 350°F (180°C/gas 4). Line two large cookie sheets with parchment paper.

2. Beat the butter and sugar using an electric mixer on medium-high speed until pale and creamy. With mixer on low speed, gradually add the flour and cocoa, beating until combined. Stir in the cornflakes and coconut by hand using a wooden or large kitchen spoon. Spoon 25 mounds of the mixture onto the prepared cookie sheets, spacing 1 inch (2.5 cm) apart.

3. Bake for 15 minutes, rotating the sheets halfway through for even baking, or until set. Let cool on the baking sheet for a few minutes. Transfer to a rack and let cool completely.

4. To prepare the frosting, combine the confectioners' sugar and cocoa in a small bowl. Add the vanilla and gradually pour in enough water to obtain a spreadable frosting. Frost the tops of the cooled cookies and top with chopped walnuts.

Gingersnaps ▷

Chocolate Chip Cookies with Candied Ginger

Makes: about 20 cookies · Prep: 15 min. · Cooking: 12–15 min. · Level 1

1²/₃	cups (250 g) all-purpose (plain) flour
1	teaspoon baking powder
⅛	teaspoon salt
1	cup (250 g) unsalted butter, softened
½	cup (100 g) firmly packed dark brown sugar
2	tablespoons light corn (golden) syrup
1	teaspoon vanilla extract (essence)
½	cup (90 g) dark chocolate chips
⅓	cup (60 g) candied ginger, chopped

1. Preheat the oven to 350°F (180°C/gas 4). Butter two large cookie sheets and line with parchment paper.

2. Mix the flour, baking powder, and salt in a medium bowl.

3. Beat the butter and brown sugar in a large bowl with an electric mixer on high speed until creamy. Beat in the corn syrup and vanilla. Stir in the mixed dry ingredients, chocolate chips, and ginger by hand until you have a soft dough. Roll the dough into walnut-sized pieces and place them on the prepared baking sheets, spacing 2 inches (5 cm) apart

4. Bake for 12–15 minutes, rotating the sheets halfway through for even baking, until lightly golden. Let cool on the cookie sheets for 5 minutes. Transfer to wire racks to cool completely.

.

Triple Chocolate Chip Cookies

These rich chocolate cookies make a wonderful treat for dessert as well as for mid-morning and mid-afternoon snacks.

Makes: about 20 cookies · Prep: 15 min. · Cooking: 12–15 min. · Level: 1

2	cups (300 g) all-purpose (plain) flour
1	teaspoon baking powder
¼	teaspoon salt
1	cup (250 g) unsalted butter, softened
¾	cup (150 g) firmly packed light brown sugar
2	tablespoons milk
1	teaspoon vanilla extract (essence)
⅓	cup (60 g) bittersweet or dark chocolate chips
⅓	cup (60 g) milk chocolate chips
⅓	cup (60 g) white chocolate chips
20	walnut halves

1. Preheat the oven to 350°F (180°C/gas 4). Butter two large cookie sheets and line with parchment paper.

2. Mix the flour, baking powder, and salt in a medium bowl.

3. Beat the butter and brown sugar in a large bowl with an electric mixer on high speed until creamy. Beat in the milk and vanilla. Stir in the mixed dry ingredients and chocolate chips by hand until you have a soft dough. Roll the dough into walnut-sized pieces and place them on the prepared baking sheets, spacing 1 inch (2.5 cm) apart. Flatten slightly and top each cookie with a walnut half.

4. Bake for 12–15 minutes, rotating the sheets halfway through for even baking, until lightly golden. Let cool on the cookie sheets for 5 minutes. Transfer to wire racks to cool completely.

Chocolate Chip Cookies with Candied Ginger ▷

White Chocolate Chunk Cookies

Be sure to use a very good quality brand of white chocolate in this recipe. The flavor will be better and the chunks of white chocolate will stay firm and attractive.

Makes: about 24 cookies • Prep: 15 min. • Cooking: 15–20 min. • Level: 1

2	cups (300 g) all-purpose (plain) flour
½	teaspoon baking soda (bicarbonate of soda)
½	teaspoon salt
1	cup (250 g) unsalted butter, softened
1¼	cups (250 g) firmly packed light brown sugar
1	large egg
2	teaspoons vanilla extract (essence)
8	ounces (250 g) best-quality white chocolate, chopped into chunks

1. Preheat the oven to 350°F (180°C/gas 4). Line two cookie sheets with parchment paper.

2. Mix the flour, baking soda, and salt in a medium bowl.

3. Beat the butter and brown sugar in a large bowl with an electric mixer on medium speed until creamy. Beat in the egg and vanilla. With mixer on low speed, beat in the mixed dry ingredients, followed by the chocolate. Shape tablespoons of the dough into balls the size of walnuts. Place on the prepared baking sheets, spacing 1 inch (2.5 cm) apart.

4. Bake for 15–20 minutes, rotating the sheets halfway through for even baking, until golden brown. Let cool on the cookie sheets for 5 minutes. Transfer to racks to cool completely.

Lemon Shortbread

Serve this shortbread with the Cardamom Ice Cream on page 228 for a superb dessert.

Makes: about 20 cookies • Prep: 30 min. + 2 hr. chilling • Cooking: 20 min. • Level: 1

½	cup (125 g) salted butter, softened
½	cup (100 g) superfine (caster) sugar, plus extra for sprinkling
4	teaspoons finely grated lemon zest
1	large egg, beaten
1⅓	cups (200 g) all-purpose (plain) flour

1. Beat the butter, superfine sugar, and lemon zest in a small bowl with an electric mixer fitted with a whisk until smooth and creamy. Gradually add the egg, beating to incorporate. Stir in the flour using a wooden spoon to form a dough. Place the dough on a sheet of plastic wrap (cling film) and shape to form a log 1½ inches (4 cm) in diameter. Wrap in plastic wrap and refrigerate for 2 hours, or until firm.

2. Preheat the oven to 325°F (170°C/gas 3). Lightly grease two cookie sheets.

3. Remove the dough from the refrigerator and slice into about twenty ¼-inch (5-mm) thick rounds. Place 1 inch (2.5 cm) apart on the prepared sheets.

4. Bake for 20 minutes, rotating the sheets halfway through for even baking, or until light golden. Remove from the oven and allow the shortbreads to cool briefly. With a palette knife, transfer the cookies to a rack to cool completely. Sprinkle with superfine sugar.

White Chocolate Chunk Cookies ▷

Walnut Brownie Cookies

These cookies have a lovely strong chocolate flavor and a satisfyingly chewy texture.

Makes: about 24 cookies · Prep: 25 min. · Cooking: 8–10 min. per batch Level: 1

- 8 ounces (250 g) bittersweet or dark chocolate
- 1/3 cup (90 g) unsalted butter
- 1 cup (200 g) sugar
- 3 large eggs
- 1 teaspoon vanilla extract (essence)
- 1/2 cup (75 g) all-purpose (plain) flour
- 1/2 teaspoon baking powder
- 1/2 teaspoon salt
- 1 cup (180 g) bittersweet or dark chocolate chips
- 1 cup (125 g) coarsely chopped walnuts

1. Preheat the oven to 350°F (180°C/gas 4). Butter two cookie sheets.

2. Melt the chocolate and butter in a double boiler over barely simmering water.

3. Combine the sugar, eggs, and vanilla in a bowl. Beat with an electric mixer on high speed until pale and creamy. With the mixer at low speed, add the chocolate mixture and beat until well mixed. Add the flour, baking powder, and salt and beat until just blended. Stir in the chocolate chips and walnuts by hand. Drop about 12 tablespoons of dough onto each cookie sheet.

4. Bake, one batch at a time, rotating the sheets halfway through for even baking, for 8–10 minutes, until the cookies have cracked a little and are still soft. Cool the cookie sheet on a rack for 5 minutes, then transfer the cookies to the rack to cool completely.

Brandy Snaps with Chantilly Cream

Makes: 8–12: · Prep: 25 min. + 1 hr. chilling · Cooking: 4 min. per batch Level: 2

BRANDY SNAPS
- 1 1/8 cups (225 g) superfine (caster) sugar
- 3/4 cup (125 g) all-purpose (plain) flour
- 1/2 cup (125 g) unsalted butter
- 1/2 cup (125 ml) light corn (golden) syrup

CHANTILLY CREAM
- 2 cups (500 ml) light (single) cream
- 1/4 cup (50 g) superfine (caster) sugar

1. To prepare the brandy snaps, combine the superfine sugar and flour in a medium bowl. Melt the butter in the corn syrup in a small saucepan. Add to the dry ingredients and combine thoroughly. Refrigerate for 1 hour.

2. Preheat the oven to 350°F (180°C/gas 4). Line two large baking sheets with parchment paper.

3. Drop large tablespoons of the batter onto the prepared baking sheet, spacing 2 inches (5 cm) apart.

4. Bake, one batch at a time, rotating the sheets halfway through for even baking, for about 4 minutes, until the cookies spread, appear lacy, and turn a golden brown. Let stand for 2 minutes.

5. Working quickly, scoop each cookie up using a metal spatula or palette knife and wrap loosely around the handle of a wooden spoon to create a tube shape. Let harden a moment, then slip off the spoon and let cool.

6. To prepare the chantilly cream, whisk the cream and superfine sugar in a medium bowl until it forms soft peaks. Spoon the cream into a piping bag fitted with a small nozzle. Fill the brandy snap tubes with cream.

◁ **Walnut Brownie Cookies**

🌿 Coconut Macaroons

Crisp on the outside and chewy within, these little cookies are delicious on their own with a cup of tea or coffee but are also good with fresh fruit and mousses (see page 172). This recipe is gluten- and dairy-free.

Makes: about 35 cookies · Prep: 10 min. · Cooking: 10–15 min. · Level: 1

2	large egg whites
¼	teaspoon cream of tartar
	Pinch of salt
¾	cup + 2 tablespoons (175 g) superfine (caster) sugar
1	cup (150 g) unsweetened coconut flakes (desiccated coconut)
1	cup (100 g) macadamia nuts, roughly chopped

1. Preheat the oven to 300°F (150°C/gas 2). Line two baking sheets with parchment paper.

2. Beat the egg whites, cream of tartar, and salt with an electric mixer on high speed until thick. Gradually add the superfine sugar, and continue beating for 3 minutes. Fold in the coconut and macadamia nuts. Place heaped teaspoons of the batter on the baking sheet, spacing 2 inches (5 cm) apart so that they can spread a little during baking.

3. Bake for 10–15 minutes, rotating the sheets halfway through for even baking, until pale golden brown. Transfer to racks to cool.

🌿 Coffee and Hazelnut Macaroons

This recipe is gluten-free. However, if you are allergic to gluten, make sure you buy reputable brands of cocoa, coffee, coconut, and other ingredients. Check online; in most countries you can download a list of reliable brands that market their products as gluten-free.

Makes: about 60 cookies · Prep: 25 min. · Cooking: 15–20 min. · Level: 2

3	large egg whites
	Pinch of salt
1	cup (200 g) superfine (caster) sugar
2	cups (300 g) finely ground hazelnuts
2	teaspoons freeze-dried coffee granules
1	tablespoon Dutch-process cocoa powder
3	ounces (90 g) white chocolate, coarsely chopped
60	coffee beans, to decorate

1. Preheat the oven to 300°F (150°C/gas 2). Line four cookie sheets with parchment paper.

2. Beat the egg whites and salt in a large bowl with an electric mixer at medium speed until frothy. With the mixer at high speed, gradually add the superfine sugar, beating until stiff, glossy peaks form. Use a large rubber spatula to fold in the hazelnuts, coffee granules, and cocoa.

3. Fit a pastry bag with a plain ½-inch (1-cm) tip. Fill the pastry bag, twist the opening tightly closed, and squeeze out mounds the size of walnuts, spacing them 1 inch (2.5 cm) apart on the prepared cookie sheets.

4. Bake, one sheet at a time, rotating the sheets halfway through for even baking, for 15–20 minutes, or until crisp and dry. Transfer to racks on the parchment paper to cool.

5. Melt the chocolate in a double boiler over barely simmering water. Drizzle the chocolate over the meringues and decorate with coffee beans.

Coffee and Hazelnut Macaroons ▷

Sacher Torte Cookies

These cookies take their flavor from the rich Viennese chocolate cake that was first invented in 1832 by a 16-year-old apprentice chef, Franz Sacher.

Makes: about 30 cookies · Prep 25 min. + 30 min. standing · Cooking: 20 min. · Level: 1

COOKIES
- 2 cups (300 g) all-purpose (plain) flour
- 2 tablespoons Dutch-process cocoa powder
- Pinch of salt
- 1 cup (250 g) salted butter, softened
- ¼ cup (50 g) sugar
- 1 large egg
- ½ cup (160 g) apricot preserves or jam

RICH CHOCOLATE GLAZE
- 7 ounces (200 g) dark chocolate, coarsely chopped
- 2 tablespoons salted butter

1. Preheat the oven to 350°F (180°C/gas 4). Butter three cookie sheets.

2. Combine the flour, cocoa, and salt in a medium bowl. Beat the butter and sugar in a large bowl with an electric mixer at high speed until creamy. Add the egg, beating until just blended. Mix in the dry ingredients to form a smooth dough.

3. Form the dough into balls the size of walnuts and place 2 inches (5 cm) apart on the prepared cookie sheets. Press your thumb into each one to make a small hollow.

4. Bake, rotating the sheets halfway through for even baking, for 12–15 minutes, or until firm to the touch. Transfer to racks to cool.

5. Fill the hollows with a small amount of preserves.

6. To prepare the glaze, melt the chocolate and butter in a double boiler over barely simmering water.

7. Spoon the glaze into a small freezer bag and cut off a tiny corner. Pipe over the cookies and let stand for 30 minutes until set.

Oatmeal Raisin Cookies

These classic cookies are deliciously soft and chewy.

Makes: about 24 cookies · Prep: 15 min. · Cooking: 15–20 min. · Level: 1

- 1½ cups (225 g) all-purpose (plain) flour
- 1 cup (125 g) unsweetened shredded (desiccated) coconut
- 1 teaspoon baking soda (bicarbonate of soda)
- ½ teaspoon ground cinnamon
- ½ teaspoon ground ginger
- ½ teaspoon salt
- 1 cup (250 g) unsalted butter, softened
- 1 cup (200 g) firmly packed light brown sugar
- ⅓ cup (90 ml) pure maple syrup
- 1 large egg
- 1½ teaspoons vanilla extract (essence)
- 3 cups (375 g) old-fashioned rolled oats
- 1 cup (180 g) raisins

1. Preheat the oven to 325°F (170°C/gas 3). Line two cookie sheets with parchment paper.

2. Mix the flour, coconut, baking soda, cinnamon, ginger, and salt in a large bowl.

3. Beat the butter and brown sugar in a large bowl with an electric mixer on medium speed until creamy. Add the maple syrup and beat until combined. Beat in the egg and vanilla. With the mixer on low speed, beat in the mixed dry ingredients, followed by the oats and raisins. Shape tablespoons of the dough into balls the size of walnuts. Place on the prepared cookie sheets, spacing 1 inch (2.5 cm) apart.

4. Bake for 15–20 minutes, rotating the sheets halfway through for even baking, until golden brown. Let cool on the cookie sheets for 5 minutes. Transfer to racks to cool completely.

Oatmeal Raisin Cookies ▷

BARS AND BROWNIES

What better way to finish a meal than with a delectable slice of warm brownie? Brownies go beautifully with ice cream, so we suggest you try the ones in this chapter with the Rich Egg-Cream Ice Cream (see page 224) or the Coconut Ice Cream (see page 228). This chapter also includes some wicked bars and squares, like the Bittersweet Caramel Squares shown here (see recipe on page 39).

◁ **Bittersweet Caramel Squares (see page 39)**

Aztec Brownies

These dense chocolate brownies will satisfy even the most craven of chocoholics. The chile adds some bite that contrasts beautifully with the sweetness of the brownie crumb. But feel free to make them without the chile; they taste just as good.

Makes: 12–16 brownies • Prep: 15 min. + 2 hr. cooling • Cooking: 25–30 min. • Level: 1

1	cup (150 g) all-purpose (plain) flour
2/3	cup (100 g) unsweetened cocoa powder
1	tablespoon apple pie spice (mixed spice)
1	teaspoon ground cinnamon
1/4	teaspoon salt
	Pinch of ground cloves
1	cup (200 g) granulated sugar
1	cup (200 g) firmly packed dark brown sugar
1	cup (250 g) unsalted butter, melted
3	large eggs
1	small dried chile pepper, crumbled
1	teaspoon vanilla extract (essence)
4	ounces (125 g) bittersweet or dark chocolate, coarsely chopped
	Confectioners' (icing) sugar, to dust

1. Preheat the oven to 350°F (180°C/gas 4). Line an 8 x 12-inch (20 x 30-cm) baking pan with aluminum foil.

2. Mix the flour, cocoa, apple pie spice, cinnamon, salt, and cloves in a medium bowl.

3. Combine the granulated and brown sugars in a large bowl. Add the butter and stir until well combined. Use a wooden spoon to beat in the eggs until well combined. Gradually beat in the flour mixture, chile pepper, vanilla, and chocolate. Spoon into the prepared baking pan.

4. Bake for 25–30 minutes, until the brownie is almost dry on top but still gooey and dense in the middle. Cool in the pan on a wire rack. Dust with confectioners' sugar. Cut into 12–16 squares.

Low-Fat Fudge Brownies

These fudgy brownies have just 5 grams of fat per serving and less than 150 calories. Indulge without sinning!

Makes: 12 brownies • Prep: 15 min. + 2 hr. cooling • Cooking: 20–25 min. Level: 1

1 2/3	cups (250 g) confectioners' (icing) sugar
2/3	cup (100 g) all-purpose (plain) flour
1/4	cup (40 g) unsweetened cocoa powder
3/4	teaspoon baking powder
1/8	teaspoon salt
1	teaspoon freeze-dried coffee granules
2	teaspoons boiling water
1 1/2	ounces (45 g) unsweetened chocolate, coarsely chopped
1 1/2	tablespoons safflower oil
2	tablespoons light corn (golden) syrup
2	teaspoons vanilla extract (essence)
2	large egg whites

1. Preheat the oven to 350°F (180°C/gas 4). Line an 8-inch (20-cm) square baking pan with aluminum foil, overlapping the foil by a few inches at two opposite ends of the pan. Spray the foil with nonstick spray coating.

2. Combine the confectioners' sugar, flour, cocoa powder, baking powder, and salt in a large bowl. Put the coffee granules in a small cup and add the boiling water. Stir until the coffee has dissolved.

3. Melt the chocolate with the oil in a double boiler over very low heat. Remove from the heat and stir in the coffee mixture, corn syrup, and vanilla.

4. Beat the egg whites until frothy, then stir them into the chocolate mixture. Gradually stir in the mixed dry ingredients until well blended. Spoon into the prepared baking pan.

5. Bake for 20–25 minutes, until the brownie is almost dry on top. Cool in the pan on a wire rack for 15 minutes. Use the overlapping foil to lift the brownie out of the pan and place on the cooling rack. Peel off the foil and let cool completely. Cut into 12 squares.

Aztec Brownies ▷

Walnut Brownies

The prefect brownie should be crisp on top and creamy and smooth in the center, without seeming gooey and underbaked.

Makes: 12–16 brownies • Prep: 25 min. + 2 hr. cooling • Cooking: 25–30 min. • Level: 1

- 1½ cups (225 g) all-purpose (plain) flour
- ½ teaspoon salt
- 1½ cups (375 g) unsalted butter
- 12 ounces (350 g) bittersweet or dark chocolate
- 6 large eggs
- 2½ cups (500 g) superfine (caster) sugar
- 1½ teaspoons vanilla extract (essence)
- 2 cups (250 g) coarsely chopped walnuts

1. Preheat the oven to 350°F (180°C/gas 4). Line an 8 x 12-inch (20 x 30-cm) baking pan with aluminum foil.

2. Mix the flour and salt in a medium bowl.

3. Combine the butter and chocolate in a medium saucepan over low heat. Cook until melted and stir to combine. Set aside to cool for 10 minutes.

4. Beat the eggs, superfine sugar, and vanilla with an electric mixer at high speed until pale than thick. With the mixer on low speed, beat in the chocolate mixture, followed by the flour mixture and walnuts. Spoon into the prepared pan.

5. Bake for 25–30 minutes, until the brownie is almost dry on top but still creamy and dense in the middle. Cool in the pan on a wire rack. Cut into 12–16 squares.

Date and Walnut Brownies

For more intensely chocolatey brownies, stir ½ cup (90 g) of dark chocolate chips or pieces into the flour with the walnuts and dates.

Makes: 12–16 brownies • Prep: 30 min. + 2 hr. cooling • Cooking: 25 min. Level: 2

- 1 cup (150 g) all-purpose (plain) flour
- 1 teaspoon baking powder
- Pinch of salt
- ½ cup (90 g) finely chopped dried dates
- ½ cup (50 g) coarsely chopped walnuts
- 1 teaspoon finely grated lemon zest
- ½ cup (125 g) unsalted butter
- 1 cup (200 g) firmly packed dark brown sugar
- 2 tablespoons unsweetened cocoa powder
- 2 tablespoons light corn (golden) syrup
- 1 large egg, lightly beaten
- 2 ounces (60 g) semisweet or dark chocolate, coarsely chopped
- Fresh strawberries, sliced, to decorate

1. Preheat the oven to 350°F (180°C/gas 4). Butter an 11 x 7-inch (28 x 18-cm) baking pan and line with parchment paper.

2. Mix the flour, baking powder, and salt in a large bowl. Mix in the dates, walnuts, and lemon zest.

3. Combine the butter, brown sugar, cocoa, and corn syrup in a small saucepan over low heat and cook, stirring constantly, until the sugar completely dissolves. Cool slightly. Beat in the egg. Stir the butter mixture into the dry ingredients until well blended. Spoon the mixture into the prepared pan, smoothing the surface.

4. Bake for about 25 minutes, or until a toothpick inserted into the center comes out clean. Cool completely in the pan.

5. Melt the chocolate in a double boiler over barely simmering water. Cut the brownie into 12–16 squares. Drizzle the chocolate over the brownies and top with the strawberries.

Walnut Brownies ▷

Chocolate Brownie Dessert

This luscious dessert is a modified, frozen version of the classic Black Forest Cake (see page 74). Serve this one on hot summer evenings.

Serves: 4–6 • Prep: 35 min. + 2 hr. cooling and 12 hr. chilling • Cooking: 25 min. • Level: 2

CHOCOLATE BROWNIE

½	cup (125 g) unsalted butter
4	ounces (125 g) unsweetened baking chocolate
2	large eggs
1	cup (200 g) sugar
1	teaspoon vanilla extract (essence)
¾	cup (125 g) all-purpose (plain) flour
¼	cup (45 g) candied (glacé) cherries

KIRSCH SYRUP

⅓	cup (90 ml) water
⅓	cup (70 g) sugar
⅓	cup (90 ml) Kirsch

CREAM FILLING

3	cups (500 ml) heavy (double) cream
8	ounces (250 g) white chocolate, coarsely chopped
2	cups (500 g) sour cherries, pitted

1. Preheat the oven to 325°F (170°C/gas 3). Line an 8-inch (20-cm) square baking pan with parchment paper.

2. To prepare the brownie, melt the butter and chocolate in a small saucepan over low heat. Beat the eggs, sugar, and vanilla in a medium bowl with an electric mixer on high speed until pale and creamy. With the mixer on low speed, pour in the chocolate mixture, beating to combine well. Add the flour and cherries and beat until just blended. Pour the batter into the prepared pan.

3. Bake for about 25 minutes, until the brownie is slightly risen around the edges and set in the center. Cool on a wire rack.

4. Remove the brownie from the pan and peel off the parchment paper. Use a long sharp knife to cut the brownie in half horizontally. Cut in half again vertically, leaving you with four brownie pieces measuring 8 x 4 inches (20 x 10 cm). Set aside.

5. To prepare the Kirsch syrup, heat the water and sugar together in a small saucepan over medium-low heat, until the sugar dissolves. Remove from the heat, add the Kirsch, and set aside.

6. To prepare the cream filling, heat the cream and chocolate together in a small saucepan over low heat, stirring until the chocolate melts.

7. To assemble the dessert, line an 8½ x 4½-inch (21 x 11-cm) loaf pan with aluminum foil, leaving enough foil overlapping at the top to enclose the top of the pan. Place a layer of the chocolate brownie on the bottom of the pan. Drizzle with a quarter of the Kirsch syrup and sprinkle with half of the cherries. Pour half of the cream filling over the top and cover with another piece of chocolate brownie. Repeat the process with the Kirsch syrup, cherries, and cream. Cover with the last piece of brownie and drizzle with the remaining syrup. Wrap the overlapping foil over the top of the dessert. Place in the freezer overnight to set.

8. To serve the dessert, remove from the pan and unwrap and discard the foil. Let rest at room temperature for 10 minutes to soften slightly, then slice and serve.

◄ **Chocolate Brownie Dessert**

Warm Chocolate Brownie with Peanut Butter Ice Cream

Serve these rich chocolate brownies still warm with scoops of peanut butter ice cream melting deliciously over the top. You will find the recipe for the Peanut Butter Ice Cream on page 226.

Serves: 6 · Prep: 30 min. · Cooking: 35–40 min. · Level: 2

³/₄	cup (180 g) salted butter
6	ounces (180 g) bittersweet or dark (70% cacao) chocolate, finely chopped
3	large eggs
1¼	cups (250 g) sugar
²/₃	cup (100 g) all-purpose (plain) flour
½	cup (75 g) unsweetened cocoa powder
8	ounces (250 g) dark chocolate, coarsely chopped
1	recipe Peanut Butter Ice Cream (see page 226)

1. Preheat the oven to 350°F (180°C/gas 4). Line a 9-inch (23-cm) square baking pan with parchment paper.

2. Combine the butter and bittersweet chocolate in a small saucepan over low heat. Heat until melted, stirring until combined. Remove from the heat and let cool for 10 minutes.

3. Beat the eggs and sugar in a medium bowl with an electric mixer on high speed until pale and creamy. Stir in the melted chocolate mixture using a wooden spoon until incorporated. Gradually add the flour, cocoa, and coarsely chopped semisweet chocolate, stirring until combined. Pour the mixture into the prepared pan.

4. Bake for 35–40 minutes, until crisp on the outside and still slightly soft in the center. Cool the brownie in the pan on a wire rack for 10 minutes. Then remove from the pan and slice into six portions.

5. Place the warm brownies on individual serving plates and top each with a scoop of the Peanut Butter Ice Cream.

Marbled Cream Cheese Brownies

Makes: 12–16 brownies · Prep: 35 min + 2 hr. cooling · Cooking: 25–30 min. · Level: 2

CREAM CHEESE MIXTURE

1	cup (250 ml) cream cheese, softened
¼	cup (50 g) sugar
2	tablespoons finely grated orange zest
3	tablespoons freshly squeezed orange juice
1	teaspoon cornstarch (cornflour)
1	large egg

CHOCOLATE MIXTURE

7	ounces (200 g) semisweet or dark chocolate, coarsely chopped
4	tablespoons unsalted cold butter, cut up
³/₄	cup (150 g) sugar
2	teaspoons vanilla extract (essence)
2	large eggs, lightly beaten with 2 tablespoons cold water
½	cup (75 g) all-purpose (plain) flour

1. Preheat the oven to 350°F (180°C/gas 4). Butter a 9-inch (23-cm) square baking pan and line with parchment paper.

2. To prepare the cream cheese mixture, beat the cream cheese and sugar in a large bowl with an electric mixer at high speed until creamy. With the mixer on low speed, beat in the orange zest, orange juice, and cornstarch. Add the egg, beating until just blended.

3. To prepare the chocolate mixture, melt the chocolate and butter in a double boiler over barely simmering water. Remove from the heat and stir in the sugar and vanilla. Add the beaten eggs, followed by the flour, beating until just blended.

4. Pour the chocolate mixture into the prepared pan. Drop tablespoons of the cream cheese mixture over the chocolate base. Use a thin metal spatula to swirl the mixtures together to create a marbled effect.

5. Bake for 25–30 minutes, or until the brownie is slightly risen around the edges and set in the center. Cool completely in the pan. Cut into 12–16 squares.

Warm Chocolate Brownie with Peanut Butter Ice Cream ▷

Chocolate Mint Squares

This classic combination of chocolate and mint never goes out of style. This creative recipe provides a refreshing and delicious finish to any meal.

Makes: about 16 squares • Prep: 20 min. + 30 min. setting • Cooking: 15–20 min. • Level: 1

BASE
- $^2/_3$ cup (100 g) all-purpose (plain) flour
- 2 tablespoons unsweetened cocoa powder
- 1 teaspoon baking powder
- $^1/_4$ teaspoon salt
- $^1/_3$ cup (70 g) granulated sugar
- 2 tablespoons unsalted butter, chilled and diced
- 1 large egg, lightly beaten with $^1/_3$ cup (90 ml) water

FILLING
- $2^1/_4$ cups (330 g) confectioners' (icing) sugar
- 1 tablespoon mint liqueur
- 1–2 tablespoons milk

FROSTING
- 4 ounces (125 g) semisweet or dark chocolate, coarsely chopped
- $^1/_3$ cup (90 g) unsalted butter

1. Preheat the oven to 350°F (180°C/gas 4). Butter an 8-inch (20-cm) square baking pan.

2. To prepare the base, mix the flour, cocoa, baking powder, and salt in a large bowl. Stir in the granulated sugar. Cut in the butter until the mixture resembles fine crumbs. Mix in the egg mixture. Firmly press the mixture into the prepared pan to form a smooth layer.

3. Bake for 15–20 minutes, or until firm to the touch.

4. To prepare the filling, mix the confectioners' sugar and mint liqueur until well blended. Stir in enough milk to achieve a spreadable consistency. Spread the peppermint mixture over the base.

5. To prepare the frosting, melt the chocolate and butter over barely simmering water. Stir until smooth. Spread the frosting over the mint layer. Let stand for 30 minutes until set. Cut into squares.

◁ **White Chocolate Almond Squares**

White Chocolate Almond Squares

Many people don't consider "white chocolate" to be chocolate at all because, unlike dark chocolate or milk chocolate, it doesn't contain any cocoa solids. Be sure to buy a good quality product that contains at least 20 percent cocoa butter.

Makes: 12–16 squares • Prep: 30 min. + 4 hr. chilling • Level: 1

- 10 ounces (300 g) white chocolate, coarsely chopped
- $^2/_3$ cup (150 g) salted butter, cut up
- $^1/_4$ cup (60 ml) heavy (double) cream
- 1 cup (90 g) amaretti cookies, crushed
- 2 tablespoons unsweetened shredded (desiccated) coconut
- 1 cup (100 g) coarsely chopped candied (glacé) cherries
- $^1/_2$ cup (50 g) flaked almonds, toasted

1. Line an 8-inch (20-cm) square baking pan with parchment paper.

2. Combine the white chocolate, butter, and cream in a double boiler over barely simmering water. Heat until the chocolate is melted and stir until smooth. Mix in the amaretti cookies, coconut, cherries, and almonds until well coated.

3. Spoon into the prepared pan, spreading evenly. Refrigerate for 4 hours, or until set. Use a knife dipped in hot water to cut into 12–16 squares.

Chocolate Orange Squares

The zesty orange and chocolate combination makes a colorful presentation.

Makes: 16–20 squares • Prep: 40 min. + 1 hr. 30 min. chilling • Cooking: 30–35 min. • Level: 2

CHOCOLATE COOKIE BASE
- 1 cup (150 g) all-purpose (plain) flour
- 2 tablespoons unsweetened cocoa powder
- Pinch of salt
- 1 cup (250 g) unsalted butter, softened
- ⅓ cup (70 g) granulated sugar
- ⅓ cup (50 g) confectioners' (icing) sugar

ORANGE FILLING
- Finely grated zest of 1 orange
- ½ cup (125 ml) freshly squeezed orange juice
- 4 tablespoons water
- ⅓ cup (50 g) cornstarch (cornflour)
- 1 teaspoon fresh lemon juice
- 1 tablespoon butter, softened
- ½ cup (160 ml) orange marmalade

CHOCOLATE CREAM GLAZE
- 3 tablespoons heavy (double) cream
- 1½ teaspoons light corn (golden) syrup
- 3 ounces (90 g) semisweet or dark chocolate, coarsely chopped

1. Preheat the oven to 325°F (170°C/gas 3). Line an 8-inch (20-cm) baking pan with aluminum foil, letting the edges overhanging.

2. To prepare the cookie base, mix the flour, cocoa, and salt in a medium bowl. Beat the butter, granulated sugar, and confectioners' sugar in a large bowl with an electric mixer at high speed until creamy. With the mixer on low speed, gradually beat in the dry ingredients.

3. Firmly press the mixture into the prepared pan to form a smooth, even layer. Prick all over with a fork.

4. Bake for 25–30 minutes, or until firm to the touch. Let cool on a rack for 10 minutes.

5. To prepare the filling, mix the orange zest, orange juice, water, cornstarch, and lemon juice in a small saucepan over medium heat. Bring to a boil and simmer, stirring constantly, for 1 minute, or until thickened. Remove from the heat and mix in the butter and marmalade until well blended.

6. Pour the filling evenly over the cookie base. Bake for 5 minutes. Cool completely in the pan. Refrigerate for 1 hour, or until set.

7. To prepare the glaze, combine the cream and corn syrup in a small saucepan and bring to a boil. Remove from the heat and stir in the chocolate until melted and smooth. Spoon the glaze into a small freezer bag and cut off a tiny corner. Pipe over the filling in a decorative manner. Refrigerate for 30 minutes.

8. Transfer the brownie to a cutting board and cut into squares.

Moist Mocha Bars

For a slightly different but equally delicious dessert, replace the milk chocolate in the frosting with the same quantity of dark or bittersweet chocolate.

Makes: 16–20 bars • Prep: 30 min. + 2 hr. cooling • Cooking: 25–35 min. Level: 1

BASE
1½ cups (225 g) all-purpose (plain) flour
1 teaspoon baking powder
   Pinch of salt
2 tablespoons very strong hot coffee
4 tablespoons unsweetened cocoa powder
1 cup (250 g) salted butter, softened
1 cup (200 g) granulated sugar
4 large eggs

MILK CHOCOLATE FROSTING
4 ounces (125 g) milk chocolate, coarsely chopped
¼ cup (60 g) salted butter, softened
1 tablespoon milk
1¼ cups (180 g) confectioners' (icing) sugar

1. Preheat the oven to 350°F (180°C/gas 4). Butter an 11 x 7-inch (28 x 18-cm) baking pan.

2. To prepare the base, mix the flour, baking powder, and salt in a medium bowl. Mix the coffee and cocoa in a large bowl. Add the butter, granulated sugar, eggs, and dry ingredients and beat until well blended. Pour the batter into the prepared pan.

4. Bake for 25–35 minutes, or until the brownie is dry on top and almost firm to the touch. Do not overbake. Cool completely in the pan.

5. To prepare the frosting, combine the milk chocolate, butter, and milk in a double boiler over barely simmering water. Heat until the chocolate melts. Remove from the heat and beat in the confectioners' sugar until smooth.

6. Spread the frosting over the top of the brownie. Cut into 16–20 bars.

Bittersweet Caramel Squares

Makes: about 30 squares • Prep: 20 min. + 30 min. setting • Cooking: 10–15 min. • Level: 2

BASE
1 cup (150 g) all-purpose (plain) flour
1 teaspoon baking powder
⅛ teaspoon salt
½ cup (125 g) salted butter, softened
½ cup (50 g) sugar

TOPPING
½ cup (125 g) salted butter
½ cup (100 g) sugar
2 tablespoons light corn (golden) syrup
1 14-ounce (400-g) can sweetened condensed milk

FROSTING
8 ounces (250 g) bittersweet or dark chocolate, coarsely chopped

1. Preheat the oven to 325°F (170°C/gas 3). Line a 9-inch (23-cm) square baking pan with aluminum foil.

2. To prepare the base, mix the flour, baking powder, and salt in a large bowl. Beat the butter and sugar in a large bowl with an electric mixer on high speed until pale and creamy. With the mixer on low speed, mix in the dry ingredients. Spread the mixture evenly in the prepared pan.

3. Bake for 10–15 minutes, or until golden brown.

4. To prepare the topping, melt the butter with the sugar, corn syrup, and condensed milk in a medium saucepan over low heat, stirring constantly. Bring to a boil and boil for 5 minutes. Remove from the heat and let cool slightly. Spread the caramel topping evenly over the cookie base.

5. To prepare the frosting, melt the chocolate in a double boiler over barely simmering water. Pour the chocolate over the caramel topping and let stand for 30 minutes until set. Cut into squares.

CUPCAKES

Cupcakes are small, sponge-like cakes that are usually baked in paper liners. In the United Kingdom they are also known as fairy cakes, presumably because they are tiny, delicate, and pretty—just like the fairies who were thought to feast on them. Cupcakes have been around for many years, but they are enjoying a revival at the moment. They used to be baked in fluted tin or ceramic molds, but the modern alternative of colored paper liners makes them even more attractive.

◁ Orange Poppy-Seed Cupcakes (see page 42)

Banoffee Cupcakes

The word "banoffee" is a combination of "banana" and "toffee." The word— and the original pie—are said to have been invented by British chefs Ian Dowding and Nigel MacKenzie in their East Sussex restaurant in 1972. Banoffee is now a popular flavor for many different cakes and pies.

Makes: 12 cupcakes · Prep: 30 min. + 1 hr. cooling · Cooking: 20 min. Level: 1

½	cup (125 g) salted butter, softened
¾	cup (150 g) firmly packed light brown sugar
2	large eggs
2	medium, overripe bananas, mashed + 1 ripe banana, sliced
⅓	cup (90 ml) sour cream
1	teaspoon baking soda (bicarbonate of soda)
3	tablespoons hot milk
¾	cup (125 g) self-rising flour
¾	cup (125 g) all-purpose (plain) flour
1	teaspoon ground nutmeg
1	cup (180 g) caramel-filled chocolate candies, coarsely chopped
½	cup (125 ml) heavy (double) cream, whipped
1	cup (250 ml) caramel sauce (see page 276)

1. Preheat the oven to 325°F (170°C/gas 3). Line a 12-cup muffin pan with paper liners.

2. To prepare the cupcakes, beat the butter and brown sugar in a large bowl with an electric mixer on medium-high speed until pale and creamy. Beat in the eggs, one at a time, beating until just blended after each addition. Beat in the mashed banana. With the mixer on low speed, add the baking soda and hot milk. Beat in both flours and the nutmeg. Stir in the candies. Spoon the batter into the prepared pan, filling each cup three-quarters full.

3. Bake for about 20 minutes, or until the cupcakes spring back when lightly touched or a skewer inserted into the center of one of the cupcakes comes out clean. Let cool in the pan on a wire rack for 5 minutes, then invert onto the rack. Turn right side up and let cool completely.

4. Top the cupcakes with a dollop of whipped cream, banana slices, and a drizzle of caramel sauce.

Orange Poppy Seed Cupcakes

Makes: 12 cupcakes · Prep 40 min. + 1 hr. cooling · Cooking: 15–20 min. Level 1

CUPCAKES

1	cup (150 g) self-rising flour
⅓	cup (30 g) finely ground almonds
¼	cup (30 g) poppy seeds
½	cup (125 g) unsalted butter, softened
¾	cup (150 g) superfine (caster) sugar
1	tablespoon finely grated orange zest
2	large eggs
½	cup (125 ml) freshly squeezed orange juice

POPPY SEED FROSTING

1	cup (150 g) confectioners' (icing) sugar
¼	cup (30 g) poppy seeds
1–2	tablespoons freshly squeezed orange juice, strained
½	cup (100 g) candied orange peel (see page 277)

1. Preheat the oven to 325°F (170°C/gas 3). Line a 12-cup muffin pan with paper liners.

2. To prepare the cupcakes, mix the flour, almonds, and poppy seeds in a small bowl. Beat the butter and superfine sugar in a large bowl with an electric mixer on medium-high speed until pale and creamy. Add the orange zest and beat in the eggs, one at a time, beating until just blended after each addition. With the mixer on low speed, gradually beat in the dry ingredients, alternating with the orange juice. Spoon the batter into the prepared pan, filling each cup three-quarters full.

3. Bake for 15–20 minutes, or until the cupcakes spring back when lightly touched or a skewer inserted into the center of a cupcake comes out clean. Cool the cupcakes in the pan on a wire rack for 5 minutes, then invert onto the rack. Turn the cupcakes right side up and let cool completely.

4. To prepare the frosting, combine the confectioners' sugar and poppy seeds in a small bowl. Gradually add the orange juice, stirring until it is at pouring consistency. Spoon over the cupcakes, allowing it to drizzle down the sides. Top each cupcake with candied orange zest.

Banoffee Cupcakes ▷

Lemon Meringue Cupcakes

For a slightly different flavor, replace the finely grated lemon zest with the same amount of orange or lime zest, and use orange or lime curd instead of the lemon curd.

Makes: 12 cupcakes • Prep: 25 min. + 1 hr. cooling • Cooking: 15–20 min. Level: 2

LEMON CUPCAKES
- ½   cup (125 g) unsalted butter, softened
- ¾   cup (150 g) superfine (caster) sugar
- 2   teaspoons finely grated lemon zest
- 3   large eggs, lightly beaten
- ¼   cup (30 g) shredded (desiccated) coconut
- 1¼ cups (180 g) self-rising flour
- ¼   cup (60 ml) milk
- 1   cup (250 ml) lemon curd (see page 276)

MERINGUE
- 3   large egg whites
- ¾   cup (150 g) superfine (caster) sugar

1. Preheat the oven to 325°F (170°C/gas 3). Line a 12-cup muffin pan with paper liners.

2. To prepare the cupcakes, beat the butter and sugar in a large bowl with an electric mixer on medium-high speed until pale and creamy. Add the lemon zest and the eggs, one at a time, beating until just blended after each addition. With the mixer on low speed, add the coconut, flour, and milk alternately, mixing until incorporated. Spoon the batter into the prepared pan, filling each cup three-quarters full.

3. Bake for 15–20 minutes, or until a cupcake springs back when lightly touched. Let cool in the pan on a wire rack for 5 minutes, then invert onto the rack. Turn right side up and let cool completely.

4. When cool enough to handle, cut a 1-inch (2.5-cm) hole out of the top of each cupcake. Discard the cake tops and fill the hole with the lemon curd and set aside.

5. To prepare the meringue, beat the egg whites in a medium bowl with an electric mixer on medium-high speed until soft peaks form. Gradually add the superfine sugar, beating until thick and glossy. Spoon the meringue into a piping bag fitted with a ½-inch (1-cm) plain tip. Pipe spiral mounds on top of each cupcake. Bake for 10 more minutes, or until meringue has set and slightly colored.

Coconut Cakes with Lime Syrup

These moist, coconut-lime cupcakes make an excellent dessert. For a sweeter touch, replace the yogurt with the same quantity of Chantilly Cream (see page 86).

Makes: 8 cupcakes • Prep: 25 min. + 1 hr. • Cooking: 15–20 min. • Level: 2

COCONUT CAKES
- 2   cups (300 g) all-purpose (plain) flour
- ¾   teaspoon baking powder
- 1⅓   cups (270 g) sugar
- 1   cup (125 g) shredded (desiccated) coconut
- 2   large eggs, lightly beaten
- 1   cup (250 ml) cream of coconut
- 1   cup (250 g) unsalted butter, melted and cooled
- 2   teaspoons finely grated lime zest
- 1   cup (250 ml) plain yogurt

LIME SYRUP
- ¾   cup (150 g) sugar
- ¾   cup (180 ml) freshly squeezed lime juice
- 5   teaspoons finely grated lime zest
- ½   cup (125 ml) water

1. Preheat the oven to 350°F (180°C/gas 4). Lightly grease eight muffin cups

2. To prepare the coconut cakes, mix the flour and baking powder in a large bowl. Add the sugar and coconut, stirring to combine. Combine the eggs, coconut cream, butter, and lime zest in a medium bowl. Whisk until blended to a smooth liquid. Add to the dry ingredients and stir with a wooden spoon until just combined. Pour the batter into prepared muffin cups.

3. Bake for 15–20 minutes, until the tops spring back when touched. Let cool in the pan on a wire rack for 5 minutes, then invert onto the rack. Turn right side up and let cool completely.

4. To prepare the lime syrup, combine the sugar, lime juice, lime zest, and water in a small saucepan over medium-low heat. Cook until the sugar dissolves. Increase the heat to medium-high and simmer for 5–10 minutes, until thickened to the consistency of honey. Pour a few spoonfuls of syrup over each cupcake. Allow to cool and absorb the lime syrup. Serve with a dollop of yogurt on the side.

Lemon Meringue Cupcakes ▷

Chocolate Butterfly Cakes

The cupcakes on these pages are named for the pieces of cake sticking out of the filling or topping in the shape of a butterfly's wings.

Makes: 12 cupcakes · Prep 20 min. + 1 hr. cooling · Cooking: 15–20 min. Level 1

1⅓	cups (200 g) all-purpose (plain) flour
⅔	cup (100 g) unsweetened cocoa powder
2	teaspoons baking powder
¼	teaspoon salt
⅔	cup (150 g) salted butter, softened
1	cup (200 g) sugar
2	large eggs
½	cup (125 ml) milk
1	tablespoon orange liqueur
½	cup (125 g) raspberry preserves (jam)
1	cup (250 ml) heavy (double) cream, whipped
	Fresh raspberries, to decorate

1. Preheat the oven to 350°F (180°C/gas 4). Line a 12-cup muffin pan with paper liners.

2. Mix the flour, cocoa, baking powder, and salt in a medium bowl. Beat the butter and sugar in a large bowl with an electric mixer at high speed until creamy. Add the eggs, one at a time, beating until just blended after each addition. With the mixer at low speed, gradually add the dry ingredients, alternating with the milk and liqueur. Spoon the batter into the cups, filling each one two-thirds full.

3. Bake for 15–20 minutes, until the cupcakes spring back when lightly touched or until a skewer inserted into the center of one of the cupcakes comes out clean. Cool the cupcakes in the pan on a wire rack for 5 minutes, then invert onto the rack. Turn right side up and let cool completely.

4. Cut a small circle about ½ inch (1 cm) deep from the top of each cupcake. Cut each piece in half and set aside. Fill the hollow in each cupcake with 1 teaspoon of preserves and top with whipped cream and 1–2 fresh raspberries. Arrange pairs of cupcake tops on the top of each cupcake like butterfly wings.

Butterfly Cupcakes

Makes: 12 cupcakes · Prep 20 min. + 1 hr. cooling · Cooking: 15–20 min. Level 1

½	cup (125 g) salted butter, softened
¾	cup (150 g) superfine (caster) sugar
1	teaspoon vanilla extract (essence)
2	large eggs
1½	cups (225 g) self-rising flour
½	cup (125 ml) milk
½	cup (125 ml) heavy cream, whipped
2	tablespoons raspberry preserves (jam)
12	fresh raspberries
	Confectioners' (icing) sugar, for dusting

1. Preheat the oven to 325°F (170°C/gas 3). Line a 12-cup muffin pan with paper liners.

2. Beat the butter, superfine sugar, and vanilla in a large bowl with an electric mixer on medium-high speed until pale and creamy. Beat in the eggs, one at a time, beating until just blended after each addition. With the mixer on low speed, add the flour and milk alternately, mixing until incorporated. Spoon the batter into the prepared pans.

3. Bake for 15–20 minutes, or until a cupcake springs back when lightly touched or a skewer inserted into the one of the cupcakes comes out clean. Let cool in the pan on a wire rack for 5 minutes, then invert onto the rack. Turn right side up and let cool completely.

4. Cut a small circle about ½ inch (1 cm) deep from the top of each cupcake. Cut each piece in half and set aside. Spoon 2 teaspoons of whipped cream into the hollow in each cupcake. Place a small dollop of raspberry preserves in the center. Arrange pairs of cupcake tops on the top of each cupcake like butterfly wings. Place a fresh raspberry in between the "wings" and dust with confectioners' sugar.

Chocolate Butterfly Cakes ▷

Frosted Nutty Cupcakes

If you prefer, replace the milk chocolate in the frosting with the same quantity of bittersweet, dark, or white chocolate.

Makes: 16 cupcakes • Prep: 20 min. + 1 hr. cooling • Cooking: 20–25 min. • Level: 1

CUPCAKES

- 2 cups (300 g) all-purpose (plain) flour
- 2 teaspoons baking powder
- 1/2 teaspoon baking soda (bicarbonate of soda)
- 1/4 teaspoon salt
- 1/2 cup (125 g) salted butter, softened
- 1/2 cup (100 g) sugar
- 1 teaspoon rum or butterscotch extract (essence)
- 2 large eggs
- 1 cup (250 ml) heavy (double) cream
- 4 ounces (125 g) chocolate nut candy bar, coarsely chopped

FROSTING

- 6 ounces (180 g) milk chocolate, coarsely chopped
- 16 pecan halves

1. Preheat the oven to 350°F (180°C/gas 4). Line a 16-cup muffin pan with paper liners or set out 16 foil cups.

2. To prepare the cupcakes, mix the flour, baking powder, baking soda, and salt in a medium bowl.

3. Beat the butter, sugar, and rum extract in a large bowl with an electric mixer at high speed until creamy. Add the eggs, one at a time, beating until just blended after each addition. With the mixer at low speed, gradually beat in the dry ingredients, alternating with the cream. Stir in the nut chocolate. Spoon the batter into the prepared cups, filling each one two-thirds full.

4. Bake for 15–20 minutes, until the cupcakes spring back when lightly touched or a skewer inserted into the center comes out clean, Cool the cupcakes in the pan on wire racks for 15 minutes, then invert onto the racks. Turn right side up and let cool completely.

5. To prepare the frosting, melt the milk chocolate in a double boiler over barely simmering water. Set aside to cool for 15 minutes. Spread over the cupcakes and top each one with a pecan.

◁ **Frosted Nutty Cupcakes**

Chocolate Marshmallow Cupcakes

These pretty cupcakes are perfect for a little girl's birthday party and they make a striking addition to the dessert section of any buffet spread.

Makes: 12 cupcakes • prep: 25 min. + 1 hr. cooling • Cooking: 15–20 min. Level: 1

CHOCOLATE CUPCAKES

- 2 ounces (60 g) bittersweet or dark chocolate, coarsely chopped
- 2/3 cup (150 ml) light (single) cream
- 1/3 cup (90 g) unsalted butter, softened
- 1 cup (200 g) superfine (caster) sugar
- 2 large eggs
- 1 cup (150 g) self-rising flour
- 2 tablespoons unsweetened cocoa powder
- 1 cup (75 g) coarsely chopped marshmallows, + extra for decoration

CHOCOLATE GANACHE

- 4 ounces (125 g) bittersweet or dark chocolate, coarsely chopped
- 1/2 cup (125 ml) light (single) cream

1. Preheat the oven to 325°F (170°C/gas 3). Line a 12-cup muffin pan with paper liners.

2. To prepare the cupcakes, combine the chocolate and cream in a double boiler over barely simmering water. Heat until the chocolate is melted and smooth. Set aside to cool a little.

3. Beat the butter and sugar in a large bowl with an electric mixer on medium-high speed until pale and creamy. Add the eggs, one at a time, beating until just blended after each addition. With the mixer on low speed, gradually add the flour and cocoa. Add the melted chocolate and marshmallows, stirring until combined. Spoon the batter into the prepared pans, filling each cup three-quarters full.

4. Bake for 15–20 minutes, or until the cupcakes spring back when lightly touched or a skewer inserted into the center of a cupcake comes out clean. Let cool in the pan on a wire rack for 5 minutes, then invert onto the rack. Turn right side up and let cool completely.

5. To prepare the chocolate ganache, combine the chocolate and cream in a double boiler over barely simmering water and heat until melted and smooth. Set aside to cool a little. Refrigerate for 30 minutes, or until thickened. Place a large dollop of ganache on top of each cupcake and spread using a small spatula or knife. Top with one or two marshmallows.

Orange Sour Cream Cupcakes

Buying brightly-colored paper liners will make your cupcakes' appearance reflect their zesty taste.

Makes: 12 cupcakes · Prep: 25 min. + 1 hr. cooling · Cooking: 20 min. Level: 1

CUPCAKES
- ½ cup (75 g) self-rising flour
- ½ cup (75 g) all-purpose (plain) flour
- ¼ cup (125 g) unsalted butter, softened
- ¾ cup (150 g) superfine (caster) sugar
- 2 teaspoons finely grated orange zest
- ¾ cup (180 g) sour cream
- 3 large eggs

FROSTING
- 2 tablespoons butter, softened
- 3 ounces (90 g) cream cheese, softened
- 1 teaspoon finely grated orange zest
- ½ teaspoon vanilla extract (essence)
- 1½ cups (225 g) confectioners' (icing) sugar
- 6 slices candied (glacé) orange, halved

1. Preheat the oven to 325°F (170°C/gas 3). Line a 12-cup muffin pan with paper liners.

2. To prepare the cupcakes, mix both flours in a small bowl. Beat the butter and superfine sugar with an electric mixer on medium-high speed until pale and creamy. Add the orange zest and ½ cup (125 ml) of the sour cream, mixing until incorporated. Beat in the eggs, one at a time, beating until just blended after each addition. With the mixer on low speed, gradually beat in the flours.

3. Spoon half the batter into the prepared pans and place a small dollop of the remaining ¼ cup (60 ml) sour cream into the center of each. Spoon in the remaining batter. Bake for 15–20 minutes, or until the cakes spring back when lightly touched. Let cool in the pan on a wire rack for 5 minutes, then invert on the rack. Turn right side up and let cool completely.

4. To prepare the frosting, beat the butter, cream cheese, orange zest, and vanilla in a small bowl until light and fluffy. Gradually add the confectioners' sugar, beating until fully incorporated. Place a large dollop of icing on each cupcake and spread with a small spatula or knife. Top with a piece of candied orange.

🌿 Low-Fat Chocolate Cupcakes

These cupcakes have just five grams of fat and less than 150 calories each.

Makes: 16 cupcakes · Prep: 20 min. + 1 hr. cooling · Cooking: 15–20 min. Level: 1

- 1¾ cups (270 g) all-purpose (plain) flour
- ½ cup (75 g) unsweetened cocoa powder
- 1 teaspoon baking powder
- 1 teaspoon baking soda (bicarbonate of soda)
- ½ teaspoon salt
- 1 cup (250 g) reduced-fat margarine or butter
- ¾ cup (150 g) sugar
- 2 large eggs
- 1½ cups (325 g) unsweetened applesauce

1. Preheat the oven to 350°F (180°C/gas 4). Line a 16-cup muffin pan with paper liners or set out 16 foil cups.

2. Place the flour, cocoa, baking powder, baking soda, and salt in a medium bowl.

3. Beat the margarine or butter and sugar in a large bowl with an electric mixer on medium speed until pale. Add the eggs, one at a time, beating until just combined after each addition. With the mixer on low speed, gradually beat in the applesauce and flour mixture. Spoon the batter into the prepared cups, filling each one two-thirds full.

4. Bake for 15–20 minutes, or until the cupcakes spring back when touched lightly or a skewer inserted into the center of a cupcake comes out clean. Cool the cupcakes in the pan on wire racks for 5 minutes, then invert onto the racks. Turn right side up and cool completely.

Orange Sour Cream Cupcakes ▷

Chocolate Cherry Cupcakes

Makes: 12 cupcakes • Prep: 30 min. + 1 hr. cooling • Cooking: 20 min. • Level: 2

CHOCOLATE CHERRY CUPCAKES

2	ounces (60 g) bittersweet or dark chocolate, coarsely chopped
2/3	cup (150 ml) light (single) cream
1/3	cup (90 g) unsalted butter, softened
1	cup (200 g) firmly packed light brown sugar
2	large eggs
1	cup (150 g) self-rising flour
2	tablespoons unsweetened cocoa powder
3/4	cup (135 g) candied (glacé) cherries, coarsely chopped

TOPPING

1	cup (125 g) shredded (desiccated) coconut
3/4	cup (135 g) candied (glacé) cherries, finely chopped
1	tablespoon heavy (double) cream
3½	ounces (100 g) bittersweet or dark chocolate, melted

1. Preheat the oven to 325°F (170°C/gas 3). Line a 12-cup muffin pan with paper liners.

2. To prepare the cupcakes, combine the chocolate and cream in a double boiler over barely simmering water and heat until the chocolate melts. Remove from the heat and let cool. Beat the butter and brown sugar in a large bowl with an electric mixer on medium-high speed until pale and creamy. Add the eggs, one at a time, beating until just blended after each addition. With mixer on low speed, beat in the flour and cocoa. Add the melted chocolate and cherries, stirring until combined. Spoon the batter into the prepared pan, filling each cup three-quarters full.

3. Bake for 15–20 minutes, or until the cupcakes spring back when lightly touched. Let cool in the pan on a wire rack for 5 minutes, then invert onto the rack. Turn right side up and let cool completely.

4. To prepare the topping, combine the coconut, cherries, and cream in a small bowl, stirring until combined and coconut is a reddish color. Spoon some of the mixture over each cupcake. Drizzle with the chocolate.

Raspberry Pastry Cream Cupcakes

If you prefer, replace the pastry cream with white chocolate. Follow the instructions below but add a small square of white chocolate (instead of the pastry cream) to each cupcake and top up with the remaining batter.

Makes: 12 cupcakes • Prep: 40 min. + 1 hr. cooling • Cooking: 20 min. • Level: 1

RASPBERRY CUPCAKES

1/2	cup (125 g) unsalted butter, softened
3/4	cup (150 g) superfine (caster) sugar
1	teaspoon vanilla extract (essence)
2	large eggs
1½	cups (180 g) self-rising flour
1/3	cup (50 g) cornstarch (cornflour)
1/2	cup (125 ml) milk
1/2	cup (125 g) fresh or frozen raspberries, thawed if frozen, + 1 cup (250 g) fresh raspberries for garnish
1/2	cup (125 ml) Vanilla Pastry Cream (see page 277)

BUTTER FROSTING

1/2	cup (125 g) salted butter, softened
1½	cups (225 g) confectioners' (icing) sugar
2	tablespoons milk
1/2	teaspoon vanilla extract (essence)

1. Preheat the oven to 325°F (170°C/gas 3). Line a 12-cup muffin pan with paper liners.

2. To prepare the cupcakes, beat the butter, sugar, and vanilla in a large bowl with an electric mixer on medium-high speed until pale and creamy. Add the eggs, one at a time, beating until just blended after each addition. With the mixer on low speed, beat in the flour and cornstarch alternately with the milk. Stir in ½ cup (125 g) raspberries. Spoon half the batter into the pan and top each cup with a dollop of pastry cream. Spoon the remaining batter into the pan.

3. Bake for 15–20 minutes, or until the cupcakes spring back when lightly touched. Let cool in the pan on a wire rack for 5 minutes, then invert onto the rack. Turn right side up and let cool completely.

4. To prepare the frosting, beat the butter in a bowl with an electric mixer on medium speed until pale. Add the confectioners' sugar, milk, and vanilla, beating until combined. Top each cupcake with frosting and garnish with raspberries.

Chocolate Cherry Cupcakes ▷

Ginger Marmalade Cupcakes

Decorate these little cakes with candied orange instead of candied ginger, if preferred. You can also vary the flavor by replacing the orange marmalade with lemon marmalade.

Makes: 12 cupcakes • Prep: 40 min. + 1 hr. cooling • Cooking: 20 min. Level: 2

CUPCAKES

1½	cups (225 g) self-rising flour
1	tablespoon ground ginger
½	cup (125 g) unsalted butter, softened
¾	cup (150 g) firmly packed light brown sugar
2	large eggs
⅓	cup (90 g) orange marmalade
½	cup (125 ml) milk

FROSTING

⅓	cup (100 g) orange marmalade
2	tablespoons unsalted butter
1	cup (150 g) confectioners' (icing) sugar
	Candied ginger, to decorate

1. Preheat the oven to 325°F (170°C/gas 3). Line a 12-cup muffin pan with paper liners.

2. To prepare the cupcakes, mix the flour and ginger in a small bowl. Beat the butter and brown sugar with an electric mixer on medium-high speed until pale and creamy. Add the eggs, one at a time, beating until just blended after each addition. Beat in the marmalade. Add the flour mixture and milk alternately, stirring until incorporated. Spoon the batter into the prepared pan, filling each cup three-quarters full.

3. Bake for 15–20 minutes, until the cupcakes spring back when lightly touched. Cool in the pan on a wire rack for 5 minutes, then invert onto the rack. Turn right side up and let cool completely.

4. To prepare the frosting, melt the marmalade in a small saucepan over medium-low heat. Remove from the heat and add the butter, stirring to combine. Add the confectioners' sugar and stir until fully incorporated. Set aside for 1–2 minutes until it firms slightly, then spread over the tops of the cupcakes. Top the cupcakes with pieces of candied ginger.

◁ **Nutty White Chocolate Cupcakes**

Nutty White Chocolate Cupcakes

While these cupcakes are ever popular with children, adults may enjoy them after dinner with a glass of pear liqueur or brandy.

Makes: 12 cupcakes • Prep: 20 min. + 30 min. cooling • Cooking: 15–20 min. • Level: 2

CUPCAKES

1⅓	cups (200 g) all-purpose (plain) flour
1	teaspoon baking powder
¼	teaspoon salt
⅓	cup (90 g) unsalted butter
1	cup (200 g) sugar
1	large egg
2	tablespoons pear liqueur
1	teaspoon vanilla extract (essence)
⅔	cup (150 ml) milk
½	cup (60 g) finely chopped toasted hazelnuts

CREAM CHEESE FROSTING

4	ounces (125 g) white chocolate
¼	cup (60 g) unsalted butter, softened
3	ounces (90 g) cream cheese, softened
1	tablespoon finely grated lemon zest
1	tablespoon pear liqueur
1½	cups (225 g) confectioners' (icing) sugar
24	toasted hazelnuts and 6 strawberries, sliced, to decorate

1. Preheat the oven to 350°F (180°C/gas 4). Line a 12-cup muffin pan with paper liners. To prepare the cupcakes, mix the flour, baking powder, and salt in a medium bowl. Beat the butter and sugar in a medium bowl with an electric mixer at high speed until pale and creamy. Add the egg and beat until just combined. With the mixer at low speed, gradually beat in the dry ingredients, alternating with the pear liqueur, vanilla, and milk. Stir in the hazelnuts. Divide the batter evenly among the muffin cups, filling each one about two-thirds full.

2. Bake for 15–20 minutes, until a skewer inserted into the center comes out clean. Cool the cupcakes on a wire rack for 5 minutes, then invert onto the rack. Turn right side up and let cool completely.

3. To prepare the frosting, melt the chocolate in a double boiler over barely simmering water. Let cool a little. Combine the chocolate, butter, cream cheese, lemon zest, liqueur, and confectioners' sugar in a medium bowl and beat until smooth. Spread on the cupcakes. Top with the hazelnuts and strawberries.

Minty Chocolate Cupcakes

These mint-flavored cupcakes make a refreshing end to a meal. Serve with cups of small, espresso-style coffee.

Makes: 18 cupcakes • Prep: 20 min. + 1 hr. cooling • Cooking: 15–20 min. • Level: 1

CUPCAKES
2	cups (300 g) all-purpose (plain) flour
1/2	cup (75 g) unsweetened cocoa powder
1	teaspoon baking powder
1/2	teaspoon baking soda (bicarbonate of soda)
1/4	teaspoon salt
2/3	cup (165 g) unsalted butter, softened
1 1/2	cups (300 g) sugar
3	large eggs
3/4	cup (200 ml) milk
1	teaspoon peppermint extract (essence)
15	chocolate mint thins

CHOCOLATE GLAZE
6	ounces (180 g) bittersweet or dark chocolate, coarsely chopped
1/2	cup (125 g) unsalted butter
1	teaspoon peppermint extract (essence)

1. Preheat the oven to 350°F (180°C/gas 4). Line 18 muffin-pan cups with foil or paper liners.

2. To prepare the cupcakes, mix the flour, cocoa, baking powder, baking soda, and salt in a large bowl.

3. Beat the butter and sugar in a large bowl with an electric mixer at high speed until creamy. Beat in the eggs, one at a time, beating until just blended after each addition. With the mixer at low speed, beat in the dry ingredients, alternating with the milk and peppermint extract. Stir in the chopped chocolate mints. Spoon the batter into the prepared cups, filling each one two-thirds full.

4. Bake for 15–20 minutes, until the cupcakes spring back when touched lightly or a skewer inserted into the center of a cupcake comes out clean. Cool the cupcakes in the pan on wire racks for 5 minutes, then invert onto the racks. Turn right side up and cool completely.

5. To prepare the chocolate glaze, melt the chocolate and butter in a double boiler over barely simmering water. Stir in the peppermint extract. Drizzle the glaze over the cupcakes.

Gluten-Free Cupcakes

Xanthan gum is used in gluten-free baking to add the "stickiness" usually given by the gluten in wheat flour. It is available in health food stores and from online suppliers. Ensure that the baking powder, baking soda, and vanilla extract are gluten-free. Spread these moist cupcakes with Chocolate Frosting (see page 14).

Makes: 18 cupcakes • Prep: 20 min. + 1 hr. cooling • Cooking: 15–20 min. • Level: 1

3/4	cup (120 g) superfine rice flour
1/2	cup (75 g) brown rice flour
1/2	cup (75 g) sorghum flour
1/2	cup (75 g) tapioca flour
1	tablespoon baking powder
1	teaspoon baking soda (bicarbonate of soda)
1/2	teaspoon salt
1	teaspoon xanthan gum
4	large eggs
1 1/4	cups (250 g) sugar
3/4	cup (180 g) mayonnaise
1	cup (250 ml) milk
2	teaspoons gluten-free vanilla extract (essence)

1. Preheat the oven to 350°F (180°C/gas 4). Line 18 muffin-pan cups with foil or paper liners.

2. Mix both rice flours, the sorghum flour, baking powder, tapioca flour, baking soda, salt, and xanthan gum in a large bowl.

3. Combine the eggs, sugar, and mayonnaise in a large bowl and beat with an electric mixer on medium speed until fluffy. With the mixer on low speed, gradually add the flour mixture, milk, and vanilla. Spoon the batter into the prepared cups, filling each one two-thirds full.

4. Bake for 15–20 minutes, or until the cupcakes spring back when touched lightly or a skewer inserted into the center of a cupcake comes out clean. Cool the cupcakes in the pan on wire racks for 5 minutes, then invert onto the racks. Turn right side up and cool completely. Let cool completely.

Minty Chocolate Cupcakes ▷

SIMPLE CAKES

These are hearty dessert cakes just right for family meals at the end of busy days of sporting activities and play. Try our delicious German Cheesecake with Streusel Berry Topping (see page 64) or the White Chocolate and Almond Cheesecake (see page 62). Many of these cakes can be served just out of the oven with whipped cream, yogurt, ice cream, or creamy, warm custard. The Frosted Zucchini Cake (see page 68) is a healthy alternative.

◁ Apple Streusel Cake (see page 60)

Frosted White Chocolate and Pear Ring

Serves: 8–10 · Prep: 30 min. + 1 hr. cooling · Cooking: 50 min. · Level: 1

CAKE

4	ounces (125 g) white chocolate, coarsely chopped
1½	cups (225 g) all-purpose (plain) flour
1½	teaspoons baking powder
¼	teaspoon salt
½	cup (125 g) unsalted butter, softened
½	cup (100 g) sugar
3	large eggs, separated
½	cup (125 ml) milk
1	(15-ounce/450-g) can pear halves, drained and sliced (syrup reserved)

FROSTING

3	cups (450 g) confectioners' (icing) sugar
⅓	cup (90 g) unsalted butter, melted
	Reserved pear syrup

1. Preheat the oven to 325°F (170°C/gas 3). Butter and flour a 9-inch (23-cm) tube pan.

2. To prepare the cake, melt the chocolate in a double boiler over barely simmering water. Set aside to cool.

3. Mix the flour, baking powder, and salt in a medium bowl. Beat the butter and sugar in a large bowl with an electric mixer at medium speed until creamy. Add the egg yolks, one at a time, beating until just blended after each addition. With mixer at low speed, gradually beat in the chocolate and dry ingredients, alternating with the milk. With mixer at high speed, beat the egg whites in a large bowl until stiff peaks form. Use a large rubber spatula to fold them into the batter. Spoon half the batter into the prepared pan. Top with the sliced pears. Spoon the remaining batter over the pears.

4. Bake for about 50 minutes, or until a toothpick inserted into the center comes out clean. Cool the cake in the pan for 10 minutes. Turn out onto a rack to cool completely.

5. To prepare the frosting, mix the confectioners' sugar and butter in a medium bowl. Beat in enough of the reserved pear syrup to make a spreadable frosting. Spread over the top and sides of the cake.

Apple Streusel Cake

Bake this cake using Cox, Golden Delicious, or Gala apples. Serve it hot or warm with sweetened whipped cream. It makes a perfect family dessert for cold winter evenings.

Serves: 6–8 · Prep: 25 min. + 10 min. cooling · Cooking: 55–70 min. · Level: 1

CAKE

4	large sweet apples, peeled, cored, and cubed
1	tablespoon freshly squeezed lemon juice
¼	cup (60 g) unsalted butter
2	tablespoons granulated sugar
1	teaspoon finely grated lemon zest
⅔	cup (150 g) unsalted butter, softened
¾	cup (150 g) firmly packed light brown sugar
1	teaspoon vanilla extract (essence)
2	large eggs
1	cup (100 g) ground almonds
⅔	cup (100 g) self-rising flour
½	teaspoon baking powder
1	tablespoon milk

STREUSEL TOPPING

⅔	cup (100 g) all-purpose (plain) flour
5	tablespoons (75 g) butter, chilled
¼	cup (50 g) Demerara or firmly packed light brown sugar
2	tablespoons coarsely chopped toasted almonds

1. Preheat the oven to 325°F (170°C/gas 3). Lightly butter and line an 8-inch (20-cm) springform pan with parchment paper.

2. To prepare the cake, drizzle the apples with the lemon juice. Heat the butter in a large skillet over medium heat. When hot, add the granulated sugar and stir until dissolved. Add the apples and lemon zest, and sauté for 5–10 minutes, until slightly softened. Set aside.

3. Beat the butter, brown sugar, and vanilla in a medium bowl with an electric mixer until light and fluffy. Beat in the eggs, one at a time, until just combined. Stir in the almonds. Fold in the flour and baking powder with the milk. Stir in the apples and spoon into the prepared pan.

4. To prepare the topping, process all the streusel ingredients in a food processor, until it resembles breadcrumbs. Sprinkle the mixture over the apple batter in the pan in an even layer.

5. Bake for 45–60 minutes, until well risen and golden brown. Leave for 10 minutes. Serve warm.

Frosted White Chocolate and Pear Ring ▷

White Chocolate and Almond Cheesecake

For a lighter and less calorie-laden cheesecake, use half reduced-fat cream and half fat-free fromage frais, instead of the cream cheese.

Serves: 6–8 • Prep: 30 min. + 1–2 hr. cooling and setting + 2 hr. chilling Cooking: 1 hr. 30 min. • Level: 2

CRUST

1¼	cups (150 g) finely crushed amaretti cookie crumbs
3	tablespoons unsalted butter, melted

FILLING

2	pounds (1 kg) cream cheese, softened
¼	cup (50 g) sugar
4	large eggs
	Seeds from 2 vanilla pods, or 2 teaspoons vanilla extract
1	tablespoon amaretto (almond liqueur)
10	ounces (300 g) white chocolate, broken into pieces
¾	cup (75 g) blanched almonds, toasted and finely ground
1	teaspoon finely grated lemon zest

TOPPING

3	tablespoons flaked almonds
	Raspberry coulis (see page 278) and whipped cream, to serve (optional)

1. Preheat the oven to 300°F (150°C/gas 2). Butter a 9-inch (23-cm) springform pan.

2. To prepare the crust, combine the cookie crumbs with the melted butter and press the mixture into the bottom of the prepared pan. Refrigerate while you prepare the filling.

3. To prepare the filling, beat the cream cheese and sugar in a large bowl with an electric mixer on low speed until smooth. Add the eggs, vanilla, and amaretto, and beat until well combined. Melt the chocolate in a double boiler over barely simmering water, stirring often. Leave to cool for a few minutes, then add to the cream cheese mixture. Stir in the ground almonds and lemon zest. Pour the filling over the cookie crust in the pan and sprinkle the top with the flaked almonds.

4. Bake for 1½ hours, or until lightly firm on top. Turn off the oven and leave the cheesecake in to cool and set for 1–2 hours. Chill in the pan in the refrigerator for 2 hours. Serve with coulis and cream, if liked.

Ricotta and Almond Cheesecake

This is an old-fashioned Italian cheesecake. For best results, bake it the day before and keep it in the refrigerator for 12 hours before serving.

Serves: 8–10 • Prep: 50 min. + 2 hr. setting + 2 hr. chilling • Cooking: 80 min. • Level: 2

CRUST

8	ounces (250 g) amaretti cookie crumbs or graham crackers, finely crushed
⅓	cup (90 g) butter, melted

FILLING

1	pound (500 g) ricotta cheese, drained
1	pound (500 g) mascarpone
1	cup (250 ml) sour cream
1	tablespoon vanilla extract (essence)
	Zest of 1 lemon, finely grated
2	tablespoons freshly squeezed lemon juice
3	tablespoons cornstarch (cornflour)
6	large eggs, separated
1	cup (200 g) sugar

1. Preheat the oven to 300°F (150°C/gas 2).

2. To prepare the crust, butter a 10-inch (25-cm) springform pan. Mix the crumbs with the butter and press firmly into the bottom of the pan. Refrigerate while you prepare the filling.

3. To prepare the filling, beat the ricotta in a large bowl with an electric mixer at medium speed until creamy. Add the mascarpone, sour cream, vanilla, lemon zest, and lemon juice, and beat again. Sprinkle with the cornstarch and mix thoroughly. Beat in the egg yolks and half the sugar with mixer at low speed until well blended.

4. Whisk the egg whites in a clean bowl until they form soft peaks. Whisk in the remaining sugar until stiff and glossy. Fold the egg whites into the cheese mixture with a large metal spoon. Spoon the mixture onto the crust.

5. Bake for 80 minutes without opening the oven door, or until the edges are golden brown and the center set. Turn off the heat and leave the cheesecake in the oven for 2 more hours.

6. Chill in the refrigerator for at least 2 hours—best overnight.

White Chocolate and Almond Cheesecake ▷

German Cheesecake with Streusel Berry Topping

Genuine German cheesecake is made with quark, now available in some supermarkets. If you can't find quark, use cream cheese or curd cheese instead. Streusel is a crumble mix that is sprinkled on top of cakes before baking. Replace the berries in the crumbly streusel topping here with any of the fruit toppings given below.

Serves: 8–10 • Prep: 35–40 min. + 1 hr. setting + 3 hr. chilling • Cooking: 60–90 min. • Level: 2

BASE
4	ounces (125 g) ladyfingers, finely crushed, or 10-inch (25-cm) store-bought sponge flan base
1/2	cup (120 g) salted butter (optional; for ladyfinger crust)

FILLING
3	large eggs
3/4	cup (150 g) granulated sugar
1 1/2	pounds (750 g) quark or cream cheese
1	pound (500-g) crème fraîche
2	teaspoons vanilla extract (essence)
1	teaspoon finely grated lemon zest
2	tablespoons freshly squeezed lemon juice
3	tablespoons semolina
3	tablespoons golden raisins (sultanas) (optional)
8	ounces (250 ml) heavy (double) cream

STREUSEL BERRY TOPPING
2/3	cup (100 g) all-purpose (plain) flour
1/3	cup (75 g) firmly packed light brown or Demerara sugar
3/4	cup (75 g) blanched hazelnuts, roughly chopped
1/3	(90 g) salted butter, melted
1	pound (500 g) cherries, pitted, or 1 pound (500 g) bottled or canned black cherries, well drained, or 1 cup (250 g) blueberries

1. To prepare the base, butter the bottom and sides of a 10-inch (25-cm) springform pan. If you are using ladyfinger crumbs, melt the butter in a saucepan, stir in the crumbs, and mix together. Press the crumbs into the bottom and around the sides of the springform pan. Chill in the refrigerator while you are making the filling. If you are using a sponge flan, press the sponge round into the base of the pan, so it fits tightly. Make sure the sponge covers the rim around the pan bottom, so the filling mixture doesn't seep out during baking.

2. Preheat the oven to 325°F (170°C/gas 3).

3. To prepare the filling, beat the eggs and sugar with an electric mixer until creamy. Beat in the quark, crème fraîche, vanilla, lemon zest, lemon juice, and semolina until smooth. Stir in the golden raisins, if using. Whisk the cream in a separate bowl, until thickened. Fold the whipped cream into the quark mixture with a large metal spoon. Pour the mixture into the pan and spread evenly on the base.

4. To prepare the topping, mix the flour, brown sugar, and hazelnuts in a small bowl. Drizzle the melted butter into the flour mix. Stir with a fork until the mixture comes together in small buttery lumps. Sprinkle over the cake top.

5. Bake for 60–90 minutes on the lowest oven rack, until the top is golden brown. Turn the oven off and leave the door ajar. Let the cake rest in the oven for 1 hour, to set. Refrigerate for at least 3 hours, or overnight, until very firm.

6. Loosen the cake by running a knife inside the rim of the pan. Slide a palette knife under the base and transfer to a cake plate.

APPLE TOPPING
3	apples, peeled, cored, and thinly sliced
1–2	tablespoons flaked almonds

Arrange the apple slices, close together and overlapping, on top of the cake. Sprinkle with almonds. Bake as directed above.

PLUM TOPPING
1 1/2	pounds (750 g) plums, pitted (stoned) and halved or quartered
1–2	tablespoons flaked almonds

Arrange the plums, cut side up, in circles on top. Sprinkle with almonds. Bake as directed above.

APRICOT OR PEACH TOPPING
12	ripe apricots, pitted (stoned) and halved or 4–6 peaches, pitted (stoned) and thickly sliced

Arrange the fruit rounded side up. Bake as directed above.

PEAR TOPPING
4–5	pears, peeled, cored, and quartered

Arrange the pears, rounded side up and overlapping. Bake as directed above.

German Cheesecake with Streusel Berry Topping ▷

Upside-Down Rhubarb Cake

Rhubarb is native to Asia and it is mentioned in Chinese books on herbal medicine dating to almost 5,000 years ago. Ginger is often used in rhubarb recipes because it enhances the flavor. Serve this cake warm with whipped cream or crème fraîche.

Serves: 4–6 • Prep: 20 min. + 10 min. cooling • Cooking: 25–35 min. Level: 2

¼	cup (60 g) unsalted butter
1	cup (200 g) firmly packed light brown sugar
½	teaspoon ground ginger
12	ounces (350 g), trimmed rhubarb stalks, cut into 1-inch (2.5-cm) pieces
1⅓	cups (200 g) all-purpose (plain) flour
1	teaspoon baking powder
¼	teaspoon baking soda (bicarbonate of soda)
¼	teaspoon salt
¾	cup (180 ml) buttermilk
2	tablespoons sour cream
2	large eggs
⅓	cup (90 ml) vegetable oil
1	teaspoon vanilla extract (essence)
2	tablespoons candied ginger, finely chopped

1. Preheat the oven to 350°F (180°C/gas 4).

2. Melt the butter in a 9½-inch (24-cm) cast-iron frying pan or tarte tatin dish over medium heat. Add ½ cup (100 g) of the brown sugar and the ground ginger and simmer for 3–5 minutes, stirring constantly. Remove from the heat and spoon the rhubarb on top of the caramelized sugar.

3. Mix the flour, baking powder, baking soda, and salt in medium bowl. Beat the remaining ½ cup (100 g) brown sugar with the buttermilk, sour cream, eggs, oil, and vanilla extract in electric mixer fitted with a wire whisk until well mixed. Stir in the candied ginger. Beat in the flour mixture with the mixer on low speed until well combined. Pour over the rhubarb in the pan and smooth the top.

4. Bake for 20–30 minutes, until the cake is golden brown and springy when you press it in the center. Allow to cool for 10 minutes.

5. Run a knife around the edges of the pan, place a large dish on top, and then swiftly turn it over, so the cake is turned upside down onto the serving plate.

◄ **Upside-Down Rhubarb Cake**

Chocolate Cookie Torte

Serves: 6–8 • Prep: 20 min. + 4 hr. chilling • Cooking: 6–8 min. • Level: 2

14	marshmallows (pink and white preferred)
¼	cup (50 g) golden raisins (sultanas)
¼	cup (50 g) candied (glacé) cherries, halved
¼	cup (45 g) dried apricots, coarsely chopped
1	tablespoon candied orange peel
1	cup (100 g) hazelnuts or almonds, coarsely chopped
1	tablespoon brandy
1½	cups (185 g) oatmeal (sweet oat) cookies or graham crackers, roughly crushed
8	ounces (200 g) bittersweet or dark chocolate, broken into pieces
½	cup (125 g) unsalted butter
	Unsweetened cocoa powder, for dusting
⅔	cup (150 ml) heavy (double) cream, whipped

1. Lightly oil an 8-inch (20-cm) springform pan. Line with waxed paper.

2. Snip each marshmallow with oiled kitchen scissors into 4 or 5 pieces and place in a large bowl. Add the golden raisins, candied cherries, apricots, orange peel, and nuts. Sprinkle with the brandy and stir together. Stir in the cookies.

3. Combine the chocolate and butter in double boiler over barely simmering water. Stir occasionally until melted, 6–8 minutes. Remove the pan from the heat and give the chocolate mixture a good stir. Let it cool for 2 minutes and then pour it over the fruit and cookie mixture. Mix together well with a spatula or wooden spoon.

4. Spoon the mixture into the cake pan as evenly as possible and press the mixture down firmly. Cover with plastic wrap (cling film) and refrigerate for at least 4 hours.

5. Loosen the pan sides and peel off the paper. Place on a serving plate and dust the top with cocoa powder. Serve with the whipped cream.

Frosted Zucchini Cake

If you are using mature zucchini (or courgettes, as they are also known outside of North America), with well developed seeds, cut each zucchini in half lengthwise and scrape out the seeds before grating. Do not peel the zucchini before grating.

Serves: 8–10 • Prep: 25 min. + 1 hr. cooling • Cooking: 45 min. • Level: 1

CAKE

1	cup (150 g) all-purpose (plain) flour
1/2	cup (75 g) whole-wheat (wholemeal) flour
1	teaspoon baking powder
1	teaspoon baking soda (bicarbonate of soda)
1/4	teaspoon salt
1/2	cup (125 g) unsalted butter, softened
1	cup (150 g) sugar
1	tablespoon finely grated lemon zest
1	teaspoon lemon extract (essence)
2	large eggs
1 1/2	cups (225 g) grated zucchini (courgette)
1/4	cup (30 g) dried apricots, finely chopped
1/4	cup (60 ml) milk

FROSTING

1/2	cup (60 g) finely chopped dried apricots
3/4	cup (180 ml) water
8	ounces (250 g) cream cheese, softened
1	cup (150 g) confectioners' (icing) sugar
2	tablespoons freshly squeezed lemon juice

1. Preheat the oven to 350°F (180°C/gas 4). Butter a 9-inch (23-cm) square baking pan. Line with waxed paper. Butter the paper.

2. To prepare the cake, mix both flours, baking powder, baking soda, and salt in a bowl. Beat the butter, sugar, lemon zest, and lemon extract with an electric mixer at medium speed until creamy. Add the eggs, one at a time, beating until just blended after each addition. With mixer at low speed, beat in the zucchini, apricots, and dry ingredients, alternating with the milk. Spoon the batter into the pan.

3. Bake for about 45 minutes, or until a toothpick inserted into the center comes out clean. Cool the cake in the pan for 10 minutes. Turn out onto a rack. Remove the paper and let cool completely.

4. To prepare the frosting, simmer the apricots and water over low heat until the apricots are soft. Set aside to cool. Beat the cream cheese, confectioners' sugar, and lemon juice in a large bowl. Stir in the apricot mixture. Spread the cake with the frosting.

Citrus Honey Cake

If you don't have the time to prepare the Vanilla Crème Anglaise (custard), beat 1 cup (250 ml) of heavy (double) cream with 2 tablespoons of confectioners' (icing) sugar and 1/2 teaspoon vanilla extract. Spread this mixture over the finished cake instead of the custard.

Serves: 8–10 • Prep: 30 min. + 5 min. cooling • Cooking: 40 min. • Level: 1

CAKE

2	cups (300 g) all-purpose (plain) flour
2	teaspoons baking powder
1/2	teaspoon salt
1	cup (250 g) unsalted butter, softened
1	cup (150 g) sugar
2	tablespoons finely grated orange zest
3	large eggs

TOPPING

1/3	cup (90 ml) honey
1	cup (125 g) chopped mixed candied peel
1/2	cup (120 g) slivered almonds
1	teaspoon ground ginger

2	cups (500 ml) Vanilla Crème Anglaise (see page 279)

1. Preheat the oven to 375°F (190°C/gas 5). Butter a 9-inch (23-cm) square baking pan.

2. To prepare the cake, mix the flour, baking powder, and salt in a large bowl. Beat the butter, sugar, and orange zest in a large bowl with an electric mixer at medium speed until creamy. Add the eggs, one at a time, beating until just blended after each addition. With mixer at low speed, beat in the dry ingredients. Spoon the batter into the prepared pan.

3. Bake for about 35 minutes, or until a toothpick inserted into the center comes out clean.

4. While the cake is baking, prepare the topping. Warm the honey in a medium saucepan over medium heat. Stir in the candied peel, almonds, and ginger.

5. Spread the cake with the topping and bake for 5 more minutes. Cool the cake in the pan on a rack for 5 minutes. Cut into portions and place on individual serving plates. Spoon a little of the custard over each dish and serve warm.

Frosted Zucchini Cake ▷

Apple and Blackberry Dessert Cake

This is a hearty cake, just right for cold winter evenings. Serve it warm with the yogurt and fresh berries to enhance the flavors.

Serves: 8 • Prep: 25 min. + 15 min. cooling • Cooking: 1 hr. • Level: 1

2	large eggs
1	cup (200 g) granulated sugar
⅓	cup (150 g) unsalted butter, melted and cooled
1½	cups (225 g) all-purpose (plain) flour
2	teaspoons baking powder
½	teaspoon salt
3	medium apples, peeled, cored and thinly sliced
1½	cups (250 g) fresh blackberries
¼	cup (40 g) hazelnuts, coarsely chopped
2	tablespoons Demerara sugar
1	cup (250 ml) plain yogurt

1. Preheat the oven to 325°F (170°C/gas 3). Lightly grease an 8-inch (20-cm) round springform cake pan with oil or nonstick cooking spray.

2. Beat the eggs and granulated sugar with an electric mixer fitted with a whisk until pale and creamy. Pour in the melted butter and stir using a wooden spoon to combine. Sift in the flour, baking powder, and salt and stir to combine until it forms a batter.

3. Pour half the batter into the prepared pan. Arrange the apples and 1 cup of the blackberries on top. Pour the remaining batter over the fruit layer and sprinkle the top with the hazelnuts and Demerara sugar.

4. Bake for 1 hour, or until the cake springs back when touched. Allow to cool for 15 minutes in the pan. Remove from the pan and slice into eight wedges.

5. To serve, place the wedges onto serving plates with a dollop of yogurt to the side and a few of the reserved fresh blackberries to garnish.

Nutty Pear Sheet Cake

Serves: 8–10 • Prep: 30 min. + 1 hr. cooling • Cooking: 50 min. • Level: 1

TOPPING

½	cup (100 g) firmly packed brown sugar
⅓	cup (50 g) all-purpose (plain) flour
1	teaspoon ground cinnamon
¼	cup (60 g) unsalted butter
1	cup (100 g) hazelnuts, coarsely chopped

CAKE

1½	cups (225 g) all-purpose (plain) flour
1	teaspoon baking powder
1	teaspoon ground cinnamon
½	teaspoon baking soda (bicarbonate of soda)
¼	teaspoon salt
½	cup (125 g) unsalted butter, softened
1	cup (200 g) sugar
½	teaspoon lemon extract (essence)
2	large eggs
1	cup (250 ml) sour cream
2	large firm-ripe pears, peeled, cored, and diced

1. Preheat the oven to 350°F (180°C/gas 4). Butter and flour a 13 x 9-inch (33 x 23-cm) baking pan.

2. To prepare the topping, stir together the brown sugar, flour, and cinnamon in a medium bowl. Use a pastry blender to cut in the butter until the mixture resembles fine crumbs. Stir in the hazelnuts.

3. To prepare the cake, mix the flour, baking powder, cinnamon, baking soda, and salt in a medium bowl. Beat the butter, sugar, and lemon extract in a large bowl with an electric mixer at medium speed until creamy. Add the eggs, one at a time, beating until just blended after each addition. With mixer at low speed, beat in the dry ingredients, alternating with the sour cream. Stir in the pears. Spoon the batter into the prepared pan. Sprinkle with the topping.

4. Bake for about 50 minutes, or until a toothpick inserted into the center comes out clean. Cool the cake completely in the pan on a rack.

Apple and Blackberry Dessert Cake ▷

LAYER CAKES
AND ROLLS

These light, creamy cakes and rolls make ideal desserts.

Studded with fruit and layered with creamy fillings, they

make an eye-catching finish to any meal. In this chapter

you will learn how to bake and prepare a perfect sponge

roll (see page 81). Here you will find our recipe for the

creamy classic Black Forest Cake (see page 74). For

those with gluten intolerance, we have included a

delicious recipe for a Gluten-Free Lemon Layer Cake

(see page 87).

◁ Raspberry Almond Torte (see page 76)

Black Forest Cake

This scrumptious chocolate layer cake comes from the Black Forest region of southern Germany. There are many variations, but the classic recipe consists of several layers of chocolate cake interspersed with cherries and cream. Kirsch, a clear, cherry brandy, is also used to flavor the cake.

Serves: 12 · Prep: 1 hr. + 1 hr. chilling and cooling · Cooking: 30 min. Level: 2

CAKE
- 1 cup (225 g) unsalted butter, softened
- 1 cup (225 g) superfine (caster) sugar
- 4 large eggs, beaten
- 2 tablespoons cocoa powder
- 1 teaspoon instant espresso powder
- 2 tablespoons water
- 1⅓ cups (200 g) self-rising flour

CHERRY FILLING
- 1 (24-ounce/680-g) jar pitted morello cherries
- 1½ teaspoons arrowroot
- 2 tablespoons Kirsch

CREAM FILLING
- 2 cups (500 ml) heavy (double) cream
- 1 tablespoon confectioners' (icing) sugar
- 1 teaspoon vanilla sugar
- 1 teaspoon Kirsch

TOPPING
- 1 cup (250 ml) heavy (double) cream
- 1 tablespoon confectioners' (icing) sugar
- 1 teaspoon Kirsch
- 2 tablespoons black cherry jam
- 4 ounces (125 g) bittersweet or dark chocolate, flaked or coarsely grated

1. Preheat the oven to 350°F (180°C/gas 4). Lightly butter and line the bottom of two 8-inch (20-cm) round cake pans with parchment paper.

2. Beat the butter and the superfine sugar with an electric mixer in a large mixing bowl until pale and fluffy. Gradually add the eggs, beating well after each addition. Blend the cocoa and espresso powder with the water to form a paste, and beat in alternately with the flour. Divide the mixture equally between the two pans and smooth the tops.

3. Bake for 30 minutes, until the cakes are firm but springy to the touch. Cool for 5 minutes, then turn out onto a rack to finish cooling.

4. To prepare the cherry filling, drain the cherries, reserving the juice in a bowl. Blend the arrowroot with ½ cup (125 ml) of the reserved cherry juice. Pour into a small saucepan and gradually bring to a boil, stirring. Remove from the heat and stir continuously until the mixture thickens. Add the Kirsch and allow to cool. Mix with the cherries, reserving 12 for decoration. Keep chilled in the refrigerator until needed.

5. To prepare the cream filling, beat the cream in a large bowl with an electric mixer on high speed until thickened. Add the confectioners' sugar and vanilla sugar. Continue to beat until soft peaks form. Fold in the Kirsch.

6. To assemble the cake, trim the dome from both cake tops to level the surface. Slice the cakes horizontally in half. Place one layer crumb-side upward; this will be the bottom layer. Divide the cherry mixture among three layers (including the bottom layer), spreading it on evenly. The fourth cake layer remains plain for now. Top each cherry mixture with whipped cream. Warm the cherry jam and spread it over the uncut side of the plain layer.

7. Place the bottom layer on a serving plate with a spatula, and top with the two cherry and cream layers, cut side down, cream side up. Finally, top with the fourth layer, cut side down and jam side up. Refrigerate the assembled cake for 30 minutes to firm the filling.

8. Meanwhile, beat the cream for the topping with the confectioners' sugar and the Kirsch until stiff. Spread the side and jam-covered top of the cake evenly with cream. If you have a piping bag, fit it with a star nozzle and pipe swirls around the top edge. Mark the cake with the back of a knife into twelve triangular portions and pipe twelve stars around the top edge—one for each slice. Place a cherry on each piped star. Alternatively, just pile the cherries up on top of the cake.

9. Decorate with chocolate, pressing it all around the side and sprinkling the top. Chill until you are ready to serve.

Black Forest Cake ▷

Cream Sponge with Passion Fruit Frosting

If you prefer a smooth and creamy frosting, strain the passion fruit pulp through a fine metal sieve before combining with the confectioners' sugar and butter.

Serves: 6–8 • Prep: 30 min. + 30 min. cooling • Cooking: 20 min. • Level: 2

SPONGE CAKE
- 1 cup (150 g) cornstarch (cornflour)
- 3 tablespoons all-purpose (plain) flour
- 1/2 teaspoon baking powder
- 1/4 teaspoon salt
- 4 large eggs, separated
- 3/4 cup (150 g) sugar

FROSTING
- 1 1/2 cups (225 g) confectioners' (icing) sugar
- 6 tablespoons passion fruit pulp
- 1 tablespoon unsalted butter, melted
- 1 cup (250 g) Chantilly Cream (see page 86)

1. Preheat the oven to 375°F (190°C/gas 5). Butter two 8-inch (20-cm) round cake pans. Line with parchment paper.

2. Combine the cornstarch, flour, baking powder, and salt in a small bowl.

3. Beat the egg yolks and sugar in a large bowl with an electric mixer at high speed until pale and thick. Use a large rubber spatula to fold in the dry ingredients.

4. Beat the egg whites in a clean, large bowl with an electric mixer on high speed until stiff peaks form. Fold them into the batter. Divide the batter between the prepared pans.

5. Bake for about 20 minutes, or until a toothpick inserted into the center comes out clean. Cool the cakes in the pans for 5 minutes. Turn out onto racks. Carefully remove the paper and let cool completely.

6. To prepare the frosting, combine the confectioners' sugar, passion fruit pulp, and butter in a medium bowl until smooth and spreadable. Place one cake layer on a serving plate. Spread with the Chantilly Cream. Top with the remaining cake layer. Spread with the frosting.

Raspberry Almond Torte

This handsome torte tastes as good as it looks (see the photograph at the beginning of the chapter). For the best taste, use fresh raspberries.

Serves: 6–8 • Prep: 35 min. + 30 min. cooling • Cooking: 40–45 min. Level: 2

- 1/2 cup (75 g) all-purpose (plain) flour
- 1 tablespoon cornstarch (cornflour)
- 3 large eggs
- 1/2 cup (100 g) superfine (caster) sugar
- 1 tablespoon vanilla sugar
- 3/4 teaspoon almond extract (essence)
- 1 cup (110 g) finely ground almonds
- 2 cups (500 g) Chantilly Cream (see page 21)
- 4–5 cups (750 g) fresh raspberries (or 1 1/2 pounds/750 g) frozen raspberries, thawed and well drained
- 2 1/2 cups (250 g) almonds, toasted and coarsely chopped, to decorate

1. Preheat the oven to 350°F (180°C/gas 4). Butter an 8-inch (20-cm) deep cake pan and line the bottom with parchment paper.

2. Mix the flour and cornstarch in a small bowl and set aside. Combine the eggs with the superfine sugar, vanilla sugar, and almond extract in a large bowl. Beat with an electric mixer at high speed for about 5 minutes. When the mixture is thick enough to hold its shape for just a second, fold in the flour mixture with a metal spoon. Sprinkle with the ground almonds and fold in. Spoon the batter into the prepared pan and smooth the surface.

3. Bake for 40–45 minutes, until the cake is lightly golden, springy to the touch, and shrinks from the side of the pan. Leave to cool in the pan for 5–10 minutes, then turn out onto a wire rack to cool completely.

4. To assemble the cake, cut the sponge horizontally into three even layers. Place the bottom layer on a serving plate. Mix one-third of the Chantilly Cream with the raspberries. Reserve some raspberries for decoration.

5. Spread the first and second layers of the sponge with the raspberry cream. Top with the last layer of cake. Spread the Chantilly Cream over the cake. Press the almonds onto the side and sprinkle on top. Decorate with the reserved raspberries.

Cream Sponge with Passion Fruit Frosting ▷

Walnut Layer Cake

Serve this cake with strong black coffee. The walnuts and cream cheese filling blend beautifully with the aroma of coffee.

Serves: 6–8 · Prep: 25 min. + 30 min. cooling · Cooking: 25 min. · Level 1

CAKE

4	large eggs
2/3	cup (130 g) superfine (caster) sugar
3/4	cup (120 g) all-purpose (plain) flour
1	teaspoon baking powder
1/4	teaspoon salt
1½	cups (150 g) walnuts, finely chopped
1/2	teaspoon vanilla extract (essence)
1/4	teaspoon rum extract (essence)
2	tablespoons (30 g) unsalted butter, melted

FROSTING

8	ounces (250 g) white chocolate, coarsely chopped
1/4	cup (60 g) unsalted butter
1	package (8 ounces/250 g) cream cheese, softened
2/3	cup (100 g) confectioners' (icing) sugar
4	tablespoons toasted walnuts, finely chopped
12	walnut halves, to decorate

1. Preheat the oven to 350°F (180°C/gas 4). Lightly butter three 7-inch (18-cm) cake pans and line the bottoms with parchment paper.

2. Beat the eggs and sugar with an electric mixer fitted with a whisk in a large bowl set over hot water for 5–8 minutes, until the beater leaves a trail across the surface. Combine the flour, baking powder, salt, and walnuts in a bowl. Fold into the egg and sugar mixture, and stir in the vanilla, rum extract, and butter with sweeping movements, making sure the mixture remains airy. Divide the batter among the pans.

3. Bake for 25–30 minutes, until a skewer inserted in the center of one comes out clean. Leave in the pans for 5 minutes, then turn out onto wire racks to cool. Carefully peel off the parchment paper.

4. To prepare the frosting, melt the chocolate and butter in a double boiler over barely simmering water. Let cool. Whip the cream cheese until smooth in a separate bowl, and gradually beat in the confectioners' sugar. Add to the chocolate and beat again. Refrigerate for 10 minutes. Place one cake on a plate, cover with frosting and sprinkle with chopped walnuts. Repeat with the next two cakes. Spread the rest of the frosting over the top and sides. Decorate with walnut halves.

Caramel Layer Cake

Keep this cake chilled in the refrigerator. Take out about 30 minutes before serving.

Serves: 10-12 · Prep: 35 min. + 30 min. cooling · Cooking: 50 min. · Level: 2

CAKE

3	cups (450 g) all-purpose (plain) flour
2	teaspoons baking powder
1	teaspoon baking soda (bicarbonate of soda)
1/2	teaspoon salt
1	cup (250 g) unsalted butter, softened
1½	cups (300 g) firmly packed brown sugar
2	teaspoons caramel or butterscotch flavoring
5	large eggs, separated
1	cup (250 ml) milk

CARAMEL FROSTING

2	cups (400 g) firmly packed brown sugar
1¼	cups (310 ml) milk
5	tablespoons unsalted butter

FILLING

1	cup (250 ml) Chantilly Cream (see page 86)

1. Preheat the oven to 350°F (180°C/gas 4). Butter a deep 10-inch (25-cm) springform pan.

2. Combine the flour, baking powder, baking soda, and salt in a large bowl and mix well. Beat the butter, brown sugar, and caramel flavoring in a large bowl until creamy. Add the egg yolks, beating until just blended. Gradually beat in the dry ingredients and milk. Beat the egg whites in a large bowl with an electric mixer on high speed until stiff peaks form. Fold into the batter. Spoon the batter into the pan.

3. Bake for 40–45 minutes, until golden brown. Cool in the pan for 15 minutes. Remove the sides and place on a rack to cool.

4. To prepare the frosting, bring the brown sugar and milk to a boil over medium heat. Stir until the sugar has dissolved. Cook until it registers 234–240°F (112–115°C) on a candy thermometer. Remove from the heat. Stir in the butter and let cool slightly.

5. Split the cake in three horizontally. Spread one layer with half the filling. Top with a second layer and spread with the remaining filling. Top with the remaining layer. Spread the top and sides with frosting.

Walnut Layer Cake ▷

Rich Chocolate Roulade

This delicious cake has no flour so is perfect for people with gluten intolerance. Be sure to use a good-quality chocolate from a reliable manufacturer of gluten-free chocolate. Keep the cake chilled in the refrigerator and take out about 30 minutes before serving.

Serves: 6–8 · Prep: 25 min. + 30 min. cooling · Cooking: 25 min. · Level 3

ROLL
- 8 ounces (250 g) bittersweet chocolate, coarsely chopped
- 8 large eggs, separated
- 1¼ cups (250 g) sugar
- ¼ teaspoon salt

RICH CHOCOLATE FROSTING
- 1 pound (500 g) bittersweet chocolate, coarsely chopped
- 1 cup (250 ml) heavy (double) cream
- 1 teaspoon vanilla extract (essence)
- 2 cups (300 g) confectioners' (icing) sugar

1. Preheat the oven to 350°F (180°C/gas 4). Butter a 10 x 15-inch (25 x 35-cm) jelly-roll pan. Line with parchment paper.

2. To prepare the roll, melt the chocolate in a double boiler over barely simmering water. Let cool.

3. Beat the egg yolks and sugar in a large bowl until pale and thick. Gradually beat in the chocolate. Beat the egg whites and salt in a large bowl until stiff peaks form. Fold them into the chocolate mixture. Spoon the batter into the prepared pan.

4. Bake for about 20 minutes, or until springy to the touch. Cool the cake in the pan for 5 minutes.

5. To prepare the frosting, melt the chocolate, cream, and vanilla together in a double boiler over barely simmering water. Sift in the confectioners' sugar and stir until combined. Strain the frosting through a sieve to remove lumps and refrigerate for 30 minutes, or until cooled and thickened.

6. Roll up the cake following the instructions here. Unroll the cake and spread with half the frosting. Reroll the cake and spread with the remaining frosting.

ROLLING A JELLY ROLL STEP-BY-STEP

Rolling a roulade or jelly roll is not difficult but it does require a gentle touch and a little patience. Rolled up and filled with whipped cream, a liqueur cream, or simple preserves, roulades always make a wonderful presentation.

1 Lay out a large kitchen towel or cloth on a flat surface. Sprinkle with 2–3 tablespoons of confectioners' (icing) sugar.

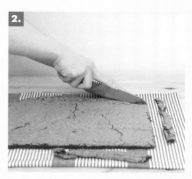

2 Carefully remove the parchment paper from the cake and use a knife to cut away the crisp edges.

3 Use the cloth as a guide to roll up the cake. Stand seam-side down until cooled.

4 Unroll the cake and use a spatula to spread the filling, leaving a border around the edges. Reroll the cake using the cloth as a guide and stand seam-side down.

5 Spread the roll with frosting or remaining filling, as required by the recipe.

Spiced Jelly Roll with Apple Filling

This is a lovely sponge roll. The ginger and cinnamon in the cake go beautifully with the lemon-flavored apple filling.

Serves: 6–8 Prep: 25 min. + 30 min. cooling · Cooking: 15 min. · Level: 2

SPICED JELLY ROLL
- 1 cup (150 g) cake flour
- 1 teaspoon baking powder
- 1 teaspoon ground cinnamon
- 1 teaspoon ground ginger
- 3 large eggs, separated
- ½ cup (100 g) sugar
- ¼ teaspoon salt

FILLING
- 2 large tart green apples, peeled, cored, and chopped
- ¼ cup (60 ml) water
- 2 tablespoons sugar
- 1 tablespoon freshly squeezed lemon juice
- 1 cup (250 ml) heavy (double) cream
- 6 tablespoons confectioners' (icing) sugar

1. Preheat the oven to 375°F (190°C/gas 5). Butter a 10 x 15-inch (25 x 35-cm) jelly-roll pan. Line with parchment paper. Mix the cake flour, baking powder, cinnamon, and ginger in a medium bowl.

2. Combine the egg yolks and sugar in a large bowl and beat with an electric mixer at high speed until pale and thick. Beat the egg whites and salt in a clean, large bowl with an electric mixer on high speed until stiff peaks form. Fold them into the egg yolk mixture. Gradually fold the dry ingredients into the batter. Spoon the batter into the pan.

3. Bake for about 15 minutes, or until the top is springy to the touch.

4. Dust a clean kitchen towel with confectioners' sugar. Turn the cake out onto the towel. Roll up the cake, following the instructions on page 81. Leave, seam side down, until cool.

5. To prepare the filling, bring the apples and water to a boil in a saucepan. Cover and simmer until tender, 10–15 minutes. Stir in the sugar and lemon juice. Drain off almost all the juice and let cool.

6. Beat the cream in a large bowl until stiff. Unroll the cake and spread with the cream. Spoon the apples over the cream. Reroll the cake. Dust with the confectioners' sugar.

Coffee Cream Jelly Roll

Both of the rolls on this page are best if filled about an hour or two before serving (just before beginning the meal). This allows the filling to penetrate the cake a little; but don't leave them for much longer otherwise they can become soggy.

Serves: 6–8 · Prep: 30 min. + 1 hr. cooling · Cooking: 20 min. · Level: 2

COFFEE CREAM ROLL
- 1 cup (150 g) all-purpose (plain) flour
- 1 teaspoon baking powder
- ¼ teaspoon salt
- 3 large eggs
- 1 cup (200 g) sugar
- ¼ cup (60 g) unsalted butter, melted
- 1 tablespoon instant coffee granules, dissolved in 2 tablespoons water

FILLING
- 2 tablespoons instant coffee granules
- 2 cups (500 ml) Chantilly Cream (see page 21)

1. Preheat the oven to 400°F (200°C/gas 6). Butter a 10 x 15-inch (25 x 35-cm) jelly-roll pan. Line with parchment paper.

2. Combine the flour, baking powder, and salt in a large bowl and mix well.

3. Beat the eggs and 1 cup (200 g) of the sugar in a large bowl with an electric mixer at high speed until pale and thick. With the mixer at low speed, gradually beat in the dry ingredients, alternating with the melted butter and coffee mixture. Spoon the batter into the prepared pan.

4. Bake for about 20 minutes, or until the top is springy to the touch.

5. Dust a clean kitchen towel with confectioners' sugar. Turn the cake out onto the towel. Roll up the cake, following the instructions on page 81. Leave, seam side down, until cool.

5. To prepare the filling, stir the coffee into the Chantilly Cream. Unroll the cake and spread evenly with the coffee-flavored Chantilly Cream. Reroll the cake.

Spiced Jelly Roll with Apple Filling ▷

Chocolate Roll with Lemon Curd

This cake is gluten-free. Be sure to use a good-quality chocolate from a reliable manufacturer of gluten-free chocolate. If you are using store-bought lemon curd, add 2-3 teaspoons of freshly squeezed lemon juice to add extra flavor.

Serves: 6–8 • Prep: 30 min. + 30 min. chilling + 2 hr. cooling • Cooking: 12–15 min. • Level: 3

CHOCOLATE ROLL
- 4 large eggs
- $3/4$ cup (150 g) superfine (caster) sugar
- $1/3$ cup (50 g) unsweetened cocoa powder
- 2 tablespoons rice flour
- $1/4$ cup (60 g) butter, melted
- 2 tablespoons grated dark chocolate
  Confectioners' (icing) sugar, for dusting

FILLING
- 1 package (8 ounces/250 g) cream cheese, softened
- $2/3$ cup (100 g) confectioners' (icing) sugar, sifted
- 2 tablespoons freshly squeezed lemon juice + 2–3 teaspoons extra if using store-bought curd
- $1/4$ cup (60 g) lemon curd (see page 276)

1. Preheat the oven to 350°F (180°C/gas 4). Line the bottom and sides of a 13 x 9-inch (33 x 23-cm) baking pan or jelly-roll pan with parchment paper. Oil the paper lightly.

2. Beat the eggs, superfine sugar, and vanilla in a bowl with an electric mixer fitted with a whisk until pale and thick. Sift the rice flour and cocoa together and fold into the egg mixture. Gently fold in the melted butter. Spoon the batter into the pan.

3. Bake for about 20 minutes, or until springy when pressed in the center. Leave the cake in the pan for 5 minutes to cool. Dust a clean kitchen towel with confectioners' sugar. Turn the cake out onto the towel. Roll up the cake, following the instructions on page 81. Leave, seam side down, until cool.

4. To prepare the filling, beat the cream cheese until smooth. Add the confectioners' sugar, lemon juice, and lemon curd (with additional juice if required) beating well. Spread the lemon curd cream over the cake and roll up. Transfer to a serving plate and dust with confectioners' sugar and sprinkle with the grated chocolate. Chill for 30 minutes before serving.

◁ **Chocolate Roll with Lemon Curd**

Vanilla Roulade with Chocolate Hazelnut Filling

Serves: 6–8 • Prep: 30 min. + 1 hr. cooling + 2 hr. chilling • Cooking: 15 min. • Level: 3

- 4 large eggs, separated
- 1 cup (150 g) confectioners' (icing) sugar + extra, for dusting
- 1 teaspoon vanilla extract (essence)
- $1/3$ cup (50 g) all-purpose (plain) flour
- 2 tablespoons cornstarch (cornflour)
- $1/4$ teaspoon salt
- 3 tablespoons (45 ml) rum
- $3/4$ cup (180 g) chocolate hazelnut spread (Nutella)
- 4 tablespoons shaved or grated dark chocolate

1. Preheat the oven to 350°F (180°C/gas 4). Line a 10 x 15-inch (25 x 35-cm) jelly-roll pan with parchment paper.

2. Beat the egg yolks, confectioners' sugar, and vanilla in a large bowl until pale and creamy. Fold in the flour and cornstarch.

3. Combine the egg whites and salt in a clean, large bowl and beat with an electric mixer at high speed until stiff. Gently fold them into the batter. Spoon the batter into the prepared pan.

4. Bake for about 15 minutes, or until risen and golden.

5. Dust a clean kitchen towel with confectioners' sugar. Turn the cake out onto the towel. Roll up the cake, following the instructions on page 81. Leave, seam side down, until cool.

6. Unroll the sponge. Drizzle with the rum and cover with the chocolate spread. Roll up using the towel as a guide. Wrap the roulade in foil. Chill for 2 hours.

7. Unwrap and transfer to a serving dish. Dust with the confectioners' sugar and sprinkle with the flakes of chocolate.

Chocolate Sponge with Chantilly Filling

Classic and simple, serve this chocolate sponge after lunch or dinner with a fresh fruit coulis (see Raspberry Coulis on page 278).

Serves: 6–8 · Prep: 25 min. + 1 hr. cooling · Cooking: 30 min. · Level: 2

SPONGE

1	cup (150 g) all-purpose (plain) flour
4	tablespoons unsweetened cocoa powder
1	teaspoon baking powder
1/4	teaspoon salt
4	large eggs, separated
3/4	cup (150 g) sugar
1/4	cup (60 ml) milk
2	cups (500 g) Rich Chocolate Frosting (see page 81)

CHANTILLY CREAM

1/2	cup (125 ml) heavy (double) cream
2	tablespoons confectioners' sugar
1/2	teaspoon vanilla extract (essence)

1. Preheat the oven to 375°F (190°C/gas 5). Butter two 8-inch (20-cm) round cake pans. Line with parchment paper.

2. Combine the flour, cocoa, baking powder, and salt in a medium bowl and mix well.

3. Beat the egg yolks and sugar in a large bowl with an electric mixer at high speed until pale and thick. With the mixer at low speed, gradually beat in the dry ingredients, alternating with the milk.

4. With mixer at high speed, beat the egg whites in a clean, large bowl until stiff peaks form. Fold them into the batter. Divide the batter between the prepared pans.

5. Bake for about 30 minutes, or until the cakes are springy to the touch and shrink from the pan sides.

6. Cool the cakes in the pans for 5 minutes. Turn out onto racks. Carefully remove the paper and let cool completely.

7. To prepare the chantilly cream, beat the cream confectioners' sugar, and vanilla in a medium bowl with an electric mixer on high speed until soft peaks form.

8. Place one cake layer on a serving plate and spread with the chantilly cream. Top with the remaining cake layer. Spread the top and sides with the frosting.

Raspberry Cream Roulade

Serves: 6–8 · Prep 25 min. + 1 hr. cooling · Cooking: 25 min. · Level: 2

ROLL

1	cup (150 g) all-purpose (plain) flour
1 1/2	teaspoons baking powder
1/4	teaspoon salt
3	large eggs, separated
3/4	cup (150 g) sugar
1	teaspoon vanilla extract (essence)
1/4	cup (60 ml) milk
1/4	teaspoon cream of tartar

FILLING

1	cup (250 g) fresh raspberries
1 1/2	cups (375 ml) heavy (double) cream
1/4	cup (50 g) sugar
1/4	cup (25 g) pistachios, coarsely chopped
4	tablespoons confectioners' (icing) sugar, to dust

1. Preheat the oven to 400°F (200°C/gas 6). Butter and flour a 10 x 15-inch (25 x 35-cm) jelly-roll pan. Line with parchment paper.

2. Combine the flour, baking powder, and salt in a medium bowl. Combine the egg yolks, sugar, and vanilla in a large bowl and beat with an electric mixer at high speed until pale and thick. With the mixer at low speed, gradually beat in the dry ingredients, alternating with the milk. Beat the egg whites and cream of tartar in a clean, large bowl with an electric mixer at high speed until stiff peaks form. Gently fold them into the batter. Spoon the batter into the pan.

3. Bake for about 15 minutes, or until the top is springy to the touch.

4. Dust a clean kitchen towel with confectioners' sugar. Turn the cake out onto the towel. Roll up the cake, following the instructions on page 81. Leave, seam side down, until cool.

5. To prepare the filling, purée the raspberries in a food processor until smooth. Strain out the seeds. Beat the cream and sugar in a large bowl until stiff. Fold in the raspberries and pistachios. Unroll the cake and spread with the filling. Reroll the cake. Place on a serving dish and dust with the confectioners' sugar.

Gluten-Free Lemon Layer Cake

Some brands of baking powder contain wheat flour or starch. Be sure to check the label when buying.

Serves: 8–10 · Prep 25 min. + 1 hr. cooling and chilling · Cooking: 35–40 min. · Level: 2

CAKE
1	cup (150 g) brown rice flour
½	cup (75 g) white rice flour
½	cup (75 g) tapioca starch (flour)
½	cup (75 g) potato starch
½	teaspoon salt
1	tablespoon baking powder
1	teaspoon xanthan gum
1	cup (250 ml) milk
1	cup (250 ml) canola oil
1	teaspoon vanilla extract (essence)
1	tablespoon finely grated fresh lemon zest
2	cups (400 g) sugar
4	large eggs

LEMON CURD
2	teaspoons finely grated fresh lemon zest
¼	cup (60 ml) freshly squeezed lemon juice
¼	cup (50 g) sugar
3	large egg yolks
¼	teaspoon guar gum
⅛	teaspoon salt
¼	cup (60 g) unsalted butter, cut into pieces
¼	teaspoon lemon extract (essence)

LEMON FROSTING:
1	cup (250 g) unsalted butter, softened
3½	cups (500 g) confectioners' (icing) sugar
¼	cup (60 ml) freshly squeezed lemon juice
½	teaspoon lemon extract (essence)
2	teaspoons finely grated fresh lemon zest

1. Preheat the oven to 375°F (190°C/gas 5). Butter two 9-inch (23-cm) round cake pans. Line with parchment paper. Oil the paper.

2. To prepare the cake, combine both rice flours, the tapioca starch, potato starch, salt, baking powder, and xanthan gum in a large bowl. Stir the milk, canola oil, vanilla, and zest in another bowl.

3. Beat the sugar and eggs in a large bowl with an electric mixer at medium speed just until combined, about 1 minute. With mixer on low speed, add the flour and milk mixtures alternately in batches, mixing until just combined. Divide the batter evenly between the prepared cake pans, smoothing the tops.

4. Bake for 35–40 minutes, until a wooden pick or skewer inserted into the center comes out clean.

5. Cool the cakes in pans on racks 10 minutes. Remove from the pan, peel off the parchment paper, and let completely.

6. To prepare the lemon curd, beat the lemon zest, lemon juice, sugar, yolks, salt, and guar gum in a 4-cup (1-liter) saucepan. Add butter and simmer over low heat, whisking constantly, until the curd is thick enough to hold marks of the whisk and tiny bubbles appear on the surface, about 5 minutes. Beat in the lemon extract. Pour the curd into a bowl. Cover the surface with plastic wrap (cling film) and chill until cold, about 30 minutes.

7. To prepare the frosting, beat the butter with an electric mixer at high speed until light and fluffy, about 1 minute. With mixer on low, add the confectioners' sugar, lemon juice, extract, and zest, and mix until creamy and smooth, about 2 minutes.

8: Use a long serrated knife to cut each layer in half horizontally. Spread the bottom half of each cake layer with half the lemon curd, then top with the remaining cake layers to form two sandwiched cakes. Put one sandwiched cake on a plate and spread with ½ cup (125 g) of frosting. Cover with the remaining sandwiched cake. Frost the top and sides of the cake with the remaining frosting.

PIES AND TARTS

Tarts and pies are classic desserts and favorites throughout the year. Their fillings vary according to the season, with rhubarb and fresh fruit tarts perfect for spring and summer, and apple and pumpkin pie classics for the fall and winter. Generally lighter and more sophisticated, tarts have a sweeter crust and less filling than pies. They are baked in shallow pans with removeable bottoms. Pies are usually more substantial and often have a second crust enclosing the filling.

◁ Orange Tart with Bitter Chocolate Sorbet (see page 107)

Apple Pie

Serves: 6 · Prep: 30 min. + 30 min. to chill · Cooking: 40 min. · Level 1

SHORTCRUST PASTRY
(for 1 double-crust 9-inch/23-cm pie)

2½   cups (375 g) all-purpose (plain) flour
½   teaspoon salt
⅔   cup (150 g) unsalted butter or
      ⅓ cup (90 g) butter and ⅓ cup (90 g) vegetable shortening
6–8   tablespoons ice water + more as needed

FILLING

1½   pounds (750 g) tart apples or cooking apples (6–8 medium-sized)
½   cup (100 g) sugar + 1 tablespoon, for sprinkling
1   tablespoon freshly squeezed orange juice or lemon juice
2   tablespoons all-purpose (plain) flour
½   teaspoon ground cinnamon
1–2   tablespoons milk, to glaze

1. Prepare pastry for a double-crust pie following the step-by-step instructions below. Refrigerate for at least 30 minutes.

2. Preheat the oven to 425°F (220°C/gas 7) and put a baking sheet in at the same time.

3. To prepare the filling, peel, core, and slice the apples. Mix them with the sugar, orange juice, flour, and cinnamon.

3. Divide the pastry into two disks, one slightly larger than the other. Lightly dust a work surface with flour and roll out the larger piece to fit into a 9-inch (23-cm) pie pan. Lift it into the pan by rolling it up on the floured rolling pin, then slowly unrolling it over the pan. Press the pastry into the corners and around the bottom and sides, allowing the extra pastry to overhang the edge of the pan. Spoon the filling into the pastry.

4. Roll out the smaller disk of pastry for the lid. Wet the pastry rim in the pan with water and place the pie lid on top. Press the lid firmly onto the rim and pinch the edges together to seal. Trim away any excess dough. Make two slits in the top to let the steam out. Brush with milk and sprinkle with sugar.

5. Place the pie on the baking sheet and bake for 10 minutes. Decrease the heat to 375°F (190°C/gas 5) and bake for 30 minutes, or until the pastry is golden.

6. Serve warm or cold.

SHORTCRUST PASTRY STEP-BY-STEP

Make piecrust as quickly as possible, before the ingredients have time to warm. It is best to use a food processor, if you have one. The entire mixing job should not take longer than 1 minute.

1 Place the flour and salt in the bowl of a food processor and pulse briefly to combine. Add the butter and pulse until the mixture resembles coarse crumbs, about 10 seconds. With the machine running, slowly add enough ice water to obtain a smooth dough.

1A If you are mixing by hand, combine the flour and salt in a large bowl or on a clean work surface. Use a pastry blender to cut in the butter until the mixture resembles coarse crumbs. Slowly add enough ice water to obtain a smooth dough.

2 Press the dough together into a ball and flatten into a disk shape. Wrap in plastic wrap (cling film) and chill in the refrigerator for at least 30 minutes, or up to 2 days, before rolling.

Lemon Tart

**Serves: 6-8 · Prep: 25 min. + 30 min. chilling · Cooking: 50-60 min.
Level: 1**

SWEET TART PASTRY
1⅓	cups (200 g) all-purpose (plain) flour
¼	teaspoon salt
⅓	cup (50 g) confectioners' (icing) sugar
½	cup (125 g) cold unsalted butter, cut in small cubes
1	large egg yolk
1-2	tablespoons water, as required

FILLING
	Freshly squeezed juice of 6-8 lemons
6	large eggs
1¼	cups (250 g) superfine (caster) sugar
	Finely grated zest of 3 lemons
¾	cup (200 ml) heavy (double) cream

1. To prepare the pastry, mix the flour, salt, and confectioners' sugar in a medium bowl. Cut in the butter with a pastry blender, until the mixture resembles fine bread crumbs. Add the yolk and knead lightly until the ingredients come together and form a firm dough. Add enough water to obtain a smooth dough. Press into a log, wrap in plastic wrap (cling film), and chill in the refrigerator for at least 30 minutes.

2. Preheat the oven to 400°F (200°C/gas 6). Lightly oil a 9-inch (23-cm) fluted tart pan with a removeable bottom.

3. To line the pan, unwrap the dough and place on a lightly floured work surface. Roll the dough out until it is about 2 inches (5 cm) larger than the tart pan. Roll the dough loosely onto the rolling pin and unroll it evenly over the tart pan. Press the pastry evenly around the bottom and sides to a thickness of ⅛-¼ inch (3-5 mm). Pinch the edges to rise ⅛ inch (3 mm) above the edge of pan. Prick the bottom with a fork. Refrigerate for 30 minutes.

4. Line the tart shell with parchment paper and fill with pie weights or dried beans. Bake for 10 minutes, remove the parchment and beans, and bake for another 5-10 minutes, until light brown and dry to the touch. Remove from the oven and leave to cool.

5. Decrease the oven temperature to 300°F (150°C/gas 2) and place a baking sheet in the oven.

6. To prepare the filling, strain the lemon juice and measure out ¾ cup (180 ml). Break the eggs into a bowl, add the superfine sugar, and beat for a few seconds—the mixture shouldn't be frothy. Pour in the lemon juice, zest, and cream, and whisk lightly until smooth.

7. Transfer the filling to a large pitcher (jug) that holds 1¼ quarts (1.2 liters). Pour into the cooled pastry shell. Bake for 35-40 minutes, until the tart is just set but still trembles a little in the center.

8. Leave to cool completely before removing from the pan.

LINING A TART PAN AND BAKING THE TART SHELL STEP-BY-STEP

1 When the dough is rolled to the desired size, roll it loosely around the rolling pin and drape it over the prepared tart pan.

2 Lift up the edges of the dough and press with your fingertips so that the dough adheres to the pan.

3 Cover the dough with a large piece of parchment paper and fill with dried beans or pie weights.

4 Pour the filling into the baked tart crust ready for final baking.

Red Currant Meringue Tart

Red currants make a striking filling in this pie, but if they are not available use black currants or gooseberries instead.

Serves: 8 • Prep: 50 min. + 30 min. chilling • Cooking: 35–45 min. • Level: 2

ALMOND PASTRY
2/3 cup (150 g) unsalted butter, softened
1/2 cup (100 g) superfine (caster) sugar
1 tablespoon vanilla sugar
1/4 teaspoon almond extract (essence)
4 large egg yolks, beaten
1 cup (100 g) finely ground almonds
1 3/4 cups (275 g) all-purpose (plain) flour
Pinch of salt

FILLING
3 cups (500 g) red currants, stems removed
1/2 cup (100 g) superfine (caster) sugar

MERINGUE TOPPING
4 large egg whites
2/3 cup (125 g) superfine (caster) sugar

1. Lightly butter and flour a 9-inch (23-cm) deep round tart pan with a removeable bottom.

2. To prepare the pastry, combine all the pastry ingredients in a food processor and process to form a stiff dough. Firmly press the dough into the bottom and sides of the pan. Prick all over with a fork. Chill in the refrigerator for 30 minutes.

3. Preheat the oven to 375°F (190°C/gas 5). Bake for 25–30 minutes, until firm and golden. Leave to cool. Increase the oven temperature to 425°F (220°C/gas 7).

4. To prepare the filling, mix the red currants with the superfine sugar in a bowl and set aside. To prepare the meringue, beat the egg whites in a large bowl with an electric mixer with a whisk attachment until stiff peaks form. Gradually beat in the superfine sugar.

5. Pile spoonfuls of meringue around the edges of the pastry. Pile the red currant mixture up in the middle and spoon the remaining meringue on top. Bake for 10–15 minutes, until the tips of the meringue are lightly browned and the crust is just firm. Serve warm or cold.

Chocolate Cherry Tart

Serves: 6–8 • Prep: 30 min. + 3 hr. chilling • Cooking: 8–10 min. Level: 1

CHOCOLATE PASTRY
1 cup (250 g) salted butter, softened
1 cup (250 g) superfine (caster) sugar
1/2 teaspoon vanilla extract (essence)
1 2/3 cup (250 g) all-purpose (plain) flour
2/3 cup (100 g) unsweetened cocoa powder

CHERRY FILLING
1 1/2 cups (185 g) shredded (dessicated) coconut
1/2 cup (50 g) finely ground almonds
1 cup (180 g) candied (glacé) cherries, coarsely chopped
2 tablespoons light rum
1/2 cup (125 ml) sweetened condensed milk

8–12 whole candied (glacé) cherries, for garnish

1. To prepare the pastry, beat the butter and superfine sugar in an electric mixer on medium-high speed, stopping and scraping down the sides occasionally, until pale and creamy. Mix in the vanilla. Sift together the flour and cocoa into a medium bowl. Stir into the butter mixture to form a dough.

2. Lightly grease a 9 1/2-inch (24-cm) tart pan with a removeable bottom. Press the dough into the tart pan to create a 1/8-inch (3-mm) thick shell. Cover and refrigerate for 1 hour.

3. Preheat the oven to 325°F (170°C/gas 3).

4. Line the tart shell with parchment paper and fill with pie weights or dried beans. Bake for 8–10 minutes, until almost firm. Let cool.

5. To prepare the filling, combine the coconut, ground almonds, chopped cherries, rum, and condensed milk in a medium bowl and mix well. Spoon into the tart shell, pressing down with the back of a wooden spoon to level. Refrigerate for 2 hours, or until firm.

6. To serve, slice the tart into six to eight wedges and place onto serving plates with a candied cherry to garnish.

Red Currant Meringue Tart ▷

Grapefruit Meringue Pie

For an attractive pinkish-red filling, use ruby red grapefruit juice.

Serves: 6–8 • Prep: 30 min. + 1 hr. cooling • Cooking: 10 min. Level: 2

1	recipe Sweet Tart Pastry (see page 92)

FILLING AND TOPPING

½	cup (100 g) superfine (caster) sugar
1	tablespoon (15 ml) lemon juice, strained
1	teaspoon finely grated ruby red grapefruit zest
¼	cup (60 ml) freshly squeezed grapefruit juice, strained
3	large eggs, separated
¼	cup (60 g) cold unsalted butter, cubed
¼	teaspoon vanilla extract (essence)
¾	cup (180 ml) heavy (double) cream, whipped

1. Prepare the pastry and bake the tart shell as explained in the text in steps 1–4 on page 92.

2. To prepare the filling, increase the oven temperature to 375°F (190°C/gas 5). Combine ¼ cup (50 g) of the superfine sugar with the lemon juice and grapefruit zest and juice in a small saucepan over medium heat and stir until the sugar has dissolved.

3. Whisk the egg yolks together in a heatproof bowl and gradually add the hot grapefruit mixture. Strain the mixture through a fine-mesh sieve and return to the heatproof bowl. Place over a saucepan of simmering water and cook, stirring continuously, until the mixture thickens to coat the back of a wooden spoon. Do not allow the mixture to boil. Remove from the heat and stir in the butter cubes, one at a time, until fully combined. Pour the hot mixture into the prepared tart shell and set aside.

4. To prepare the meringue topping, beat the egg whites and vanilla with an electric mixer with a whisk until stiff peaks form. Gradually add the remaining ¼ cup (50 g) superfine sugar a little at a time, beating until the meringue becomes thick and glossy. Spoon the meringue topping over the grapefruit filling, using a spatula to create wave-like peaks.

5. Bake for 10 minutes, or until light golden. Remove from the oven and cool to room temperature. Serve with the whipped cream.

Passion Fruit and Coconut Tart

Serves: 6–8 • Prep: 15 min. + 1 hr. cooling • Cooking: 40 min. • Level: 1

1	recipe Sweet Tart Pastry (see page 92)

FILLING

2	large eggs
1	cup (200 g) superfine (caster) sugar
½	cup (125 g) mascarpone
½	cup (125 ml) cream of coconut
½	cup (125 ml) passion fruit pulp
2½	cups (560 g) shredded (desiccated) coconut
¾	cup (180 ml) heavy (double) cream, whipped, to serve

1. Prepare the pastry and bake the tart shell as explained in the text in steps 1–4 on page 92.

2. To prepare the filling, whisk the eggs and superfine sugar together until light and fluffy. Stir in the mascarpone, cream of coconut, passion fruit pulp, and coconut with a wooden spoon until combined.

3. Pour the filling into the prepared tart shell. Bake for 40 minutes, or until golden. Allow to set and cool for 1 hour before to serving.

4. To serve, slice the tart into six or eight wedges and place onto individual serving plates with a dollop of whipped cream on the side.

Grapefruit Meringue Pie ▷

Apricot Tart

A scoop of vanilla ice cream goes well with this tart. We have given a fairly broad range in the cooking time for this tart; the time will depend on how ripe the fruit is. Ripe fruit will cook more quickly than less mature fruit.

Serves: 6–8 · Prep: 35 min. + 1½–2 hr. chilling · Cooking: 40–55 min. Level: 2

ALMOND PASTRY

½   cup (75 g) almonds, blanched
⅔   cup (150 g) unsalted butter, chilled and diced
¼   cup (50 g) superfine (caster) sugar
¼   teaspoon almond extract (essence)
1   cup (150 g) all-purpose (plain) flour
⅛   teaspoon salt

FILLING

3   pounds (1.5 kg) ripe apricots (about 16–20), halved and pitted (stoned)
1   tablespoon granulated sugar
3–4   tablespoons apricot preserves (jam)
1–2   teaspoons confectioners' (icing) sugar, for dusting (optional)

1. To make the pastry, finely chop the almonds in a food processor. Add the butter, superfine sugar, and almond extract and pulse until combined. Add the flour and salt in three batches, pulsing for 30 seconds after each batch. When the dough comes together in a ball, wrap in plastic wrap (cling film) and shape into a 6-inch (15-cm) disk. Wrap and chill in the refrigerator for 1 hour.

2. Butter and lightly flour a 10-inch (25-cm) tart pan with a removeable bottom. Unwrap the pastry and place in the center of the pan. Firmly press the pastry into the bottom and up the sides of the pan to a thickness of ¼ inch (5 mm) using the floured palms of your hands. Prick the tart shell all over with a fork. Return to the refrigerator for 30–60 minutes.

3. Preheat the oven to 425°F (220°C/gas 7). Line the pastry shell with parchment paper and fill with pie weights or dried beans. Bake for 15 minutes. Decrease the heat to 325°F (170°C/gas 3). Remove the lining paper and beans. Bake for 5–8 minutes, until golden. Let cool.

4. Increase the oven temperature to 350°F (180°C/gas 4). Arrange the apricot halves, cut side up and overlapping in the tart shell. Sprinkle with granulated sugar. Bake for 15–25 minutes, until the apricots are soft. Warm the apricot preserves in a small pan and brush or drizzle over the apricots. Bake for 2–3 minutes more. Serve warm or cold, lightly dusted with confectioners' sugar.

Gooseberry Tart

If liked, serve this pie hot with whipped cream or vanilla ice cream.

Serves: 6 · Prep: 40 min. + 1 hr. 15–30 min. chilling · Cooking: 50–60 min. · Level: 2

1   recipe Sweet Tart Pastry (see page 92)

FILLING

3   large eggs
½   cup (100 g) golden or plain superfine (caster) sugar
3   tablespoons vanilla sugar
1   cup (250 mm) heavy (double) cream
3   tablespoons sour cream or crème fraîche
1   pound (500 g) gooseberries, topped and tailed
Confectioners' (icing) sugar, for dusting

1. Prepare the pastry as explained in the text in step 1 on page 92. Set the pastry aside to chill.

2. Dust a large piece of parchment paper with flour. Place the pastry on the flour, dust with flour, and cover with another piece of parchment. Roll out the pastry to fit a deep 9- or 10-inch (23- or 25-cm) round or rectangular tart pan. Remove the paper and, lifting the pastry over the rolling pin, place it in the pan. Push the pastry into the bottom and corners of the pan and up the sides, patching any holes where necessary. Prick the pastry all over with a fork. Refrigerate for 15–30 minutes.

3. Preheat the oven to 350°F (180°C/gas 4).

4. Line the tart shell with parchment paper and fill with pie weights or dried beans. Bake for 15 minutes. Remove the lining and beans and bake for another 10 minutes, or until golden. Set aside to cool.

5. To prepare the filling, whisk the eggs, superfine and vanilla sugars, cream, and sour cream in a bowl. Fill the pastry shell with gooseberries. Pour the egg and cream mixture over the berries.

6. Bake for 25–35 minutes, until just firm in the center.

7. Leave to cool and set slightly for 10 minutes before eating. Dust with confectioners' sugar and serve warm.

Apricot Tart ▷

Blueberry Tart

Serves: 6–8 • Prep: 15 min. + 30 min. cooling • Level: 1

1   recipe Sweet Tart Pastry (see page 92)

FILLING
2   tablespoons honey
2   tablespoons crème de cassis or blueberry liqueur
1½ pounds (750 g) blueberries
1   cup (250 g) mascarpone
⅓   cup (90 ml) heavy (double) cream
¼   cup (50 g) granulated sugar

1. Prepare the pastry and bake the tart shell as explained in the text in steps 1–4 on page 92. Let the tart shell cool for 30 minutes.

2. To prepare the filling, heat the honey and liqueur in a small saucepan over medium heat, stirring until combined. Pour over the blueberries.

3. Beat together the mascarpone, cream, and sugar with an electric mixer fitted with a whisk until stiff peaks form. Spoon the mixture into the tart shell, spreading it smooth with a spatula. Pile the blueberries on top.

4. Serve as soon as possible after you have put the filling in the tart crust so that it remains crisp.

Banoffee Pie

Banoffee pie is an English dessert made from bananas, cream, and boiled condensed milk (or dulce de leche). Its name is a combination of "banana" and "toffee."

Serves: 6–8 • Prep: 30 min. + 1½ hr. chilling and cooling • Cooking: 45 min. • Level: 1

½   recipe Shortcrust Pastry (see page 91)

FILLING
1   14 ounce (400-g) can sweetened condensed milk
⅓   cup (70 g) firmly packed dark brown sugar
3   large bananas
1   cup (250 ml) heavy (double) cream
2   tablespoons confectioners' (icing) sugar

1. Prepare the pastry. Shape the dough into a ball, cover in plastic wrap (cling film), and refrigerate for at least 30 minutes.

2. Preheat the oven to 325°F (170°C/gas 3). Lightly grease a 9½-inch (24-cm) tart pan with a removeable bottom.

3. Roll out the pastry on a lightly floured surface to a thickness of ⅛ inch (3 mm). Lift it into the pan by rolling it up on the floured rolling pin, then slowly unroll it over the pan. Press the pastry into the corners and around the bottom and sides and trim away the excess. Refrigerate for 30 minutes.

4. Line the tart shell with parchment paper and fill with pie weights or dried beans. Bake for 25 minutes, or until light golden. Set aside to cool.

5. Combine the condensed milk and brown sugar in a small saucepan over medium-low heat and cook, stirring, for 20 minutes, or until it becomes a thick caramel sauce. Remove from the heat, allow to cool a little, then refrigerate until chilled.

6. Pour the chilled caramel sauce into the prepared tart shell. Peel and slice the bananas and arrange on top of the caramel.

7. Beat together the cream and confectioners' sugar with an electric mixer fitted with a whisk until it forms stiff peaks. Spoon the whipped cream on top of the banana layer and use a spatula create decorative peaks. Refrigerate until you are ready to serve.

◁ **Banoffee Pie**

Melktert

A traditional Dutch tart with a pastry cream filling. To prepare the pastry, use our Sweet Tart pastry recipe on page 92. If liked, replace the water with the same quantity of milk.

Serves: 6–8 · Prep: 40 min. + 1 hr. 15 min. cooling + infusing · Cooking: 30–40 min. · Level: 2

1	recipe Sweet Tart Pastry (see page 92)

FILLING
1²/₃	cups (400 ml) heavy (double) cream
¼	cup (60 g) unsalted butter
1	vanilla pod, split
1	2-inch (5-cm) piece cinnamon stick
4	medium eggs, separated
½	cup (100 g) firmly packed light brown sugar
1	teaspoon vanilla extract (essence)
2	tablespoons all-purpose (plain) flour
2	tablespoons cornstarch (cornflour)

TOPPING
⅓	cup (75 g) firmly packed dark brown sugar
1	tablespoon ground cinnamon
¼	teaspoon ground ginger

1. Prepare the pastry and bake the tart shell as explained in the text in steps 1–4 on page 92. Let the tart shell cool for 30 minutes.

2. To prepare the filling, combine the cream, butter, vanilla, and cinnamon in a saucepan over medium-low heat. Bring to a boil. Remove from the heat and leave to infuse for 15 minutes.

3. Beat the egg yolks, brown sugar, and vanilla with an electric mixer fitted with a whisk until very thick. Beat in the flour and cornstarch. Strain the cream into a pitcher (jug). Gradually add to the egg mixture, whisking to make a thick sauce. Pour the mixture into the pan. Bring to a boil over medium heat, stirring all the time. Lower the heat and simmer gently for 2–3 minutes, still stirring as the cream thickens. Remove from the heat and let cool a little. Whisk the egg whites into soft peaks. Fold into the cream and pour into the pastry shell.

5. To prepare the topping, mix the brown sugar, cinnamon, and ginger in a small bowl and sprinkle over the filling. Bake for 20–30 minutes, until set and crusty on top. Cool for 30 minutes before serving.

Tiramisù Tart

Serves: 6–8 · Prep: 30 min. + 30 min. cooling · Cooking: 25 min. · Level: 2

1	recipe Sweet Tart Pastry (see page 92)

FILLING
1½	cups (375 g) mascarpone cheese
½	cup (125 ml) heavy (double) cream
½	cup (100 g) superfine (caster) sugar
½	cup (125 ml) brewed espresso
¼	cup (60 ml) amaretto (almond liqueur)
10	ladyfinger cookies
3	ounces (90 g) dark chocolate

1. Prepare the pastry and bake the tart shell as explained in the text in steps 1–4 on page 92. Let the tart shell cool for 30 minutes.

2. To prepare the filling, beat the mascarpone, cream, and superfine sugar in a medium bowl with an electric mixer fitted with a whisk until stiff peaks form. Spoon one-third of the cream mixture into the prepared tart shell.

3. Combine the espresso and amaretto in a small bowl. Soak the ladyfingers in the mixture for a few seconds, then arrange on top of the cream layer. Spoon the remaining cream over the top and use a spatula or the back of a spoon to create a smooth surface.

3. Finely grate the chocolate on top of the tart just before serving.

Melktert ▷

Pear and Frangipane Tart

Serve this delicious tart with crème fraiche or vanilla ice cream.

Serves: 6–8 · Prep: 40 min. + 30 min. cooling · Cooking: 35–40 min. Level: 3

- 1   recipe Sweet Tart Pastry (see page 92)

FILLING
- ⅓   cup (90 g) butter, softened
- ½   cup (100 g) firmly packed light brown sugar
- ½   teaspoon almond extract (essence)
- 2   large eggs, beaten
- 1   cup (100 g) ground almonds
- 2   tablespoons self-rising flour
- 4   tablespoons greengage or yellow plum preserves
- 4   firm ripe pears

GLAZE
- 2   tablespoons clear apple jelly
- 1   teaspoon lemon juice
     Confectioners' (icing) sugar, to dust

1. Prepare the pastry and bake the tart shell as explained in the text in steps 1–4 on page 92. Let the tart shell cool for 30 minutes.

2. Decrease the oven temperature to 350°F (180°C/gas 4).

3. To prepare the filling, combine the butter, brown sugar, and almond extract in a medium bowl. Beat with an electric mixer at medium speed until smooth and creamy. Beat in the eggs, one at a time. Beat in the almonds and flour.

4. Spread the apple preserves over the bottom of the pastry shell and pour in the almond mixture. Smooth the surface with a palette knife.

5. Peel, halve, and core the pears. Place each half cut-side down on a cutting board. Slice thinly lengthwise. Arrange in a fan shape on top of the filling. Bake for 35–40 minutes, until the filling is set and golden.

6. To prepare the glaze, heat the jelly and lemon juice in a small saucepan over low heat for 1–2 minutes, or until bubbling. Spread the glaze over the warm tart. Leave for 10 minutes, then remove from the pan. Dust with confectioners' sugar.

Apple and Gingered Rhubarb Pie

Serves: 6–8 · Prep: 30 min. + 1 hr. 30 min. chilling · Cooking: 55 min. Level: 2

- 1   recipe Shortcrust Pastry (see page 91)

FILLING
- 8   ounces (250 g) rhubarb stalks
- ⅓   cup (70 g) firmly packed light brown sugar
- 2   tablespoons candied (glacé) ginger, finely chopped
- 1   teaspoon finely grated orange zest
- 1   teaspoon ground cinnamon
- 1   pound (500 g) tart apples, such as Granny Smith

     Milk, to glaze
     Demerara sugar, for sprinkling
- 1   cup (250 ml) heavy (double) cream, whipped

1. Prepare the pastry as explained in the text in steps 1–2 on page 91. Divide the dough in two, wrap in plastic wrap (cling film), and chill for 1 hour in the refrigerator.

2. Roll one piece of dough out to a thickness of ⅛ inch (3 mm) and use it to line a 9-inch (23-cm) pie plate. Roll out the other disk to a thickness of ⅛ inch (3 mm) and place it on a plate. Refrigerate both for 30 minutes.

3. Preheat the oven to 400°F (200°C/gas 6).

4. Roughly chop the rhubarb. Combine the rhubarb, brown sugar, ginger, orange zest, and cinnamon in a medium saucepan over medium-low heat. Cook for 15 minutes, or until the rhubarb is softened. Transfer into a large bowl.

5. Peel, core, and slice the apples. Stir into the rhubarb mixture.

6. Remove the tart shell from the refrigerator and fill with the apple and rhubarb mixture. Place the remaining piece of pastry on top and press down with your fingers around the edges to secure. Cut off any excess pastry, brush with milk, and sprinkle with Demerara sugar.

7. Bake for 40 minutes, or until the pastry is golden brown. Serve warm with the whipped cream.

Pear and Frangipane Tart ▷

Orange Tart with Bitter Chocolate Sorbet

This tart can be served by itself, but it is really superb when paired with the chocolate sorbet. The sorbet can be prepared ahead of time and kept in the freezer until you are ready to serve.

Serves: 6–8 · Prep: 30 min. + 45 min. cooling · Cooking: 35 min. · Level: 2

1   recipe Sweet Tart Pastry (see page 92)

FILLING

¼   cup (50 g) superfine (caster) sugar
1   tablespoon (15 mm) freshly squeezed lemon juice, strained
¼   cup (60 mm) freshly squeezed orange juice, strained
1   teaspoon finely grated orange zest
3   large egg yolks
¼   cup (60 g) unsalted butter, chilled and diced

   Bitter Chocolate Sorbet (see page 243), to serve

1. Prepare the pastry and bake the tart shell as explained in the text in steps 1–4 on page 92. Let the tart shell cool for 15 minutes.

2. Decrease the oven temperature to 375°F (190°C/gas 5).

3. To prepare the filling, combine the superfine sugar, lemon juice, orange juice, and orange zest in a small saucepan over medium heat and cook until the sugar has dissolved.

4. Whisk the egg yolks in a heatproof bowl and gradually add the hot orange mixture. Strain the mixture through a fine-mesh sieve. Return to heatproof bowl and place over a saucepan of barely simmering water. Cook, stirring continuously, until the mixture thickens to coat the back of a wooden spoon. Do not allow the mixture to boil. Remove from the heat and stir in the butter cubes, one at a time, until fully combined.

5. Pour the hot mixture into the prepared tart shell. Bake for 10 minutes, or until set. Remove the tart from the oven and set aside to cool to room temperature, about 30 minutes. Serve with a scoop of the sorbet on the side.

Tarte Au Chocolat

Serves: 6–8 · Prep: 40 min. + 45 min. cooling + 2 hr. chilling · Level: 2

1   recipe Sweet Tart Pastry (see page 92)

FILLING

1⅔   cups (400 ml) heavy (double) cream
12   ounces (300 g) dark chocolate (70% cacao), coarsely chopped
1   tablespoon Cointreau or brandy
1   cup (250 g) fresh raspberries, to serve

1. Prepare the pastry and bake the tart shell as explained in the text in steps 1–4 on page 92. Let the tart shell cool for 30 minutes.

2. To prepare the chocolate filling, pour the cream into a heavy saucepan and bring slowly to a boil. As soon as the first bubbles appear, remove from the heat and stir in the chocolate. Add the Cointreau and stir until all the chocolate has melted. Whisk until smooth, and let cool for 15 minutes.

3. Pour into the pastry shell and leave to set for at least 2 hours. Place some raspberries on top of the tart and serve with more raspberries.

◁ **Tarte au Chocolat**

Lemon Meringue Pies

Individual pies are a bit labor-intensive, but these meringue-topped beauties are worth their weight in custard gold.

Serves: 12 • Prep: 25 min. + 1 hr. chilling • Cooking: 35–45 min. • Level: 2

PASTRY

2	cups (300 g) all-purpose (plain) flour
	Pinch of salt
2/3	cup (150 g) unsalted butter
1	large egg, beaten
	Zest and juice of 1 lemon

FILLING

1	tablespoon finely grated lemon zest
3/4	cup (200 ml) freshly squeezed lemon juice, strained
1	teaspoon finely grated lime zest
3	tablespoons freshly squeezed lime juice, strained
1/2	cup (100 g) superfine (caster) sugar
1	cup (250 ml) cold water + 5–6 tablespoons
5	tablespoons cornstarch (cornflour)
3	large egg yolks

TOPPING

3	large egg whites
1/3	cup (75 g) superfine (caster) sugar

Vanilla ice cream, to serve (optional)

1. To prepare the pastry, combine the flour and salt in a medium bowl. Cut in the butter with a pastry blender until the mixture resembles fine bread crumbs. Mix in the egg, zest, and enough lemon juice for the mixture to form a ball. Press the dough into a disk, wrap in plastic wrap (cling film), and chill in the refrigerator for at least 30 minutes.

2. Preheat the oven to 400°F (200°C/gas 6). Set out a deep 12-cup nonstick muffin pan.

3. Roll out the pastry on a lightly floured surface to a thickness of 1/8 inch (3 mm). Use a 4 1/2-inch (11-cm) straight-edged pastry cutter and cut out 12 disks. Line the muffin cups with the pastry rounds. Prick the pastry all over with a fork. Refrigerate for 15–20 minutes.

4. Line each pastry cup with parchment paper or paper liners. Fill with pie weights or dried beans. Bake for 10 minutes. Remove the lining and beans, and return the pastry to the oven for 5–10 minutes, until golden brown. Remove from the oven and leave the pastry to cool.

5. Reduce the heat to 300°F (150°C/gas 2).

6. To prepare the filling, combine the lemon zest and juice and lime zest and juice in a saucepan. Add the superfine sugar and 1 cup water and heat slowly, stirring all the time, until the sugar has dissolved. Mix the cornstarch with enough water (5–6 tablespoons) to make a smooth paste, and gradually stir into the the lemon and lime mixture. Bring to a boil over a medium heat, stirring continuously. Simmer for 1–2 minutes, until thickened, smooth, and glossy. Remove from the heat and leave to cool slightly.

7. Beat in the egg yolks, one at a time. Drop teaspoons of the mixture into the pastry cups and level the surfaces.

8. To prepare the topping, whisk the egg whites in a large, clean bowl until soft peaks form. Gradually add the superfine sugar and whisk until stiff and glossy. Top each the lemon pie with a dollop of meringue mixture, swirling it into a peak with a skewer or fork. Alternatively, pipe the mixture over the filling.

9. Bake for 20–25 minutes, until the meringue is crisp and golden. Serve hot with a scoop of vanilla ice cream on the side.

Lemon Meringue Pies ▷

Fig Frangipane Tart

Bake this tart in late summer and early fall when fresh figs are at their best. You can use green or black figs, whichever are available.

Serves: 6–8 • Prep: 25 min. + 30 min. cooling • Cooking: 40 min. • Level: 2

  1   recipe Sweet Tart Pastry (see page 92)

FILLING
- ½ cup (100 g) superfine (caster) sugar
- 6 tablespoons (90 g) unsalted butter, softened
- ⅓ cup (50 g) all-purpose (plain) flour
- 1½ cups (150 g) ground almonds
- 2 large eggs, beaten
- 1 teaspoon vanilla extract (essence)
- 5-6 ripe figs, halved

  ¾   cup (180 ml) crème fraîche or whipped cream, to serve

1. Prepare the pastry and bake the tart shell as explained in the text in steps 1–4 on page 92.

2. Keep the oven temperature at 400°F (200°C/gas 6).

3. To prepare the filling, combine the superfine sugar, butter, flour, almonds, eggs, and vanilla in a food processor and process until a smooth paste is formed. Spoon this frangipane mixture into the prepared tart shell and smooth using a spatula or the back of a spoon. Arrange the fig halves, cut side up, decoratively over the tart.

4. Bake for 40 minutes, or until the frangipane is golden. Cool to room temperature in the pan. Serve with a dollop of whipped cream on the side.

Mixed Berry Tart

The recipe for this attractive and delicious pie was contributed by food writer and editor Andrea Chesman.

Serves: 6 • Prep: 45 min. + 30 min. chilling + 5 min. cooling • Cooking: 20 min. • Level: 1

  1   recipe Sweet Tart Pastry (see page 92)

FILLING AND TOPPING
- 4 ounces (125 g) cream cheese, softened
- ½ cup (75 g) confectioners' (icing) sugar
- 2 tablespoons double (heavy) cream
- 1 teaspoon finely grated lemon zest
- 1 tablespoon freshly squeezed lemon juice
- 4 strawberries, hulled and sliced
- 3-4 kiwifruit, peeled and sliced
- 1 cup (200 g) blackberries
- 1 cup (200 g) raspberries
- ½ cup (100 g) blueberries
- ⅓ cup (90 g) apple jelly

1. Prepare the pastry and bake the tart shell as explained in the text in steps 1–4 on page 92.

2. Keep the oven temperature at 400°F (200°C/gas 6).

3. To make the filling, beat the cream cheese, confectioners' sugar, whipping cream, lemon zest, and lemon juice until light and well blended. Spread in the cooled tart shell and smooth the tops.

4. Arrange a row of strawberry slices around the outside edge of the tart so that the tips of each slice extend beyond the crust. Lay the kiwifruit slices over the strawberries to partially overlap them. Arrange a standing row blackberries inside the circle of kiwifruit slices. Arrange a standing row of raspberries inside the blackberries. Place the blueberries in the center of the tart, covering the filling. The fruit should cover the filling with concentric circles.

5. Heat the jelly until liquid. Brush the fruit with the melted jelly. Refrigerate the tart for at least 30 minutes before serving.

◁ **Fig Frangipane Tart**

PASTRIES AND YEAST CAKES

Within this chapter you will find an array of desserts made with pastry. They include old favorites such as Baklava (see page 117), two cream puff desserts (see pages 115 and 116), and two delicious mille-feuilles, or Napoleons (see page 118). We have also included Rum Babas with Cinnamon Cream (see page 122) and Apple Crumble Kuchen (see page 124).

◁ **Baklava (see page 117)**

Hazelnut Cream Puffs with Chocolate Sauce

Serves: 6–8 · Prep: 40 min. · 1 hr. cooling · Cooking: 40 min. · Level 2

CHOUX PASTRY
1	cup (250 ml) water
⅓	cup (90 g) butter
1	cup (150 g) all-purpose (plain) flour
2	teaspoons granulated sugar
¼	teaspoon salt
4	large eggs

HAZELNUT CREAM
1	cup (250 ml) light (single) cream
2	tablespoons confectioners' (icing) sugar
2	tablespoons (30 ml) Frangelico or hazelnut liqueur

CHOCOLATE SAUCE
4	ounces (125 g) dark chocolate, coarsely chopped
1	tablespoon (15 ml) water
2	tablespoons (40 g) unsalted butter
⅓	cup (70 g) superfine (caster) sugar

1. Preheat the oven to 400°F (200°C/gas 6).

2. Prepare the choux pastry for the cream puffs following the step-by-step instructions below.

3. Bake for 10 minutes. Decrease the oven temperature to 375°F (190°C/gas 5) and bake for 20 minutes, until puffed and golden brown. Turn the oven off, remove the puffs and cut a slit in the top of each one. Return to the oven and leave to dry out for 10 minutes. Remove and transfer to a wire rack. Let cool completely.

3. To prepare the Hazelnut Cream, whisk the cream in a small bowl until it begins to thicken. Add the confectioners' sugar and Frangelico and continue whipping until the cream is thick enough to hold its shape. Follow step 3 below to fill the cram puffs with the cream.

4. To prepare the Chocolate Sauce, melt the chocolate and water in a small saucepan over low heat. Add the butter and sugar until the sugar has completely dissolved.

5. To serve, place 1–2 cream puffs on each serving plate and drizzle with chocolate sauce.

◁ **Chocolate Roll with Lemon Curd**

CHOUX PASTRY STEP-BY-STEP

Choux pastry (from the French pâte à choux) can be used to make a host of recipes, both sweet and savory. Cream puffs and éclairs are classics and sure to please everyone.

1. Bring the water and butter to a boil in a medium saucepan over medium-low heat. Combine the flour, sugar, and salt in a small bowl. Add to the saucepan, stirring constantly with a wooden spoon for about 5 minutes, or until the mixture comes away from the sides of the pan. Remove from the heat and let cool for 5 minutes. Beat the eggs in, one at a time, until each is fully absorbed. The mixture will form a glossy ball of dough.

2. Line two baking sheets with parchment paper. Fit a pastry bag with a large plain nozzle and fill with the dough. Pipe 16 mounds about the size of a golf ball 2 inches (5 cm) apart onto the prepared baking sheet.

3. Fit a pastry bag with a medium star nozzle and fill with cream. Pipe the cream into each puff and set aside until ready to serve.

Croquembouche

Croquembouche is the French name for a pile of filled cream puffs shaped into a pyramid. This is an impressive centerpiece for a special occasion. You can make the choux puffs a few days in advance and fill them on the day you plan to serve them. Whipped cream is a lighter alternative to the buttercream filling.

Serves: 10–12 • Prep: 50–60 min. + 1 hr. cooling • Cooking: 25–30 min. Level: 3

PASTRY
- 1   recipe Choux Pastry (see page 115)

BUTTERCREAM FILLING
- 4   tablespoons vanilla pudding mix (not instant) or custard powder
- 2   cups (500 ml) milk
- 2   tablespoons granulated sugar
- 1   vanilla pod, split lengthways
- 1   cup (250 g) unsalted butter, softened
- 1   cup (50 g) confectioners' (icing) sugar

FROSTING
- 3   ounces (90 g) dark chocolate, coarsely chopped
- 2   tablespoons (30 g) unsalted butter, diced

1. Preheat the oven to 350°F (180°C/gas 4). Lightly oil 2 large baking sheets or line with parchment paper.

2. Prepare the pastry as shown on page 115. Spoon teaspoonfuls of the pastry into 28–30 little rounds, each about the size of a small walnut, onto the baking sheets. Space them well apart, because they will puff up as they bake. Alternatively, pipe the rounds on, using a pastry bag fitted with 1-inch (2.5-cm) plain tip.

3. Bake for 20–25 minutes, or until golden brown. Remove from the oven and pierce a small hole or make a slit in the side of each puff with a skewer or pin, to release steam. Leave to cool in the turned-off oven with the door ajar for at least 1 hour.

4. To prepare the buttercream, mix the pudding powder with ⅓ cup (90 ml) of the milk and the granulated sugar in a small bowl until smooth. Pour the remaining 1⅔ cups (430 ml) of milk into a saucepan, add the vanilla pod, and bring slowly to a boil.

5. Remove from the heat, discard the vanilla pod, and stir the pudding mixture into the milk. Stir over low heat until the pudding comes to a boil and thickens. Simmer for 1 minute, stirring continuously. Transfer to a clean bowl and leave to cool, placing a piece of plastic wrap (cling film) on top, to prevent a skin forming.

6. Beat the butter with the confectioners' sugar until creamy. Fold spoonfuls of the butter mixture into the cooled pudding, making sure the butter and pudding are the same temperature.

7. When you are ready to fill the puffs, fit a piping bag with a small plain tip. Fill the bag with the buttercream. Insert the tip into each hole or slit (you might have to enlarge it with a small knife) and pipe some filling into each puff. As you fill the puffs, arrange them in a pyramid shape on a large flat plate.

8. To prepare the frosting, melt the chocolate and the butter in the top of a double boiler over barely simmering water. Stir until smooth.

9. Spoon the frosting over the pyramid, letting it drizzle down the sides.

Chocolate Palmiers

Palmiers, or palm leaves, are a crisp puff pastry dessert. This chocolate-flavored version is delicious by itself but can also be served with ice cream or whipped cream.

Serves: 8–10 · Prep: 30 min. + 1 hr. cooling · Cooking: 8–10 min. · Level: 1

1	tablespoon unsalted butter
3	ounces (90 g) dark chocolate, chopped
½	cup (75 g) confectioners' (icing) sugar
8	ounces (250 g) frozen puff pastry, thawed if frozen
⅓	cup (50 g) unsweetened cocoa powder

1. Preheat the oven to 400°F (200°C/gas 6). Line a baking sheet with parchment paper.

2. Melt the butter in a small saucepan over low heat. Add the chocolate and stir until smooth. Set aside to cool.

3. Dust a work surface with half the confectioners' sugar and set the pastry on top. Roll out into a 15 x 12-inch (38 x 30-cm) rectangle. Trim the pastry so that the edges are straight. Fold the pastry in half lengthways to mark the center and unfold it again, leaving a mark down the middle.

4. When the chocolate mixture is thick and cool, pour it onto the pastry, working quickly so that it doesn't set. Use a spatula to spread the chocolate evenly over the pastry. It is important that the chocolate is not too thick otherwise it will leak out during baking. Sift the cocoa over the top.

5. Begin to roll the sides of the pastry rectangle to the middle, where the mark is. Repeat for the other end, until it meets the already rolled half. Roll carefully in the remaining confectioners' sugar and transfer to a plate. Refrigerate for 15 minutes.

6. When the dough is firm, cut across the rolls in ¼-inch (5-mm) thick slices. Place on the prepared baking sheet, spacing them 1 inch (2.5 cm) apart.

7. Bake until golden, 8–10 minutes. Place on wire racks and let cool completely.

Baklava

Variations on this popular Middle Eastern dessert are made throughout the world. Food historians think that it may originally come from Azerbaijan in Central Asia. Whatever its origins, there are now many versions using different combinations of nuts and syrups.

Serves: 6 · Prep: 30 min. 1 hr. cooling · Cooking: 1 hr. · Level: 2

PASTRY

1	cup (120 g) walnuts
½	cup (80 g) pistachios
1	teaspoon ground cinnamon
½	cup (125 g) salted butter, melted
12	filo pastry sheets
2	tablespoons confectioners' (icing) sugar
3	tablespoons finely chopped pistachios

SYRUP

1¼	cups (300 ml) water
1¼	cups (250 g) granulated sugar
2	tablespoons (30 ml) orange blossom water
1	tablespoon (15 ml) rose water

1. Preheat the oven to 350°F (180°C/gas 4). Line a 10½ x 15½-inch (25 x 38-cm) jelly roll pan with parchment paper.

2. Combine the walnuts, pistachio nuts, and cinnamon in a food processor and chop finely. Cut the sheets of filo in half. Keep the pastry covered with a slightly damp cloth. Coat the pan with butter using a pastry brush and lay a sheet of pastry on top. Coat with butter and repeat to layer another 11 sheets of pastry and butter. Sprinkle the nut mixture evenly over the pastry and continue with another 12 layers of filo, coating with butter between each layer, Brush the top with butter. Use a sharp knife to score the top few pastry sheets into 12 diamond-shaped pieces.

3. Bake for 30 minutes. Decrease the oven temperature to 300°F (150°C/gas 2) and bake for 20 more minutes, or until golden.

4. To prepare the syrup, combine the water and sugar in a small saucepan over medium-high heat. Bring to a boil. Decrease the heat and simmer for 10 minutes. Stir in the orange blossom water and rose water and set aside.

5. Remove the baklava from the oven, brush the top with any remaining butter and completely cut through the scored patterns to create 12 pieces. Drizzle with the syrup and leave to cool and absorb the syrup.

6. Dust with confectioners' sugar, and sprinkle with chopped pistachios.

Chocolate Mille-Feuille

This recipe explains how to make a perfect puff pastry—not an easy task, but fun to try. If you are short of time, use 2 pounds (1 kg) of ready-rolled puff pastry instead.

Serves: 10–12 • Prep: 2 hr. • Cooking: 10–15 min. • Level: 3

3	cups (450 g) all-purpose (plain) flour
½	cup (75 g) unsweetened cocoa powder
½	teaspoon salt
1½	cups (375 g) unsalted butter, chopped into small pieces
1¼	cups (300 ml) iced water
3	cups (750 ml) Chocolate Pastry Cream (see page 279)
	Unsweetened cocoa powder, to dust

1. Mix the flour, cocoa, and salt in a large bowl. Stir the butter into the flour, without rubbing it in. Make a well in the center and add half the water. Use your hands to mix together. Add the rest of the water and bring together until it forms a soft dough. The butter should be firm and visible throughout.

2. Turn the dough out onto a floured work surface and roll out into a 6 x 12-inch (15 x 30-cm) rectangle. Take the left side and fold into the middle. Take the right side and fold over the left. You will have a 3-layered vertical rectangle. Make one turn to the left so that the rectangle is horizontal and repeat the process by rolling the dough out again, and folding in the same way. Make a mark on the left-hand side of the dough, cover, and refrigerate for 20 minutes. Remove the dough and, with the mark at the left side, repeat the rolling and folding. Refrigerate once more and repeat the rolling and folding one last time. You will still be able to see the butter layers through the pastry. Let sit for 20 minutes before using.

3. Preheat the oven to 400°F (200°C/gas 6). Oil a baking sheet. Roll out the pastry to a 10 x 12-inch (25 x 30-cm) rectangle about ½-inch (1-cm) thick. Fold the pastry in three to mark equal thirds, and cut along the marks. You will have 3 strips of pastry. Place the pastry on the baking sheet leaving space between the strips. Using a fork, prick the pastry evenly to prevent it from rising too much.

4. Bake for 10–15 minutes, until crisp and well puffed. Place on wire racks and let cool completely. Spread two layers of pastry with chocolate pastry cream. Place one layer on top of the other, and top with the plain layer. Dust with cocoa powder and refrigerate for 20 minutes. Slice with a serrated knife and serve.

Merry Berry Mille-Feuille

Mille-feuille, better known in North America as a Napoleon, is made up of layers of puff pastry, usually filled with vanilla or chocolate pastry cream. A classic French dessert, its original name can be translated as "thousand layer cake" which evokes the idea of lovely crisp sheets of pastry slathered with sweet cream. An excellent, very crisp Napoleon can also be made using phyllo pastry.

Serves: 6–8 • Prep: 50 min. + 80 min. chilling • Cooking: 10–12 min. Level: 2

PASTRY

1	sheet (about 8 ounces/250 g) puff pastry, thawed if frozen
1–2	tablespoons confectioners' (icing) sugar, sifted

FILLING

1	cup (150 g) fresh raspberries
1	cup (150 g) fresh strawberries, sliced
1	teaspoon balsamic vinegar
2	tablespoons superfine (caster) sugar
8	ounces (250 g) mascarpone cheese
3	tablespoons sweetened whipped cream

1. Preheat the oven to 400°F (200°C/gas 6). Line a large baking sheet with parchment paper.

2. Roll out the pastry on a lightly floured surface, cut into two rectangles measuring about 9 x 4 inches (23 x 10 cm), and place on the baking sheet. Prick each pastry rectangle all over with a fork.

3. Bake for 10–12 minutes, until puffed up and golden. Transfer at once to racks and sprinkle evenly with confectioners' sugar. Leave to cool. When completely cold, cut the pastry rectangles in half lengthwise with a serrated knife.

4. To prepare the filling, combine the raspberries and strawberries in a bowl. Add the vinegar and superfine sugar. Stir and set aside for 20 minutes.

5. Whisk together the mascarpone and cream in a large bowl. Stir in the fruit. Refrigerate this mixture for at least 1 hour.

6. Assemble the pastries about an hour before serving. Place a pastry sheet on a serving plate or board and spread with one-third of the filling. Top with another sheet and a layer of filling and press down gently. Repeat the process, finishing with the last pastry sheet on top. Dust with confectioners' sugar. Cut into slices with a serrated knife and serve.

Merry Berry Mille-Feuille ▷

Orange Savarin with Strawberries

Serves: 6 · Prep: 45–55 min. + 1 hr. 30 min. rising · Cooking: 45-55 min.
Level: 2

SAVARIN
- ⅓ cup (90 ml) warm (about 110°F/43°C) milk
- 2 teaspoons active dry yeast
- 3 tablespoons sugar
- 2 cups (300 g) all-purpose (plain) flour
- ½ teaspoon salt
- ⅓ cup (90 g) unsalted butter, softened
- 4 large eggs, lightly beaten

ORANGE SYRUP
- 1 large orange
- 2 cups (500 ml) water
- 1⅓ cups (250 g) sugar
- 1 cup (250 ml) dark rum

TO SERVE
- ⅓ cup (90 g) strawberry preserves (jam)
- 1 tablespoon dark rum
- 2 cups (500 g) fresh strawberries, hulled and halved

1. Prepare the savarin dough following the step-by-step instructions below.

2. Place the dough in a clean, lightly oiled bowl and cover with plastic wrap (cling film). Let rise in a warm place for 1 hour, or until doubled in bulk.

3. Butter a 10-inch (25-cm) savarin pan. Punch down the dough. Place in the prepared pan, spreading it evenly. Cover with a clean cloth and let rise in a warm place for 30 minutes, or until almost doubled in bulk. Preheat the oven to 375°F.

4. Bake for 35–45 minutes, or until golden brown. Cool the savarin in the pan for 15 minutes.

5. To prepare the orange syrup, use a sharp knife to remove the zest from the orange in one long piece. Bring the water, sugar, and orange zest to a boil in a saucepan over medium heat, stirring constantly, until the sugar has dissolved. Simmer for 8 minutes. Remove from the heat and add the rum.

6. Place the cake (still on the rack) over a large plate. Spoon the syrup over the cake until all the syrup has been absorbed. Cool the savarin completely in the pan on a rack.

7. Heat the jelly and rum in a saucepan over low heat. Remove the savarin from the pan and place on a serving plate. Spread with the warm jelly. Decorate with the strawberries.

YEAST DOUGH FOR SAVARIN AND OTHER YEAST CAKES STEP-BY-STEP

There are three main types of yeast available nowadays. Active dry, as we have suggested here, is probably the easiest to store and prepare. Compressed fresh yeast is a good alternative, but make sure it is very fresh, otherwise, the finished dessert may have a sour taste. If you wish to substitute the active dry yeast with fresh yeast for this recipe, you will need ½ ounce (15 g). There are also quick- or rapid-rising yeasts that do not have to be proofed.

1 Stir the milk, yeast, and 1 teaspoon sugar in a small bowl. Set aside for 10 minutes, or until foamy.

2 Put the flour and salt in a large bowl. Stir in the yeast mixture. Add the eggs, butter, and remaining sugar and beat until well blended. Knead in the bowl using a dough hook or flat beater for 5 minutes.

3 To knead by hand, place the sticky ball of dough on a floured work surface and press down. Flip the dough, pick it up, and slam it down on the surface. Repeat until smooth and pliable, about 10 minutes.

Rum Babas with Cinnamon Cream

This is a very old dessert and its origins are thought to pre-date the spread of Christianity in Europe. Records show that it was served at pagan festivals to celebrate the arrival of spring. The name "baba" is the colloquial word for grandma or woman in many Slavic languages.

Serves: 4 · Prep: 45 min. + 2 hr. 45 min. rising · Cooking: 12–15 min. Level: 2

BABAS

2	tablespoons warm (about 110°F/43°C) milk
½	teaspoon active dry yeast
1½	teaspoons sugar + a pinch
½	cup (75 g) all-purpose (plain) flour + 1½ teaspoons
1	large egg
¼	cup (60 g) unsalted butter, softened
2	tablespoons raisins

CINNAMON CREAM

¾	cup (200 ml) heavy (double) cream
2	tablespoons confectioners' (icing) sugar
1	teaspoon ground cinnamon

RUM SYRUP

½	cup (100 g) granulated sugar
¾	cup (180 ml) water
2	tablespoons freshly squeezed orange juice, strained
⅓	cup (90 ml) dark rum

1. To prepare the babas, combine 1 tablespoon of the milk with the yeast and a pinch of sugar in a small bowl. Set aside in a warm place for 5 minutes, or until foamy. Stir 1½ teaspoons of the flour into the yeast mixture, cover with plastic wrap (cling film) and set aside in a warm place for 45–60 minutes, until doubled in size.

2. Transfer the yeast mixture to a food processor fitted with a dough hook. Add the egg, the remaining 1½ teaspoons sugar, the remaining flour, and remaining 1 tablespoon milk. Process for 1–2 minutes, until a dough is formed. Add the butter and process until incorporated.

3. Lightly grease a large bowl. Shape the dough into a ball and add to the bowl. Cover with a clean cloth, and set in a warm place for 45–60 minutes, or until doubled in size.

4. Lightly butter four baba or dariole molds.

5. Add the raisins to the dough and "knock back" or knead for 2–3 minutes, incorporating the raisins into the dough as you knead. Divide the dough into four and place in the prepared molds, filling each one about one-third full.

6. Place the molds on a baking sheet, cover loosely with a clean cloth, and set in a warm place for 30–45 minutes, or until dough has risen to the top of the molds.

7. Preheat the oven to 425°F (220°C/gas 7).

8. Bake the babas for 12–15 minutes, until browned. Remove from the molds and place on a wire rack to cool.

9. To prepare the cinnamon cream, beat the cream with an electric mixer fitted with a whisk on high speed until thickened. Add the confectioners' sugar and cinnamon and beat until soft peaks form and the cream holds its shape. Set aside.

10. To prepare the rum syrup, combine the granulated sugar, water, and orange juice in a small saucepan over medium heat and cook until the sugar dissolves. Remove from the heat and add the rum.

11. Place a baking sheet under the wire rack that holds the babas. One by one, dip the warm babas into the rum syrup, let soak for 10 seconds, then return to the wire rack.

12. Place the babas on individual serving plates, drizzle with any remaining syrup, and place a dollop of cinnamon cream to the side.

Rum Babas with Cinnamon Cream ▷

Apple Crumble Kuchen

Kuchen is a Yiddish term used to describe a yeast dough pastry that is topped with fruit or nuts and streusel.

Serves: 8–10 • Prep: 40 min. + 2–2 hr. 30 min. rising • Cooking: 20–25 min. • Level: 2

DOUGH
- ³⁄₄ cup (200 ml) warm milk
- 2 teaspoons active dried yeast
- 3 tablespoons superfine (caster) sugar
- 2½ cups (375 g) all-purpose (plain) flour, plus extra for kneading
- 1 sachet or 1 tablespoon vanilla sugar
- ¼ teaspoon salt
- ¼ cup (60 g) unsalted butter, melted
- 1 large egg, beaten (at room-temperature)

APPLE TOPPING
- 8 large dessert apples (such as Granny Smith or Cox)
- Finely grated zest of ½ lemon, finely grated
- Freshly squeezed juice of ½ lemon
- 2 tablespoons golden raisins (sultanas)
- 1–2 tablespoons melted butter, for brushing

STREUSEL TOPPING
- 1⅓ cups (200 g) all-purpose (plain) flour
- 2 tablespoons vanilla sugar
- ⅓ cup (70 g) granulated sugar
- ½ cup (125 g) unsalted butter, chilled
- ½ cup (40 g) almonds, roughly chopped

TO SERVE
- 1 cup (250 ml) whipped cream

1. Prepare the dough following the instructions on page 115. Cover with a clean kitchen towel and leave to rise, until doubled in size, for 1–2 hours in a warm place.

2. To prepare the apple topping, peel, quarter, and core the apples, then cut into ½-inch (1-cm) slices, and sprinkle with lemon juice and the zest.

3. To prepare the streusel topping, put the flour and sugars into a bowl and rub in the butter until crumbly. Then stir in the almonds.

4. Lightly butter a 15½ x 11½-inch (40 x 30 cm) baking sheet or 10½ x 15½-inch (26 x 40-cm) jelly roll pan. Dust your hands with flour, punch the risen dough down, and take it out of the bowl. Briefly knead it on a lightly floured surface and roll it out.

5. Place the dough on the baking sheet or in the pan, and stretch and pull to fill it. Pat to a thickness of ¼ inch (5 mm).

6. Brush the top of the dough with melted butter and arrange the apple slices, close together and overlapping on top. (Any leftover apple juices can be mixed into the topping with a fork.) Scatter with the golden raisins. Sprinkle the streusel crumble over the apple topping and press it down lightly.

7. Leave to rise for a further 30–60 minutes in a warm place, until doubled in bulk.

8. Preheat the oven to 400°F (200°C/gas 6). Bake for 10 minutes. Turn down the oven to 350°F (180°C/gas 4) and bake for 10–15 more minutes, until well risen, golden brown at the edges, and pale golden on top.

9. Leave for 10 minutes on the sheet before slicing. Serve warm with the whipped cream.

Apple Crumble Kuchen ▷

COBBLERS AND STRUDELS

Cobblers and crisps (or crumbles, in British English) make great family desserts. Strudels are made by wrapping fruit, sugar, and spices in the thinnest possible dough layers of strudel pastry or phyllo pastry. In this chapter we explain how to make strudel pastry (see Viennese Apple Strudel, page 137), although you may choose to use ready-made phyllo pastry instead.

◁ **Plum and Sour Cream Cobbler (see page 139)**

Apple and Blackberry Crisp

If you like plenty of crisp topping, double the topping ingredients below and bake in a slightly larger pan.

Serves: 4–6 • Prep: 25 min. • Cooking: 30–40 min. • Level: 1

3	medium cooking apples, peeled, cored, and sliced
12	ounces (350 g) fresh blackberries
¼	cup (50 g) firmly packed light brown sugar
1	tablespoon dark brown sugar
	Freshly squeezed juice of 1 lemon

TOPPING
1	cup (150 g) all-purpose (plain) flour
3	tablespoons old-fashioned rolled (porridge) oats
½	cup (125 g) salted butter, chilled and diced
3	tablespoons vanilla sugar
3	tablespoons light brown sugar
1	tablespoon dark brown sugar

1) Preheat the oven to 350°F (180°C/gas 4). Butter a 9-inch (23-cm) pie pan or ovenproof dish.

2) Put the fruit in the prepared pan. Sprinkle with the light and dark brown sugars and lemon juice and toss together.

3) To make the topping, combine the flour and oats in a bowl. Rub in the butter with your fingertips, until you have a lumpy, buttery mixture. Stir in the vanilla sugar, light brown sugar, and dark brown sugar with a fork. Sprinkle the topping over the fruit.

4) Bake for 30–40 minutes, until the topping is crisp and golden. Serve warm.

Blackberry Clafoutis

Clafoutis is a specialty from the Limousin region of France. Traditionally it consists of cherries baked in a custard or flan, but many other types of fruit can also be used.

Serves: 6 • Prep: 10 min. • Cooking: 35 min. • Level: 1

⅔	cup (100 g) all-purpose (plain) flour
2	large eggs, lightly beaten
½	cup (100 g) superfine (caster) sugar
1	cup (250 ml) milk
2	tablespoons butter, melted
2	cups (500 g) fresh blackberries
	Confectioners' (icing) sugar, for dusting
¾	cup (180 ml) heavy (double) cream, whipped

1) Preheat the oven to 350°F (180°C/gas 4). Lightly brush a 1½-quart (1.5-liter) ovenproof dish with butter and set aside.

2) Combine the flour and eggs in a medium bowl. Add the superfine sugar, milk, and melted butter, stirring with a wooden spoon to form a smooth batter. Pour into the prepared dish. Sprinkle the blackberries on top.

3) Bake for 35 minutes, or until a skewer comes out clean when inserted into the center. Remove from the oven and dust with confectioners' sugar.

4) Serve hot, with a dollop of whipped cream on the side.

Apple and Blackberry Crisp ▷

Boysenberry and Apple Cobbler

Try this cobbler with blackberries or gooseberries instead of the boysenberries. If using gooseberries, you may need a little more sugar in the filling. Taste and add more as needed.

Serves: 6 · Prep: 30 min. · Cooking: 35 min. · Level: 1

1½	pounds (650 g) tart apples, such as Granny Smith
4	cups (750 g) boysenberries, fresh or frozen (thawed, if frozen)
½	cup (100 g) granulated sugar
1	cup (150 g) all-purpose (plain) flour
1	teaspoon baking powder
¼	teaspoon baking soda (bicarbonate of soda)
1	tablespoon superfine (caster) sugar
3	tablespoons (45 g) butter, chilled and diced
¾	cup (180 ml) buttermilk
	Confectioners' (icing) sugar, for dusting
1	recipe Vanilla Crème Anglaise (see page 279)

1) Preheat the oven to 400°F (200°C/gas 6).

2) To prepare the filling, peel, core, and thinly slice the apples. Combine the apples, boysenberries, and granulated sugar in a large saucepan over medium-low heat and cook, stirring occasionally, until the apples begin to soften, 10 minutes. Remove from the heat, spoon the fruit into a medium ovenproof dish, and set aside.

3) Combine the flour, baking powder, baking soda, and superfine sugar in a medium bowl. Rub in the butter, using your fingers, until the mixture begins to resemble fine crumbs. Pour in the buttermilk and stir with a wooden spoon until combined. Sprinkle the dough over the fruit; it will not cover the fruit completely.

4) Bake for 25 minutes, or until the topping has risen and is golden brown. Remove from the oven and set aside to cool for 10 minutes.

5) Serve warm with the Vanilla Crème Anglaise poured over the top.

Austrian Apple Delight

Serves: 4 · Prep: 25 min. · Cooking: 30 min. · Level: 1

1½	pounds (750 g) Golden Delicious or Gala apples, peeled, cored, and cut into ¼-inch (7-mm) dice
¼	cup (50 g) granulated sugar
¼	cup (50 g) unsalted butter
¼	cup (50 g) firmly packed dark brown sugar
2½	cups (150 g) fresh white bread crumbs
2	tablespoons grated dark chocolate, for sprinkling (optional)
	Plain yogurt or fresh cream, to serve

1) Cook the apples with the granulated sugar in a heavy-bottomed skillet over medium-low heat until softened, 5–8 minutes. Do not add any water. Mash roughly and leave to cool.

2) Preheat the oven to 375°F (190°C/gas 5). Butter an 8-inch (20-cm) pie pan or small gratin dish.

3) While the apples are cooking, melt the butter in a large frying pan over low heat. When the butter has turned golden brown, add the brown sugar and stir over medium to low heat for 2–3 minutes, until the sugar has dissolved. Add the bread crumbs to the caramelized sugar and increase the heat to medium-high. Fry the crumbs for 5 minutes, until they are toffee-coated.

4) Spread a layer of the bread crumbs over the bottom of the prepared pan, followed by a layer of apple mash and top with bread crumbs.

5) Bake for 20 minutes, or until the mixture is bubbling and golden brown.

6) Let cool to warm, then sprinkle with grated chocolate, if using. Serve with plain yogurt or cream.

Boysenberry and Apple Cobbler ▷

Cherry Clafoutis

This cherry batter pudding from Limousin in France is traditionally made with unpitted sour cherries, which have a bitter almond flavor. But pitting is advisable (though tedious) if you don't want to risk anyone swallowing a pit. If you are using bottled cherries, drain them well. Serve this classic dessert warm with crème fraîche or vanilla ice cream.

Serves: 4 • Prep: 20 min + 1 hr. soaking • Cooking: 25–30 min • Level: 1

1	pound (500 g) black cherries, stems removed
¼	cup (60 ml) Kirsch or dark rum, for soaking
½	cup (75 g) all-purpose (plain) flour or amaranth flour (for a gluten-free dish)
⅓	cup (75 g) superfine (caster) sugar
2	large eggs, separated
1¼	cups (300 ml) milk
4	tablespoons unsalted butter, melted
1–2	tablespoons confectioners' (icing) sugar, for dusting

1. Put the cherries into a bowl and sprinkle with 2 tablespoons of the Kirsch. Let soak for 1 hour.

2. Combine the flour and superfine sugar in a medium bowl. Beat in the egg yolks, milk, and 3 tablespoons of the melted butter until smooth.

3. Drain the cherries, and add the Kirsch juice to the batter. In a clean bowl, whisk the egg whites until stiff. Fold into the batter.

4. Preheat the oven to 375°F (190°C/gas 5). Brush the remaining butter on the bottom and sides of a 9-inch (23-cm) pie pan or an ovenproof dish with a pastry brush. (The dish should be large enough to hold the cherries in one layer.)

5. Put the cherries in the prepared pan and shake the pan to distribute them evenly. Pour in the batter and shake again, so everything is level.

6. Bake for 25–30 minutes, until golden, puffed, and set in the center.

7. Remove from the oven and sprinkle immediately with the remaining 2 tablespoons Kirsch. Let cool for 15 minutes. Dust generously with confectioners' sugar before serving straight from the dish.

🌿 Gluten-Free Plum Clafoutis

Amaranth flour is available in health food stores. This recipe is gluten-free.

Serves: 4–6: Prep: 20 min. (+ optional resting) • Cooking: 25–35 min. Level: 1

⅓	cup (50 g) amaranth flour
5	tablespoons superfine (caster) sugar
	Pinch of salt
½	cup (50 g) ground almonds
3	large eggs
1	cup (250 ml) light (single) cream or milk
3	tablespoons (45 g) unsalted butter, melted
1	tablespoon rum
1¼	pounds (600 g) small fresh plums, pitted (stoned) and cut in half
1–2	tablespoons granulated sugar, for sprinkling
	Fresh cream, to serve

1. Combine the amaranth flour, superfine sugar, salt, and almonds in a large bowl. Mix well.

2. Beat together the eggs and cream with an electric mixer fitted with a whisk. Add to the dry ingredients, whisking until smooth. Stir in 2 tablespoons of the melted butter and the rum. (The batter can be prepared in advance and rested for a few hours or overnight.)

3. Preheat the oven to 375°F (190°C/gas 5). Brush the inside of a 9-inch (23-cm) gratin dish or shallow baking pan with the remaining 1 tablespoon butter.

4. Put the plums in the baking dish. Beat the batter until smooth and pour over the plums.

5. Bake for 25–35 minutes, or until puffed up and golden brown. It should be set, but still slightly gooey. Sprinkle with granulated sugar and serve hot with plenty of fresh cream.

◁ **Cherry Clafoutis**

Almond and Plum Crisp

It is easier to control the crumbly consistency of the topping if you make it by hand. If you do use a food processor, pulse the flour and butter for a few seconds only, until the mixture resembles coarse bread crumbs. Then stir in the sugar and any other ingredients. You can freeze crumble topping in a plastic bag for up to 2 months.

Serves: 6 · Prep: 20 min. · Cooking: 40–45 min. · Level: 1

2	tablespoons (30 g) unsalted butter
2	pounds (1 kg) plums, halved and pitted (stoned)
2	tablespoons honey
¼	cup (50 g) firmly packed light brown sugar

TOPPING
1	cup (150 g) all-purpose (plain) flour
	Pinch of salt
½	cup (125 g) salted butter, chilled and diced
⅓	cup (70 g) firmly packed light brown sugar
½	cup (50 g) ground almonds
2	tablespoons flaked almonds

1. Preheat the oven to 350°F (180°C/gas 4). Butter an 8-inch (20-cm) pie pan or ovenproof dish.

2. Melt the butter in a large frying pan over medium heat. When the butter is bubbling, add the plums, honey, and brown sugar. Cook over high heat for 4–5 minutes, until the plums are soft but still hold their shape, and the juices are beginning to darken. Spoon the plums and their juices into the prepared dish.

3. To make the topping, mix the flour and salt in a medium bowl. With your fingertips, rub the butter into the flour, until the mixture resembles coarse bread crumbs. Stir in the brown sugar and ground almonds. Spoon the crumble topping loosely over the plums but don't press it down. Sprinkle with the flaked almonds.

4. Bake for 35–40 minutes, or until the topping is golden and the juices are bubbling. Serve hot.

Rhubarb Crisp

Although both topping and fruit can be prepared in advance, only assemble the crumble when you are ready to bake it. A baked crisp can always be reheated in the oven. Serve warm or cold with custard, cream, vanilla ice cream, or yogurt.

Serves: 4 · Prep: 20 min. · Cooking: 35–45 min. · Level: 1

1	tablespoon unsalted butter
1½	pounds (750 g) rhubarb stalks, cut into short lengths
3	tablespoons superfine (caster) sugar
	Finely grated zest of 1 orange
1	tablespoon fresh orange juice
1	tablespoon vanilla extract (essence)
1½	teaspoons cornstarch (cornflour)

TOPPING
⅔	cup (100 g) all-purpose (plain) flour
½	teaspoon ground ginger
½	cup (125 g) salted butter, chilled and diced
½	cup (100 g) firmly packed light brown sugar
1	cup (100 g) ground almonds
2	teaspoons water, for sprinkling

1. Preheat the oven to 350°F (180°C/gas 4). Butter a 9-inch (23-cm) pie pan or ovenproof dish.

2. Melt the butter in a large frying pan over medium heat. When the butter is bubbling, add the rhubarb, superfine sugar, orange zest, orange juice, and vanilla. Stir in the cornstarch.

3. Simmer over medium heat for 4–5 minutes, until the rhubarb is softened but still holds its shape. Spoon the rhubarb and its juices into the prepared dish.

4. To prepare the topping, mix together the flour and ginger in a bowl. Rub the butter into the flour mixture, using the tips of your fingers, until the mixture resembles coarse bread crumbs. Stir in the brown sugar and almonds.

5. Spoon the crumble topping on top of the rhubarb. Spread it out loosely, so it covers all the fruit, and sprinkle with the water. Bake for 30–40 minutes, until the topping is golden brown and the juices are bubbling. Serve hot.

Almond and Plum Crisp ▷

Viennese Apple Strudel

Serves: 6–8 · Prep: 25 min. + 30 min. resting · Cooking: 25 min. · Level 1

STRUDEL DOUGH
1½ cups (250 g) all-purpose (plain) flour + more as needed
½ teaspoon salt
1 large egg
2 tablespoons sunflower oil
5 tablespoons warm water
¼ cup (50 g) butter, melted, for brushing

FILLING
5 large tart apples, peeled, cored, and thinly sliced
1 cup slivered almonds
½ cup (60 g) finely chopped hazelnuts
1 cup golden raisins (sultanas)
2 tablespoons finely grated lemon zest
½ cup (100 g) granulated sugar
1 teaspoon ground cinnamon
1 tablespoon fresh lemon juice
2 tablespoons rum or Calvados
¼ cup (60 g) butter, for the bread crumbs
1 cup (150 g) fine dry bread crumbs

GLAZE
3 tablespoons light cream
2 teaspoons granulated sugar
Confectioners' (icing) sugar, for dusting

1. Prepare the dough following the step-by-step instructions.

2. To prepare the filling, mix the apples, almonds, hazelnuts, golden raisins, lemon zest, sugar, cinnamon, lemon juice, and rum in a large bowl. Set aside. Melt the butter in a frying pan, add the crumbs, and fry for 4 minutes, or until light golden.

3. Preheat the oven to 375°F (190°C/gas 5). Generously butter a baking sheet.

4. Roll out the dough following the step-by-step instructions.

5. Fill and roll up the dough following the step-by-step instructions.

6. Position the baking sheet so that you can slip the strudel onto it. Curl the roll into a horseshoe shape if it is too big for the sheet. Brush all over with the melted butter. Place the strudel in the oven to begin baking.

7. To prepare the glaze, mix the cream and granulated sugar. Brush the strudel following the step-by-step instructions. Bake for a total of 40–45 minutes, until crisp and golden.

8. Leave to rest on the baking sheet for 10 minutes before carefully lifting with a spatula onto a serving dish. Dust with confectioners' sugar and serve warm.

PREPARING A STRUDEL STEP-BY-STEP

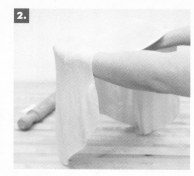

MAKING THE DOUGH

1 Combine the flour and salt in a bowl. Beat the egg, 1 tablespoon of oil, and 5 tablespoons of warm water in a small bowl. Pour into the flour and mix until the dough comes away from the sides of the bowl. Turn out onto a floured board and knead until little blisters appear. Form into a disk, brush with oil, and cover with a cloth. Let rest for 30 minutes.

2 Sprinkle a board with flour and roll the dough out to an oblong

PREPARING THE STRUDEL

3 Place the dough on a clean kitchen towel. Brush with melted butter and sprinkle with bread crumbs. Spread the filling over the front half of the short side, keeping a 1½-inch (4-cm) border. Pick up the two nearest corners

shape. When you can't roll it any thinner, begin stretching it with your hands. Brush the dough with the remaining oil. Dip your hands in flour and curl your fingers. Standing at the short side, lift the dough from the center with the back of your hands. Gently pull it toward you from under-neath, pulling and stretching in all directions. The dough is ready when it measures about 28 x 18 inches (70 x 45 cm).

of the kitchen towel and roll up the strudel from the filled side. Fold in the top edge and sides to seal.

4 Brush two or three times during baking.

Rhubarb Strudel

This recipe makes two rolls, using five phyllo pastry sheets for each. Always remember when working with phyllo pastry to keep the sheets you are not working on covered with a damp cloth. This will keep them from drying out.

Serves: 6–8 • Prep: 25 min. • Cooking: 30–35 min. + 10 min. resting Level: 2

FILLING
- 2 pounds (1 kg) rhubarb stalks, cut into short lengths
- 2 tablespoons freshly squeezed orange juice
- 1½ cups (75–100 g) firmly packed light brown sugar
- 1 cup (150 g) crushed amaretti cookies
- ½ cup (75 g) golden raisins (sultanas)
  Finely grated zest of 1 orange
- 1 teaspoon vanilla extract (essence)
- 2 tablespoons (30 g) butter, chilled and diced

- 10 sheets phyllo pastry
- ½ cup (125 g) unsalted butter, melted
- ½ cup (75 g) toasted wheat germ, for sprinkling
  Confectioners' (icing) sugar, for dusting
- ⅔ cup (150 ml) heavy (double) cream, to serve

1. To prepare the filling, combine the rhubarb, orange juice, and brown sugar in a medium saucepan over medium heat. Simmer for 3–5 minutes, until the rhubarb is soft but keeps its shape. Drain over a bowl, reserving the juice. Let cool.

2. Preheat the oven to 375°F (190°C/gas 5). Generously butter a large baking sheet. Mix the amaretti crumbs with the golden raisins, orange zest, vanilla, and diced butter in a large bowl. Stir in the rhubarb.

3. To assemble, lay a sheet of phyllo pastry on a clean surface. Brush with butter and sprinkle with wheat germ. Repeat this layering, buttering, and sprinkling with five sheets of phyllo. Spread half the filling over the front half, nearest to you, within 1 inch (2.5 cm) of the pastry edges. Roll it up, away from you, tucking in the sides. Using a spatula, lift the strudel onto the baking sheet, seamside down. Brush with butter and sprinkle with wheat germ. Use the remaining phyllo, filling, and butter to make another strudel in the same way.

4. Bake for 30–35 minutes, until golden and crisp. Let rest for 10 minutes. Whip the cream with the reserved rhubarb juice, until it forms soft peaks. Sprinkle the strudel with confectioners' sugar and serve warm with the whipped cream.

Apricot and Almond Strudel

Serves 6–8 • Prep: 25 min. • Cooking: 40 min. • Level: 2

FILLING
- 3 pounds (1.5 kg) ripe apricots, halved, pitted, and thinly sliced
- ½ cup (50 g) ground almonds
- ½ cup (30 g) fresh bread crumbs
- ½ cup (80 g) flaked almonds, lightly toasted
- ¼ cup (80 g) apricot preserves (jam)
- 2 tablespoons butter

- 12 sheets phyllo pastry
- ½ cup (125 g) butter, melted

  Confectioners' (icing) sugar, for dusting
- 1 cup (250 ml) light (single) cream, to serve

1. Preheat the oven to 350°F (180°C/gas 4). Line a 25½ x 17½-inch (65 x 45-cm) baking sheet with parchment paper.

2. To prepare the filling, combine the apricots, ground almonds, bread crumbs, and flaked almonds in a large bowl. Melt the apricot preserves and 2 tablespoons butter in a small saucepan over low heat. Pour over the apricot and almond mixture and stir to combine.

3. To assemble the strudel, flour a clean work surface and lay out a sheet of phyllo pastry. Brush lightly with melted butter and lay another sheet out overlapping one-third of the original sheet to create a longer rectangle. Repeat the process, brushing with butter in between, with another four sheets, creating three layers of pastry. Spread the apricot and almond filling down the center line of the pastry. Wrap the pastry around the filling. Layer the remaining pastry in the same way as before, brushing with butter in between each layer. Place the filling wrapped in phyllo down the center and wrap the pastry around the strudel, using melted butter to seal the edges. Brush the top with melted butter and carefully transfer onto the prepared tray, placing seam-side down, and creating a horseshoe shape so it can fit.

4. Bake for 40 minutes, or until apricots are cooked and the pastry is crisp and golden. Let rest for 10 minutes before serving. Serve warm with the cream.

Plum and Sour Cream Cobbler

This colorful cobbler should be served while still warm. If you like, serve with vanilla ice cream instead of fresh cream.

Serves: 6–8 • Prep: 30 min. • Cooking: 35–35 min. • Level: 1

FILLING

2½	pounds (1.2 kg) red, yellow, and green plums
1	cup (250 g) fresh blackberries, blueberries, or black currants
3	tablespoons granulated sugar or unrefined cane sugar
1	tablespoon cornstarch (cornflour)
1	tablespoon all-purpose (plain) flour
2	teaspoons finely grated lemon zest
2–3	tablespoons freshly squeezed lemon juice
1	teaspoon unsalted butter, chilled and diced

CRUST

1	cup (150 g) all-purpose (plain) flour
½	teaspoon salt
2	tablespoons granulated sugar
2	teaspoons baking powder
¼	cup (60 g) unsalted butter
½–⅔	cup (125–150 ml) sour cream
1–2	tablespoons milk, optional

GLAZE

1	tablespoon light (single) cream
1	teaspoon Demerara or unrefined cane sugar
	Pinch of ground cinnamon

Fresh cream, to serve

1. Preheat the oven to 375°F (190°C/gas 5). Lightly butter a round 10-inch (25-cm) ovenproof dish.

2. To prepare the filling, cut the small plums in half and remove the pits (stones). Slice the large plums and remove the pits. Combine the plums with the blackberries, sugar, cornstarch, flour, lemon zest, lemon juice, and butter in a large bowl. Transfer to the prepared baking dish.

3. To prepare the crust, combine the flour, salt, granulated sugar, and baking powder in a large bowl. Rub in the butter with your fingertips until the mixture resembles coarse bread crumbs. Stir in enough sour cream to make a soft dough. Add more sour cream or 1–2 tablespoons of milk if the dough is brittle.

4. Break off walnut-sized pieces of the dough, flatten them slightly, and place on top of the fruit, in about 10 rounds. Don't cover all the fruit.

5. To prepare the glaze, mix the cream, Demerara sugar, and cinnamon in a small bowl. Brush the mixture over the top of the dough rounds with a pastry brush.

6. Bake for 25–35 minutes, until the crust is golden and the juices are bubbling up through the crust.

7. Let stand for 10 minutes. Serve warm with the cream.

MERINGUES

Versatile, light-as-air meringue can be baked as cookies and served with whipped cream and fresh fruit, rolled into exquisite filled roulades, or baked in disks, spread with creamy fillings and piled up high to make elegant layer cakes. Many meringue recipes—but not all—contain no flour or wheat, making them suitable for people with gluten intolerances. The gluten-free meringues in this chapter are all marked.

◁ Strawberry Meringue Cake (see page 149)

Almond and Apricot Dacquoise

Serves: 6–8 · Prep: 30 min. + 1 hr. cooling · Cooking: 80–90 min. · Level: 2

DACQUOISE

6	large egg whites
¼	teaspoon salt
1½	cups (300 g) granulated sugar
1½	cups (225 g) finely ground almonds
1	tablespoon cornstarch (cornflour)

FILLING

5	large egg yolks
½	cup (100 g) granulated sugar
½	cup (125 ml) milk
1	cup (250 g) unsalted butter, softened and cut in cubes
1	teaspoon almond extract (essence)
1	(15-ounce/450-g) can apricot halves, drained
¾	cup (100 g) flaked almonds
2	tablespoons confectioners' (icing) sugar

1. Preheat the oven to 300°F (150°C/gas 1). Line two baking sheets with parchment paper and mark three 9-inch (23-cm) circles on them. Turn pencil-side down.

2. Prepare the dacquoise following steps 1 and 2 in the step-by-step instructions below.

3. Bake for 80–90 minutes, until crisp. Cool the disks for 10 minutes with the oven door ajar. Transfer to racks. Carefully remove the paper and let cool completely.

4. To prepare the filling, beat the egg yolks and granulated sugar in a large bowl with an electric mixer at high speed until pale and thick.

5. Bring the milk to a boil in a large saucepan over medium heat. Slowly beat the hot milk into the egg mixture. Return the mixture to the saucepan. Simmer over low heat, stirring constantly with a wooden spoon, until the mixture lightly coats a metal spoon. Gradually stir in the butter and almond extract. Transfer to a bowl. Press plastic wrap (cling film) directly on the surface, and refrigerate until chilled, at least 1 hour.

6. Reserve 3–4 apricot halves to decorate and coarsely chop the rest. Spoon half the filling into another bowl and fold in the chopped apricots.

7. Place one dacquoise round on a serving plate and spread with half the apricot filling. Top with another dacquoise round and spread with the remaining apricot filling. Place the remaining dacquoise on top. Spread with the plain filling. Sprinkle with the almonds and decorate with the reserved apricots. Dust with the confectioners' sugar.

PREPARING A DACQUOISE STEP-BY-STEP

A dacquoise is a baked meringue made with finely ground nuts. Layers of dacquoise can be sandwiched together with pastry creams to make exquisite desserts. To vary the recipe on this page, replace the canned apricots with raspberries or ½ cup (125 ml) strained fresh passion fruit.

1 Beat the egg whites and salt in a bowl with an electric mixer at medium speed until frothy. With the mixer at high speed, gradually add the sugar, beating until stiff, glossy peaks form. Use a spatula to fold in the almonds and cornstarch.

2 Spoon the meringue into a pastry bag fitted with a ½-inch (1-cm) plain tip. Pipe the meringue in a spiral to fill the circles. Bake according to the directions above.

3 Spread the filling over the dacquoise, leaving a ½-inch (1-cm) border.

🌿 Hazelnut Meringue Gâteau

Always assemble meringue cakes just before serving them. This will prevent the meringue from melting on contact with the various cream fillings and toppings. This recipe is gluten-free. Some types of chocolate do contain traces of gluten; always buy reputable brands of gluten-free chocolate.

Serves: 6–8 • Prep: 30 min. + 1 hr. cooling • Cooking: 1 hr. • Level: 2

4	large egg whites
1⅛	cups (225 g) superfine (caster) sugar
¼	cup (25 g) ground hazelnuts
8	ounces (250 g) milk chocolate chips
½	cup (125 ml) light (single) cream
1¼	cups (300 ml) heavy (double) cream
1	cup (150 g) hazelnuts, lightly toasted
	Confectioners' (icing) sugar, to dust

1. Preheat the oven to 300°F (150°C/gas 2). Line two baking sheets with parchment paper and mark three 8-inch (20-cm) circles on the paper. Turn pencil-side down.

2. Beat the egg whites in a medium bowl with an electric mixer fitted with a whisk on high speed until they begin to foam. Gradually whisk in the superfine sugar until the stiff glossy peaks form. Fold in the ground hazelnuts.

3. Spread one-third of the meringue onto each of the parchment rounds, smoothing them with a spatula or knife. Bake for 1 hour, or until meringue is dry and crisp. Cool the disks of meringue for 10 minutes. Transfer to racks. Carefully remove the paper and let cool completely.

4. Heat the chocolate and light cream together in a small saucepan over low heat, stirring, until the chocolate is melted and the mixture is smooth.

5. Beat the heavy cream with an electric mixer fitted with a whisk on high speed until stiff peaks form. Fold the cream into the chocolate mixture and set aside.

6. Just before serving the gâteau, spread half of the chocolate cream over one of the meringue disks and sprinkle with half of the hazelnuts. Place another disk on top and repeat the process. Top with the remaining disk. Dust with confectioners' sugar. Serve immediately, before the meringue begins to melt.

🌿 Meringue Gâteau

The candied chestnuts, or marrons glacé, used to decorate this layer cake are available from specialty food stores. If preferred, substitute with coarsely grated dark chocolate. This recipe is gluten-free. Some types of chocolate do contain traces of gluten; always buy reputable brands of gluten-free chocolate.

Serves: 6–8 • Prep: 30 min. + 1 hr. cooling • Cooking: 90 min. • Level: 2

1	cup (200 g) superfine (caster) sugar
⅔	cup (100 g) confectioners' (icing) sugar
6	large egg whites
¼	teaspoon salt
2	cups (500 ml) heavy (double) cream
½	teaspoon vanilla extract (essence)
½	cup (90 g) chocolate chips
4	candied (glacé) chestnuts, crumbled or coarsely chopped

1. Preheat the oven to 300°F (150°C/gas 2). Line two baking sheets with parchment paper and mark three 9-inch (23-cm) circles on the paper. Turn pencil-side down.

2. Mix the superfine sugar and confectioners' sugar in a medium bowl.

3. Beat the egg whites with half the sugar mixture and the salt in a large bowl with an electric mixer fitted with a whisk at medium speed until soft peaks form. Gradually beat in the remaining sugar mixture until stiff, glossy peaks form. Spread a quarter of the meringue onto each parchment round.

4. Bake for about 1 hour 30 minutes, or until the meringues are crisp and firm to the touch. Turn the oven off and let cool with the door ajar, about 1 hour.

5. Beat the cream and vanilla in a large bowl until stiff. Fold in the chocolate chips and candied chestnuts.

6. Carefully remove the paper from the meringues. Place one meringue round on a serving plate. Spread with one-third of the cream. Top with another meringue round and spread with one-third of the cream. Top with the last round and spread with the remaining cream. Crumble the remaining meringue round over the cake.

Hazelnut Meringue Gâteau ▷

Meringues with Raspberry Filling

This recipe is gluten-free. Cornstarch (cornflour) is milled from corn into a fine white flour. It does not contain wheat or gluten. Some cornstarch is milled from wheat, but it is clearly labeled on the package.

Serves: 8 • Prep: 45 min. + cooling time • Cooking: 90 min. • Level: 2

MERINGUES

1¼	cups (250 g) superfine (caster) sugar
2	cups (300 g) confectioners' (icing) sugar
2	tablespoons cornstarch (cornflour)
8	large egg whites
¼	teaspoon salt

FILLING

2	tablespoons cornstarch (cornflour)
½	cup (125 ml) dry red wine
¾	cup (150 g) granulated sugar
14	ounces (400 g) raspberries, mashed with a fork
3	tablespoons raspberry liqueur
1½	cups (375 ml) heavy (double) cream
4	ounces (125 g) bittersweet or dark chocolate, melted

1. Preheat the oven to 250°F (130°C/gas ½). Line a baking sheet with parchment paper. Butter and flour the paper.

2. To make the meringues, mix the superfine sugar, confectioners' sugar, and cornstarch in a bowl. Beat the egg whites with half the sugar mixture and salt in a large bowl with an electric mixer fitted with a wire whisk at medium speed until soft peaks form. Gradually beat in the remaining sugar mixture until stiff, glossy peaks form. Spoon the mixture into a pastry bag with a ½-inch (1-cm) tip and pipe 3-inch (8-cm) spiral disks on the baking sheet. Bake for 90 minutes, or until crisp. Turn the oven off and let cool with the door ajar.

3. To make the filling, heat the cornstarch and a little wine in a medium saucepan. Stir until smooth. Add the remaining wine and ½ cup (100 g) of sugar. Bring to a boil, stirring constantly. Add two-thirds of the raspberries and return to a gentle boil. Add the liqueur and simmer, stirring constantly, for 5 minutes. Let cool.

4. Whip the cream with the remaining sugar in a large bowl. Fold in the remaining raspberries. Drizzle each of the meringues with a little chocolate. Pipe a border of raspberry cream onto half of the meringues. Spoon the raspberry sauce into the center of each one and then cover them with the remaining meringues.

Meringue with Currant Compote

A good compote really requires fresh fruit. If fresh red and black currants are not available serve this meringue with the Mixed Berry Coulis on page 188. This recipe is gluten-free.

Serves: 6–8 • Prep: 40 min. + 40 min. cooling • Cooking: 1 hr. • Level: 1

MERINGUE

4	large egg whites
¼	teaspoon cream of tartar
⅛	teaspoon salt
1¼	cups (250 g) superfine (caster) sugar
1½	teaspoons cornstarch (cornflour)
1	teaspoon freshly squeezed lemon juice, strained
¼	teaspoon vanilla extract (essence)
	Almond or peanut (groundnut) oil, for greasing

COMPOTE

1½	cups (250 g) red currants, leaves and stems removed
½	cup (125 g) black currants, leaves and stems removed
4	tablespoons granulated sugar
1–2	tablespoons water

TOPPING

¾	cup (200 ml) heavy (double) cream
1	teaspoon vanilla sugar

1. Preheat the oven to 300°F (150°C/gas 2). Lightly oil a 9-inch (23-cm) cake pan with a removable bottom. Line with parchment paper.

2. To prepare the meringue, beat the egg whites, cream of tartar, and salt in a large bowl with an electric mixer fitted with a whisk at medium speed until almost stiff. Gradually add the superfine sugar, beating until stiff peaks form. Fold in the cornstarch, lemon juice, and vanilla with a large metal spoon. Spoon into the prepared pan. Bake for 1 hour. Turn the oven off and let cool for at least 40 minutes without opening the door.

3. To prepare the compote, combine the currants in a saucepan with the sugar and 1 tablespoon of water. Bring to a boil over low heat. If the currants stick to the pan, add the remaining water. When the currants start to burst, remove from the heat and set aside to cool.

4. Beat the cream and vanilla sugar in a bowl until stiff. Fill the center of the meringue with scoops of cream. Serve with the compote.

Meringue with Currant Compote ▷

🌿 Eton Mess

This strawberry and cream dessert in a "mess" of smashed-up meringues is traditionally served at Eton College, the famous English school. No one knows if the broken meringues were originally the result of an accident, but they are certainly a great help to inexperienced meringue makers. With store-bought meringues, you can whip up this dessert in just minutes! This recipe is gluten-free.

Serves: 4–6 · Prep: 20 min. + 30 min. resting · Cooking: 50–60 min. Level 1

MERINGUES
- 2 large egg whites
- ⅛ teaspoon salt
- ½ cup (100 g) superfine (caster) sugar
- ¼ teaspoon freshly squeezed lemon juice

FILLING
- 1 pound (500 g strawberries), hulled and halved
- 1 tablespoon confectioners' (icing) sugar
- 1 cup (250 ml) light (single) cream

1. Preheat the oven to 250°F (130°C/gas ½). Line two cookie sheets with parchment paper.

2. To prepare the meringues, beat the egg whites and salt in a large bowl with an electric mixer fitted with a whisk at medium speed until soft peaks form. With the mixer at high speed, gradually add the superfine sugar and lemon juice, beating until stiff, glossy peaks form.

3. Drop rounded tablespoons of the mixture 1 inch (2.5 cm) apart on the prepared cookie sheets. Bake for 50–60 minutes, or until the meringues are crisp and dry to the touch, rotating the sheets halfway through.

4. Turn the oven off and leave the meringues for 30 minutes. Transfer to racks to cool. Don't worry if the meringues are still a bit soft inside.

5. To prepare the filling, combine a little less than half the strawberries with the confectioners' sugar in a food processor or blender and process until smooth. Whip the cream until it stands in soft peaks.

6. To serve, break the meringues into pieces. Put the pieces in a large bowl, add the strawberries, and gently stir in the cream. Fold in 2–3 tablespoons of the strawberry purée. Pile the mixture into a glass bowl or individual dishes and top with the remaining purée. Serve immediately.

🌿 Meringues with Rose Cream

This recipe is gluten-free.

Serves: 4–6 · Prep: 20 min. + 1 hr. cooling · Cooking: 1 hr. · Level: 1

MERINGUES
- 4 large egg whites
- 1 tablespoon confectioners' (icing) sugar
- Pinch of salt
- 1 cup (200 g) granulated sugar
- ½ teaspoon vanilla extract (essence)

FILLING
- 1 cup (250 ml) heavy (double) cream
- 2 tablespoons confectioners' (icing) sugar
- ½ teaspoon red food coloring
- Fresh mint leaves, to garnish (optional)

1. Preheat the oven to 250°F (130°C/gas 1/2). Line two baking sheets with parchment paper.

2. To prepare the meringues, combine the egg whites, the confectioners' sugar, and salt in a large bowl. Beat with an electric mixer fitted with a whisk until soft peaks form. Gradually beat in the granulated sugar, 1 tablespoon at a time, until stiff, glossy peaks form. Fold in the vanilla.

3. Spoon the meringue into a piping bag with a plain tip and pipe (or use a spoon) to place golf ball size blobs on the baking sheets, spacing about 1½ inches (4 cm) apart.

4. Bake until crisp and dry, about 1 hour. Turn off the oven and let cool completely with the door ajar.

5. To prepare the filling, beat the cream and confectioners' sugar in a medium bowl until stiff. Fold in the food coloring.

6. Spread half the meringues with cream and press together in pairs. Serve at once, garnishing the dish with fresh mint leaves, if liked.

Baked Almond Meringue Cake

If you are short of time, use a store-bought sponge cake.

Serves: 8–10 • Prep: 1 hr. + 12 hr. freezing • Cooking: 5 min. • Level: 3

FILLING

7	ounces (200 g) almond paste (marzipan)
3/4	cup (180 ml) water
1/4	cup (60 ml) milk
1/2	teaspoon almond extract
2	tablespoons unflavored gelatin powder
1 1/2	cups (375 ml) heavy (double) cream
	Basic Sponge Cake (see page 76), thinly sliced
3	tablespoons rum mixed with 3 tablespoons water

MERINGUE

4	large egg whites
1/2	cup (100 g) granulated sugar
1/8	teaspoon salt
2	tablespoons slivered almonds

1. To prepare the filling, crumble the almond paste into a medium saucepan. Add the water and milk. Simmer over low heat until the almond paste dissolves. Add the almond extract and gelatin and stir until dissolved. Remove from the heat and set aside to cool until it is just beginning to set around the edges, 15–20 minutes.

2. Beat the cream in a large bowl until stiff. Fold the almond mixture into the cream.

3. Line a 2-quart (2-liter) dome-shaped pudding mold with plastic wrap (cling film) and line with slices of cake. Brush with the rum mixture and fill with half the almond filling. Cover with a layer of cake and brush with rum mixture. Fill with the remaining almond filling and top with a layer of cake. Freeze for 12 hours.

4. Preheat the oven to 350°F (180°C/gas 4).

5. To prepare the meringue, beat the egg whites, granulated sugar, and salt in a large bowl with an electric mixer fitted with a whisk at high speed until stiff peaks form.

6. Unmold the cake onto an ovenproof plate, dome-side up. Spread the meringue over the cake and sprinkle with the almonds. Bake for 5 minutes, or until the meringue is pale gold. Serve immediately.

Strawberry Meringue Cake

If you can get them, use small and extra-tasty wild strawberries for this recipe. Or replace the strawberries with an equal quantity of raspberries. This recipe is gluten-free.

Serves: 6–8 • Prep: 1 hr. + 1 hr. cooling • Cooking: 60–75 min. • Level: 1

9	large egg whites
1/8	teaspoon salt
3	cups (600 g) superfine (caster) sugar
2	cups (500 ml) heavy (double) cream
1/3	cup (50 g) confectioners' (icing) sugar
1	teaspoon vanilla extract (essence)
3	cups (500 g) fresh strawberries, sliced

1. Preheat the oven to 200°F (100°C). Line two baking sheets with parchment paper and mark three 9-inch (23-cm) circles on the paper. Cut one 8 x 12-inch (20 x 30-cm) rectangle of parchment paper and place on one of the baking sheets.

2. Beat the egg whites and salt in a large bowl with an electric mixer fitted with a whisk at medium speed until frothy. With the mixer at high speed, gradually add the superfine sugar, beating until stiff, glossy peaks form.

3. Spread a quarter of the meringue onto each parchment round. Drop the remaining meringue in tablespoons onto the extra paper to make 6–8 small meringues to decorate the cake.

4. Bake for 50–60 minutes, making sure that the meringue does not turn brown. Remove the small meringues and continue baking for 10–15 minutes, or until the large meringues are crisp. Turn the oven off and let the meringues cool in the oven with the door ajar, at least 1 hour. Remove from the oven and carefully remove the paper.

5. With mixer at high speed, beat the cream, confectioners' sugar, and vanilla in a large bowl until stiff.

6. Place one meringue round on a serving plate. Spread with one-third of the cream and sprinkle with one-third of the strawberries. Top with another meringue round. Spread with one-third of the cream and sprinkle with one-third of the strawberries. Top with another round and spread with the remaining cream. Decorate with the remaining strawberries and meringues. Serve immediately.

Raspberry Meringue Roulade

A meringue roulade makes a superb dessert, although it is not especially easy to make. The filling needs to be fairly firm, and the meringue should not be too crumbly or sticky to roll. However, practice makes perfect, and you can also recycle the meringue as Eton Mess (see page 148). This recipe is gluten-free.

Serves: 6 · Prep: 40 min. + 1 hr. cooling + 5 hr. chilling · Cooking: 30 min. Level: 3

- 6 large egg whites
- 1¼ cups (250 g) superfine (caster) sugar
- 1 tablespoon cornstarch (cornflour)
- 1 teaspoon freshly squeezed lemon juice, strained
- 2 tablespoons confectioners' (icing) sugar, for dusting
- 2 tablespoons unsweetened cocoa powder, for dusting

FILLING
- 1 cup (250 ml) heavy (double) cream
- 1½ cups (375 g) fresh raspberries
- 2–3 tablespoons coarsely grated semisweet chocolate

1. Preheat the oven to 325°F (170°C/gas 3). Prepare a jelly-roll pan as explained in step 2 of the next recipe (see right).

2. To prepare the meringue, beat the egg whites in a large bowl with an electric mixer fitted with a whisk at high speed until soft peaks form. Gradually beat in half the superfine sugar. Beat in the remaining superfine sugar until stiff, glossy peaks form. Fold in the cornstarch and lemon juice.

3. Spread the meringue evenly in the prepared pan. Bake for 20 minutes, or until pale golden. Let cool for about 1 hour.

4. Place the other sheet of parchment paper on a work surface and dust with confectioners' sugar and cocoa powder, reserving some for later. Invert the baked meringue in its paper onto the parchment. Carefully remove the paper (if it sticks, brush sparingly with water).

5. To prepare the filling, beat the cream in a bowl until stands in soft peaks. Spread over the meringue with a palette knife. Sprinkle the raspberries and chocolate evenly over the cream. Use the paper to help you roll up the meringue from the short end. Lift one edge of the paper beneath the meringue and as it comes up, gently roll it over. Don't worry about any cracks as you are rolling—they will be covered up later. Dust with the remaining sugar and cocoa.

6. Ease the roulade seam-side down onto a serving dish and refrigerate until ready to serve.

Meringue Roulade with Lemon Curd Cream

This recipe is gluten-free.

Serves: 6–8 · Prep: 45 min. + 65 min. cooling · Cooking: 20 min. · Level: 3

- 1 recipe Lemon Curd (see page 276)
- ¾ cup (180 ml) light (single) cream

MERINGUE
- 4 large egg whites
- ¾ cup (150 g) superfine (caster) sugar
- 1 teaspoon vanilla extract (essence)
- 1 teaspoon white-wine vinegar
- 1 teaspoon cornstarch (cornflour)
- 4 tablespoons confectioners' (icing) sugar

1. Prepare the lemon curd and refrigerate for 1 hour, or until cooled. Whisk the light cream in a small bowl until stiff peaks form, then fold into the cooled lemon curd. Cover and refrigerate until required.

2. Preheat the oven to 325°F (170°C/gas 3). Line a 15½ x 10½-inch (38.5 x 26.5-cm) jelly-roll pan with parchment paper. Cut the paper so it comes right up the sides of the pan. Cut another parchment sheet to the same measurements, and put aside for later.

3. To prepare the meringue, beat the egg whites in a medium bowl with an electric mixer fitted with a whisk on medium-high speed until soft peaks form. Gradually add the sugar, whisking until thick and glossy. Fold in the vanilla, vinegar, and cornstarch.

4. Spread the meringue evenly in the prepared pan. Bake for 20 minutes, or until pale golden. Remove the meringue from the oven and let cool in the pan for 5 minutes.

5. Place the other sheet of parchment paper on a work surface and dust with half the confectioners' sugar. Turn the meringue out onto the paper. Carefully remove the paper.

6. Spread the lemon curd cream over the meringue. Use the paper to help you roll up the meringue from the short end.

7. Dust with the remaining confectioners' sugar, slice into six to eight even portions, and serve.

Meringue Roulade with Lemon Curd Cream ▷

🌿 Chocolate Vacherin

Vacherin is a French dessert made with meringue filled with sweetened cream, chocolate, and fruit. This recipe is gluten-free.

Serves: 6–8 • Prep: 30 min. + 1 hr. cooling • Cooking: 50–60 min. • Level: 1

5	large egg whites
1½	cups (300 g) superfine (caster) sugar
⅓	cup (50 g) unsweetened cocoa powder
1	teaspoon vanilla extract (essence)
2	cups (500 ml) chocolate ganache (see page 278)
1	cup (250 ml) heavy (double) cream
2	ounces (60 g) bittersweet or dark chocolate, grated
½	cup (100 g) fresh raspberries, to decorate

1. Preheat the oven to 275°F (140°C/gas 3). Line a baking sheet with parchment paper and mark two 9-inch (23-cm) circles on the paper. Turn pencil-side down.

2. Beat the egg whites in a large bowl with an electric mixer fitted with a whisk at medium speed until frothy. With the mixer at high speed, gradually add the superfine sugar, beating until stiff, glossy peaks form. Use a large rubber spatula to fold in the cocoa and vanilla.

3. Spoon the mixture into a pastry bag fitted with a ½-inch (1-cm) nozzle and pipe the mixture into two spiral disks, starting at the center of the drawn circles and filling each one.

4. Bake for 50–60 minutes, until crisp. Turn off the oven and leave the door ajar for about 1 hour, until the meringues are completely cool. Transfer the meringues to racks. Carefully remove the paper.

5. About 1 hour before serving, place a meringue layer on a serving plate. Spread with the ganache. Top with the remaining meringue layer.

6. With the mixer at high speed, beat the cream in a large bowl until stiff. Spread over the top of the cake. Sprinkle with chocolate and top with the raspberries. Serve immediately.

🌿 Meringues with Blueberry Cream

This recipe is gluten-free.

Serves: 6 • Prep: 25 min. + 1 hr. cooling • Cooking: 40 min. • Level: 1

4	large egg whites
1	cup (250 g) superfine (caster) sugar
2	tablespoons (30 ml) frangelico (hazelnut liqueur)
1½	cups (375 g) fresh blueberries
2	cups (500 ml) light (single) cream, lightly whipped

1. Preheat oven to 300°F (150°C/gas 2). Line two baking sheets with parchment paper. Mark twelve 3-inch (8-cm) circles, as a guide for the meringues. Turn pencil-side down.

2. Beat the egg whites in a large bowl with an electric mixer fitted with a whisk until they soft peaks form. Gradually beat in the superfine sugar until the mixture is thick and glossy. Spread the meringue onto the pencil circles on the prepared baking sheets.

3. Bake for 40 minutes, until crisp. Turn the oven off. Let the meringues cool for about 1 hour with the door slightly ajar.

4. Combine the liqueur and half the blueberries in a large bowl. Mash a little using a fork. Add the remaining blueberries and cream and fold them in.

5. Place six meringues on individual serving plates. Spread with blueberry cream and top with the remaining meringues. Serve at once.

Chocolate Vacherin ▷

BAKED CUSTARDS

Smooth, luscious baked custards are easy to prepare and can be made ahead of time and stored in the refrigerator until you are ready to serve dessert. We have included a Classic Crème Brûlée recipe here (see page 156) as well as two modern takes on this old favorite, both featuring fruit (see page 156 and 163). We have also included two other classics—Crème Caramel and Crema Catalana (see page 160 for both recipes).

◁ Surprise Truffle Cups (see page 158)

🌿 Classic Crème Brûlée

This dessert comes from France. You can prepare these little custards complete with their caramelized toppings ahead of time and chill until serving. But they are even better if chilled without their topping, then sprinkled with sugar and broiled (grilled) quickly under a very hot broiler. This gives you a chilled custard base with a hot, crisp caramel topping—delicious. This recipe is gluten-free.

Serves: 4 · Prep: 20 min. + 5 hr. cooling and chilling · Cooking: 1 hr. Level: 1

1	vanilla pod
3	large egg yolks
¼	cup (50 g) superfine (caster) sugar
1¼	cups (300 ml) light (single) or heavy (double) cream
¼	cup (60 ml) milk
½	cup (100 g) firmly packed light brown sugar

1. Preheat the oven to 375°F (190°C/gas 5). Oil four ³⁄₄-cup (180-ml) ramekins.

2. Spilt the vanilla pod lengthwise and use a knife to scrape out the seeds. Combine the seeds in a bowl with the egg yolks and superfine sugar. Whisk until pale and creamy. Gradually whisk in the cream and milk. Strain through a fine-mesh sieve into a pitcher (jug) and pour into the ramekins.

3. Place the ramekins in a baking dish. Pour enough boiling water into the baking pan to fill halfway up the sides of the ramekins.

4. Bake for 30 minutes, or until just set. Let cool to room temperature, about 1 hour. Chill in the refrigerator for at least 4 hours.

5. Sprinkle the brown sugar evenly over the top of each dish, ensuring the cream is completely covered. Light a chef's blowtorch or preheat the broiler (grill) until red-hot. Place the ramekins in a pan of ice water. Place the ramekins 3–4 inches (8–10 cm) below the heat and broil for 3–5 minutes, watching carefully, until the sugar begins to melt and turns a golden caramel.

6. Serve at once or chill and serve later.

🌿 Tropical Crème Brûlée

This recipe is gluten-free.

Serves: 6 · Prep: 20 min. + 5 hr. cooling and chilling · Cooking: 25 min. Level: 2

2	large eggs
4	large egg yolks
⅓	cup (75 g) granulated sugar
½	cup (125 g) passion fruit flesh
	Scant 1¼ cups (300 ml) heavy (double) cream
1²⁄₃	cups (400 ml) coconut milk
½	cup (100 g) firmly packed brown sugar

1. Preheat the oven to 350°F (180°C/gas 4). Oil six ³⁄₄-cup (180-ml) ramekins.

2. Beat the eggs, egg yolks, granulated sugar, and passion fruit in a large bowl until well mixed.

3. Bring the cream and coconut milk to a boil in a large saucepan over medium-low heat. Remove from the heat and gradually whisk into the egg mixture, beating well. Return the mixture to the saucepan and simmer over very low heat, stirring constantly, until thickened and the mixture will coat the back of a wooden spoon, 5–7 minutes.

4. Divide the cream among the ramekins. Arrange the ramekins in a baking pan. Pour enough hot water into the baking pan to come halfway up the sides of the ramekins.

5. Bake until the cream has set, about 25 minutes. Remove from the oven and let cool to room temperature, about 1 hour. Chill in the refrigerator for at least 4 hours.

6. Sprinkle the brown sugar evenly over the top of each dish, ensuring the cream is completely covered. Light a chef's blowtorch or preheat the broiler (grill) until red-hot. Place the ramekins in a pan of ice water. Place the ramekins 3–4 inches (8–10 cm) below the heat and broil for 3–5 minutes, watching carefully, until the sugar begins to melt and turns a golden caramel.

7. Serve at once or chill and serve later.

Classic Crème Brûlée ▷

Baked Chocolate Custard Puddings

Serve these delicious little desserts well chilled with fresh raspberries or red currents. This recipe is gluten-free.

Serves: 4 · Prep: 30 min. + 5 hr. cooling and chilling · Cooking: 45 min. Level: 1

4	ounces (125 g) best-quality dark chocolate, chopped
¼	cup (125 ml) heavy (double) cream
3	large egg yolks
⅓	cup (70 g) sugar
2	tablespoons unsweetened Dutch-process cocoa powder
	Pinch of salt
¾	cup (180 ml) whole (full cream) milk
2	teaspoons vanilla extract (essence)
2	large eggs, lightly beaten

1. Preheat the oven to 300°F (150°C/gas 2).

2. Put the chocolate in a medium heatproof bowl. Heat the cream in a small saucepan over low heat until almost boiling, stirring occasionally. Pour about half the hot cream over the chocolate. Allow to stand for a minute or two, then whisk gently until smooth. Gradually stir in the remaining hot cream.

3. In small heatproof bowl, beat the egg yolks with a fork until combined. Stirring constantly, gradually add warm chocolate mixture. Scrape the bottom and sides of the bowl with rubber spatula.

4. Combine the sugar, unsweetened cocoa powder, and salt in a small saucepan. Gradually stir in the milk. Place over low heat and, stirring frequently, bring almost to a boil. Remove from the heat. Gradually stir the hot milk mixture into the chocolate egg mixture. Strain through a fine-mesh sieve into a small pitcher (jug).

5. Pour into four ¾-cup (180-ml) ramekins. Let stand for 2 minutes; if any foam appears on the custard, gently spoon it off. Cover the ramekins with aluminum foil. Place in a baking pan. Pour enough boiling water into the pan to fill halfway up the sides of the ramekins.

6. Bake for 45 minutes. Place the custards on a cooling rack and remove the foil covers. The tops of custards should look quite dark and the custards should be firm but wobbly in the center.

7. Cool to room temperature, about 1 hour. Refrigerate for at least 4 hours before serving.

Surprise Truffle Cups

These little truffle surprises are baked in coffee cups. The hot water bath prevents the cups from cracking in the oven. Serve them hot, with a dollop of crème fraîche or whipped cream, if liked.

Serves: 4 · Prep: 20 min. · Cooking: 20–25 min. · Level: 1

COATING

1	tablespoon unsalted butter, melted
2–3	tablespoons granulated sugar

TRUFFLE

8	ounces (250 g) good-quality bittersweet or dark chocolate, broken into pieces
⅔	cup (150 g) unsalted butter
3	large eggs
⅔	cup (125 g) superfine (caster) sugar
3	tablespoons all-purpose (plain) flour
6	cocoa-dusted Chocolate Truffles (see page 266)

1. Preheat the oven to 350°F (180°C/gas 4).

2. Evenly brush the insides of six coffee cups (or small pudding molds) with the butter. Fill each buttery cup with sugar and rotate, until lined with a sugary crust. Shake out any excess. Arrange the cups in a deep baking dish.

3. To prepare the truffle mixture, melt the chocolate and butter in a medium saucepan over very low heat, watching and stirring occasionally. Leave to cool slightly.

4. Beat the eggs and superfine sugar with an electric mixer fitted with a whisk at high speed in a large bowl until pale and thick. Fold in the chocolate mixture. Sift the flour over the mixture and gently fold it in.

5. Spoon the mixture into the cups, so each one is half filled. Drop in one truffle and cover with the remaining chocolate mixture, leaving room for the pudding to rise.

6. Pour enough boiling water into the baking pan to fill one-third of the way up the sides of the cups. Bake for 20–25 minutes, or until the pudding has risen and is coming away from the edges.

7. Serve hot.

Baked Chocolate Custard Puddings ▷

🍃 Crème Caramel

This recipe is gluten-free. Replace the heavy (double) cream for a low-fat Crème Caramel.

Serves: 6 • Prep: 20 min. + 5 hr. cooling and chilling • Cooking: 30 min. Level: 1

2¼	cups (450 g) superfine (caster) sugar
2	tablespoons water
1	cup (250 ml) milk
1	cup (250 ml) heavy (double) cream
4	large eggs
1	teaspoon vanilla extract (essence)

1. Preheat the oven to 400°F (200°C/gas 6).

2. Combine 1¾ cups (350 g) of the superfine sugar with the water in a medium frying pan over medium heat, and cook, stirring occasionally, for 5 to 10 minutes, until the sugar melts and turns golden. Pour the mixture into six ovenproof ½-cup (125-ml) ramekins and place in a baking pan.

2. Combine the milk and cream in a small saucepan over medium-low heat and bring to a boil.

3. Whisk the eggs, vanilla, and remaining ½ cup (100 g) superfine sugar in a medium bowl until combined. Gradually pour in one-third of the hot cream mixture, whisking to combine. Whisk in the remaining hot cream mixture. Strain the custard into the ramekins.

4. Pour enough boiling water into the baking pan to fill it halfway up the sides of the ramekins.

5. Bake for 20 minutes, or until set. Let cool to room temperature, about 1 hour. Chill in the refrigerator for at least 4 hours.

6. Serve the crème caramels in their ramekins, or turn them out onto individual serving dishes, letting the caramel sugar run down the sides.

🍃 Crema Catalana

This is a traditional crème brûlée from Catalonia. It can be made in individual ovenproof dishes or in a large shallow dish. If liked, serve with sliced oranges sprinkled with sugar and a pinch of cinnamon. This recipe is gluten-free.

Serves: 6 • Prep: 30 min. + 14–15 hr. cooling and chilling • Cooking: 30–35 min. • Level: 2

2¼	cups (550 ml) light (single) cream
1	cinnamon stick (about 4 inches/10 cm long)
	Zest of 1 lemon, in one long piece
6	medium egg yolks
3	tablespoons superfine (caster) sugar

SUGAR CRUST
½	cup (100 g) raw (golden granular) sugar

1. Combine the cream, cinnamon stick, and lemon zest in a heavy-bottomed saucepan over low heat, and bring to the simmering point. Do not allow it to boil. Remove the pan from the heat and let the flavors infuse for 10 minutes.

2. Preheat the oven to 325°F (170°C/gas 3).

3. Beat the egg yolks and superfine sugar with an electric mixer on high speed until pale and creamy. Gradually whisk in the hot cream.

4. Pour through a fine-mesh sieve into six ½-cup (125-ml) ramekins or a shallow 1 quart (1 liter) baking dish. Place them in a baking pan and pour enough cold water into the baking pan to come halfway up the sides of the dishes.

5. Bake for 25–35 minutes, until just set and a knife inserted into the center comes out clean. (If you are using a large dish, bake for 40–50 minutes, until just set and a knife inserted into the center comes out clean.)

6. Cool to room temperature, about 1 hour. Chill in the refrigerator for at least 12 hours, preferably overnight.

7. To make the sugar crust, light a chef's blowtorch or preheat a broiler (grill) until red-hot. Sprinkle the sugar evenly over the top of each dish, ensuring the cream is completely covered. Place under the hot broiler about 3–4 inches (8–10 cm) below the heat for 2–3 minutes, watching carefully, until the sugar begins to melt and turns a golden caramel.

8. Chill again for 1–2 hours before serving.

Baked Cream of Coconut Custard

This is the ultimate dessert for coconut lovers. If liked, serve with a fruit compote or coulis—try it with our Currant Compote (see page 146) or Mixed Berry Coulis (see page 188). This recipe is gluten-free.

Serves: 4–6 • Prep: 15 min. + 5 hr. 15 min. cooling and chilling • Cooking: 1 hr. • Level: 1

5	large eggs
1	14-ounce (400-g) can sweetened condensed milk
1	12-ounce (350-ml) can evaporated milk
1	14-ounce (400-g) can cream of coconut
1	cup (150 g) unsweetened coconut flakes (desiccated coconut)
1	tablespoon vanilla extract (essence)
½	cup (125 ml) rum

1. Preheat the oven to 300°F (150°C/gas 2).

2. Beat the eggs in a large bowl until frothy. Add the condensed milk, evaporated milk, and cream of coconut and beat until smooth. Fold in the coconut flakes, vanilla, and rum. Pour the mixture into a 9 x 13-inch (23 x 32-cm) baking dish.

3. Bake for 1 hour, or until a toothpick inserted into the center comes out clean. Turn the oven off and let cool in the oven for 15 minutes.

4. Remove from the oven and let cool to room temperature. Refrigerate for 4 hours before serving.

Easy Blueberry Custard

This recipe is gluten-free.

Serves: 4–6 • Prep: 5 min. • Cooking: 20–25 min. • Level: 1

3	tablespoons unsalted butter
8	large eggs
¼	cup (60 ml) honey
2½	cups (625 ml) milk
1	teaspoon vanilla extract (essence)
⅔	cup (100 g) all-purpose (plain) flour
½	teaspoon salt
1	cup (125 g) blueberries
½	teaspoon ground nutmeg
4	tablespoons confectioners' (icing) sugar, for dusting

1. Preheat the oven to 425°F (220°C/gas 7). Put the butter in a 9 x 13-inch (23 x 32-cm) baking dish. Place in the oven to melt the butter.

2. Combine the eggs, honey, milk, vanilla, flour, and salt in a blender. Blend until smooth. Pour over the melted butter in the hot dish. Sprinkle with the blueberries.

3. Bake for 20–25 minutes, or until puffed and golden.

4. Dust with the nutmeg and confectioners' sugar and serve warm.

Lime Crème Brûlée

Kaffir lime, also known as makrut lime, is a member of the citrus family. The fruit is knobbly and bitter-tasting, and it is the leaves that are most commonly used to flavor food. If you can't find the lime leaves for this dish, it is okay to leave them out. This recipe is gluten-free.

Serves: 6 · Prep: 15 min. + 1 hr. infusing + 5 hr. cooling and chilling Cooking: 1 hr. · Level: 2

2	cups (500 ml) heavy (double) cream
3	kaffir lime leaves, finely sliced
	Finely grated zest and juice of 2 limes
5	large egg yolks
1	cup (100 g) superfine (caster) sugar

1. Preheat the oven to 275°F (140°C/gas 1).

2. Combine the cream, kaffir lime leaves, lime zest, and juice in a medium saucepan over medium heat. Bring to a boil, then remove from the heat and set aside for 1 hour to allow the flavors to infuse.

3. Beat the egg yolks and ½ cup (100 g) superfine sugar in a medium bowl and pour in the infused milk, stirring until combined. Strain the egg mixture through a fine-mesh sieve into a pitcher (jug).

4. Pour the custard mixture into six ½-cup (125-ml) ramekins and place in a baking dish. Pour enough cold water into the baking pan to fill halfway up the sides of the ramekins.

5. Bake for 1 hour, or until the custard has set but is still a little wobbly. Cool the ramekins on a rack to room temperature, about 1 hour. Chill in the refrigerator for at least 4 hours.

6. Light a chef's blowtorch or preheat a broiler (grill) on its highest setting until red-hot. Sprinkle the remaining ½ cup (100 g) superfine sugar evenly over the top of each dish, ensuring the cream is completely covered. Place the ramekins in a pan of ice water. Place under the hot broiler about 3–4 inches (8–10 cm) from the heat source and broil for 2–3 minutes, watching carefully, until the sugar begins to melt and turns a golden caramel.

7. Remove the ramekins from the iced water and dry. Serve warm.

Baked Lemon and Lime Dessert

Serves: 4–6 · Prep: 20 min. · Cooking: 40–50 min. · Level: 1

	Finely grated zest and juice of 2 lemons
	Finely grated zest and juice of 2 limes
⅓	cup (90 g) unsalted butter, softened
1½	cups (300 g) granulated sugar
3	large eggs, separated
4	tablespoons all-purpose (plain) flour
⅛	teaspoon baking powder
1¼	cups (310 ml) milk
	Confectioners' (icing) sugar, for dusting
1	cup (250 ml) heavy (double) cream, whipped

1. Preheat the oven to 350°F (180°C/gas 4).

2. Combine the lemon and lime zest, butter, and granulated sugar in a medium bowl. Beat with an electric mixer on high speed until light and creamy. Combine the lemon and lime juices and measure out ⅔ cup (165 ml). Beat the egg yolks into the butter and sugar mixture. Pour in the juice. Sift the flour and baking powder over the egg mixture and add the milk, stirring to incorporate.

3. Beat the egg whites in a medium bowl with an electric mixer on high speed until stiff peaks form. Fold the egg whites into the egg mixture to make a smooth batter.

4. Pour the batter into a 6-cup (1.5-liter) ovenproof baking dish and place in a roasting pan. Pour enough boiling water into the roasting pan to fill halfway up the sides of the baking dish. Bake for 40–50 minutes, or until golden.

5. Spoon into serving bowls while still warm. Dust with confectioners' sugar and place a dollop of whipped cream to the side.

◁ **Baked Lemon and Lime Dessert**

MOUSSES AND CREAMY DESSERTS

Smooth, cool creams, mousses, and trifles—this chapter

includes a host of new takes on some classic desserts.

Try our Fruity Tiramisù (see page 183), Chocolate Panna

Cotta (see page 174), or Chocolate Pots de Crème with

Meringues (see page 179). The desserts in this chapter

are just right for any occasion.

◁ **Bavarois au Chocolat (see page 171)**

Amaretti Lime Delights

If you are short of time, make this dessert using store-bought lime curd or lemon curd. Serve with crisp, freshly baked amaretti cookies.

Serves: 6 • Prep: 15 min. + 30 min. cooling + 2–4 hr. chilling Cooking: 15–20 min. • Level: 1

LIME CURD
- ⅓ cup (75 g) unsalted butter
- Finely grated zest of 2 limes
- Freshly squeezed juice of 3 limes
- 2 large eggs
- ¾ cup (150 g) sugar

AMARETTI CREAM
- 1 cup (250 ml) heavy (double) cream
- 1 cup (250 ml) thick Greek-style plain yogurt
- 1 cup (125 g) crushed amaretti cookie crumbs
- Zest of 1 lime, cut into thin strips, for decoration
- Small mint leaves, for decoration

1. To prepare the lime curd, melt the butter in a heavy-bottomed saucepan. Whisk in the lime zest, lime juice, eggs, and sugar. Simmer over very low heat, stirring constantly, until the mixture thickens. Do not allow the curd to boil. Alternatively, combine all the ingredients in a bowl and stir constantly in a double boiler over barely simmering water until thickened. Let cool to room temperature, about 30 minutes.

2. To prepare the amaretti cream, beat the cream until it is about to form soft peaks. Be careful not to let the cream become too thick. Fold in the yogurt and lime curd with a large spoon. Then fold in the cookie crumbs.

3. Spoon the mixture into six small ramekins, liqueur glasses, or espresso cups. Cover tightly with plastic wrap (cling film) and chill in the refrigerator for 2–4 hours.

4. Decorate with strips of zest and 1 or 2 mint leaves and serve.

Ginger Ripple Log

This is a great dessert for people who love ginger.

Serves: 6–8 • Prep: 15 min. + 30 min cooling + 12 hr. chilling • Cooking: 5 min. • Level: 1

- ½ cup (90 g) dates
- 1 cup (250 ml) water
- 2 cups (500 ml) heavy (double) cream
- 2 teaspoons vanilla extract (essence)
- 4 tablespoons confectioners' (icing) sugar
- ½ teaspoon ground ginger
- 1 (8-ounce/250-g) (about 20) package gingersnaps (gingernut biscuits), + 2 cookies reserved for garnish
- 2 tablespoons candied (glacé) ginger, finely sliced

1. Combine the dates and water in a small saucepan over medium heat and cook for 5 minutes, or until the dates have softened. Set aside to cool, about 30 minutes.

2. Purée the date mixture in a blender until it forms a smooth paste and set aside.

3. Beat the cream and vanilla in an electric mixer fitted with a whisk on medium speed until it begins to thicken. Stir in the confectioners' sugar and ground ginger and continue beating until soft peaks form.

4. Reserve two cookies for a garnish. To assemble the dessert, spread half a tablespoon of the date mixture on one side of each of the twenty gingersnaps, followed by a tablespoon of whipped cream. Stick on another cookie and repeat the layering process until twenty of the cookies have been used and a log is formed. Place the log on a large serving plate and spread the remaining whipped cream over the outside. Cover with plastic wrap (cling film) and place the log in the refrigerator overnight.

5. To serve, crumble the reserved cookies over the top of the log and garnish with slices of candied ginger. Slice the log on the diagonal into six to eight pieces and place on individual serving plates.

Amaretti Lime Delights ▷

Brandied Chocolate Pots

The good news is that many now believe that chocolate, eaten in judicious quantities, is good for your health! It should always be good-quality dark chocolate with at least 70 percent cacao.

Serves: 6 • Prep: 15 min. + 2 hr. chilling • Cooking: 15 min. • Level: 1

1	cup (250 ml) heavy (double) cream
1	cup (250 ml) half-and-half or light (single) cream
12	ounces (350 g) dark chocolate (70% cacao), coarsely chopped
6	large egg yolks
3	tablespoons (45 ml) brandy
1/2	teaspoon finely grated orange zest
3/4	cup (180 ml) light (single) cream
2	tablespoons confectioners' (icing) sugar
1	teaspoon ground cinnamon

1. Combine the cream, half-and-half, and chocolate in a double boiler over barely simmering water. Stir with a wooden spoon until smooth. Remove from the heat.

2. Whisk the egg yolks, brandy, and orange zest together in a medium bowl. Slowly pour in the chocolate mixture, continuously whisking until combined. Return the mixture to the double boiler and simmer, stirring constantly with a wooden spoon, until thickened. Remove from the heat and pour the mixture into six 6-ounce (175-g) dessert cups or individual soufflé dishes. Refrigerate for 2 hours, or until firm.

3. Whisk the cream in a small bowl until it begins to thicken. Add the confectioners' sugar and beat until the cream is thick enough to hold its shape.

4. To serve, place the chocolate cups on small plates, top with a dollop of whipped cream, and sprinkle with cinnamon.

Coffee Chocolate Pots

Serves: 4 • Prep: 10 min. + 30 min. cooling + 1 hr. chilling • Cooking: 2–3 min. • Level: 1

4	ounces (125 g) dark chocolate
3/4	cup (180 ml) heavy (double) cream
1	scant teaspoon instant espresso powder
2	tablespoons Kahlúa or other coffee-flavored liqueur
2/3	cup (150 g) Greek-style plain yogurt

1. Coarsely grate 1 ounce (30 g) of chocolate and reserve.

2. Break the remaining chocolate into small pieces and place in a heatproof bowl with 3 tablespoons of cream and the espresso powder. Place over barely simmering water for 2–3 minutes, until melted, then stir. Remove from the heat and let it cool a little.

3. Fold in the liqueur, the remaining cream, and half the yogurt, whipping it together to thicken.

4. Divide the mixture among four coffee cups or 1/2-cup (125-ml) ramekins, and spoon the remaining yogurt over the top. Sprinkle with grated chocolate and chill for 1 hour before serving.

Brandied Chocolate Pots ▷

Vanilla and Almond Bavarois

Bavarois, also known as Bavarian Cream, is a very smooth chilled cream that, as its name suggests, originally came from southern Germany. This cream is especially good with Sugar Roasted Pears (see page 212).

Serves: 6 · Prep: 20 min. · Cooking: 10 min. + 1 hr. cooling + 4 hr. chilling Level: 3

CUSTARD BASE
¾	cup (200 ml) milk
¾	cup (200 ml) heavy (double) cream
1	vanilla pod, slit lengthways
5	large egg yolks
½	cup (100 g) superfine (caster) sugar
4	sheets leaf gelatin or 1 tablespoon unflavored gelatin powder + 3 tablespoons water

FLAVORING
1¼	cups (300 ml) heavy (double) cream
1	tablespoon vanilla sugar
1½	cups (150 g) blanched almonds, toasted and finely ground

1. To prepare the custard base, combine the milk and cream in a heavy-bottomed saucepan. Scrape in the vanilla seeds, add the pod, and slowly heat almost to the boiling point, but do not let the mixture boil.

2. Whisk together the egg yolks and superfine sugar in a large bowl until pale and creamy.

3. Discard the vanilla pod. Whisk the hot milk mixture into the yolk and sugar mixture a little at a time. Return to the saucepan and simmer over very low heat, stirring constantly, for about 5 minutes, until the custard thickens and coats the back of a spoon; do not let the custard boil.

4. If using the leaf gelatin, fill a small bowl with cold water. Add the leaf gelatin and leave to soak for about 5 minutes, until softened. If using powdered gelatin, sprinkle over the 3 tablespoons cold water and leave to soften for 5 minutes.

5. If using leaf gelatin, remove from the water, squeeze out gently, and stir into the warm custard. If using powdered gelatin, stir the mixture into the warm custard. Whisk until dissolved. Strain the custard through a fine-mesh sieve into a bowl and leave to cool. Stir occasionally to prevent a skin from forming.

5. Whip the cream and vanilla sugar with an electric mixer until soft peaks form.

6. When the custard starts to set around the edges, gently fold in the ground almonds. Then fold in the whipped cream with a large metal spoon. (If the custard is too stiff, set it in a bowl over hot water and whisk until soft enough to fold in the cream.)

7. Lightly oil six individual ¾-cup (180-ml) pudding molds or ramekins and pour in the vanilla bavarois. Refrigerate for about 4 hours, until firmly set.

8. To serve, dip the molds into hot water for a few seconds and invert onto serving plates.

Bavarois au Chocolat

Serve this dark chocolate Bavarian cream with fresh berries. They will both lighten and highlight the full chocolately taste of the chilled cream. The same recipe can also be used to make a white chocolate cream by replacing the 8 ounces (250 g) of dark chocolate in the flavoring with the same amount of white chocolate.

Serves: 4 · Prep: 30 min. + 1 hr. cooling + 3–4 hr. chilling · Cooking: 20 min. · Level: 3

CUSTARD BASE
- ⅓ cup (90 ml) milk
- ⅓ (90 ml) heavy (double) cream
- 1 vanilla pod, slit lengthwise
- 3 large egg yolks
- ¼ cup (50 g) superfine (caster) sugar
- 2 sheets leaf gelatin or 1½ teaspoons unflavored gelatin powder + 3 tablespoons water

FLAVORING
- 8 ounces (250 g) dark chocolate, coarsely chopped
- ¾ cup (200 ml) heavy (double) cream

DECORATION
- 1 ounce (30 g) dark chocolate, coarsely grated
- ½ cup (125 g) fresh mixed berries (blueberries, red currants, raspberries), optional

1. To prepare the custard base, combine the milk and cream in a heavy-bottomed saucepan. Scrape in the vanilla seeds, add the pod, and slowly heat almost to the boiling point.

2. Whisk together the egg yolks and superfine sugar in a large bowl until pale and creamy.

3. Discard the vanilla pod. Whisk the hot milk mixture into the egg and sugar, a little at a time. Return the mixture to the saucepan and simmer over very low heat for about 5 minutes, stirring constantly, until the custard thickens and coats the back of a spoon; do not let the custard boil.

4. If you are using the leaf gelatin, fill a small bowl with cold water. Add the leaf gelatin and leave to soak for about 5 minutes, until softened. If you are using powdered gelatin, sprinkle it over the 3 tablespoons of cold water and leave to soften for 5 minutes.

5. If you are using leaf gelatin, remove the gelatin from the water, squeeze gently, and stir into the warm custard. If you are using powdered gelatin, stir the gelatin mixture into the warm custard. Strain the custard through a fine-mesh sieve into a bowl and leave to cool. Stir occasionally to prevent a skin from forming.

6. Melt the chocolate in a double boiler over barely simmering water. Let cool.

7. Stir the cooled chocolate into the custard, cover, and chill.

8. When the custard starts to set around the edges, whip the cream in a bowl, until thick but not stiff. Fold the cream into the chocolate bavarois. (If the custard is too stiff, set it in a bowl over hot water and whisk until soft enough to fold in the cream.)

9. Lightly oil four ramekins or other small molds and spoon in the mixture. Refrigerate for 3–4 hours, until firmly set.

10. To serve, invert each ramekin onto a plate. Decorate with grated chocolate and berries.

White Chocolate and Strawberry Mousse

Serves: 6 • Prep: 30 min. + 30 min. cooling + 12 hr. chilling • Cooking: 15 min. • Level: 1

2	cups (500 g) strawberries, hulled, + 6 additional strawberries for garnish
¼	cup (60 ml) + 3 tablespoons (45 ml) water
¼	cup (50 g) sugar
1¼	cups (300 ml) heavy (double) cream
1	vanilla bean, split lengthwise
3	large egg yolks
8	ounces (200 g) white chocolate, coarsely chopped, + additional grated for garnish
1	teaspoon unflavored gelatin powder
1¼	cups (300 ml) heavy (double) cream, whipped

1. Combine the strawberries, ¼ cup (60 ml) water, and sugar in a medium saucepan over medium heat and simmer for 15 minutes, or until the berries have softened to a jamlike consistency. Let cool.

2. Heat the cream and vanilla bean in a small saucepan over medium heat until just before it reaches boiling point. Remove from the heat. Discard the vanilla bean.

3. Whisk the egg yolks in a medium heatproof bowl. Gradually add one-third of the hot cream, whisking all the time. Whisk in the rest. Add the chocolate and place the bowl over a saucepan of barely simmering water. Cook, stirring continuously, until it thickens and coats the back of a wooden spoon. Do not allow the mixture to boil.

4. Pour the remaining 3 tablespoons water into a small cup, sprinkle the gelatin powder into the water, and allow to soak for 5 minutes. Add the softened gelatin mixture to the custard, stirring to combine. Strain the custard through a fine-mesh sieve into a medium bowl. Set aside and allow to cool to room temperature.

5. Gently fold the whipped cream into the custard and then stir in the strawberries to create a rippled effect. Pour the mousse into six dessert glasses and refrigerate overnight, or until set.

6. To serve, place the glasses on small individual serving plates and top with grated white chocolate and a strawberry, cut in half.

Frozen Honey Mousse with Caramel Dates

Serves: 6 • Prep: 30 min. + 12 hr. freezing • Cooking: 30 min. • Level: 2

MOUSSE

1	cup (250 ml) intensely-flavored honey
1	cup (250 ml) milk
4	large egg yolks
2½	cups (625 ml) heavy (double) cream

DATES

¼	cup (60 ml) water
½	cup (100 g) sugar
⅓	cup (90 ml) orange juice
½	cup (125 ml) light (single) cream
12	fresh dates, pitted and halved

1. To prepare the mousse, combine the honey and milk in a medium saucepan over medium-low heat and cook until it reaches the simmering point. Whisk the egg yolks in a medium bowl and gradually pour in the hot milk, whisking to combine. Return the mixture to the saucepan and simmer over medium-low heat for 10 minutes, until the mixture thickens. Cover and refrigerate until cool.

2. Whip the cream in a medium bowl until it forms firm peaks and fold into the cooled honey mixture.

3. Line a 13 x 9-inch (23 x 23-cm) baking pan with parchment paper. Pour in the honey mixture, cover with parchment paper, and freeze overnight, or until frozen solid.

4. To prepare the dates, combine the water and sugar in a small saucepan over low heat and cook for 5 minutes, or until the sugar has dissolved. Increase the heat to medium and boil the sugar syrup without stirring for 5–10 minutes, until it turns to caramel. Remove from the heat and stir in the orange juice and cream. Return the saucepan to the heat and simmer for 5 minutes, stirring until the mixture slightly thickens. Add the dates and stir to coat in the caramel.

5. To serve, slice the frozen honey mousse into six even portions using a hot knife. Place the slices on serving plates with some caramel dates to the side.

White Chocolate and Strawberry Mousse ▷

Vanilla Panna Cotta with Caramelized Oranges

Panna cotta, which means "cooked cream," is an Italian dessert. There are many variations; this one is served with caramelized oranges. You may also like to try it with the Raspberry Compote on page 278 or the Chocolate Sauce on page 230.

Serves: 6 • Prep: 30 min. + 12 hr. chilling • Cooking: 45 min. • Level: 2

PANNA COTTA
- 4 cups (1 liter) heavy (double) cream
- ½ cup (100 g) superfine (caster) sugar
- 2 tablespoons (30 ml) rum
- 2 vanilla pods, split lengthwise
- 1 tablespoon (15 ml) water
- 2 teaspoons unflavored gelatin powder

CARAMELIZED ORANGES
- 4 oranges
- 1½ cups (300 g) superfine (caster) sugar
- ¼ cup (60 ml) water
- 5 tablespoons (75 ml) brandy

1. To prepare the panna cotta, combine the cream, superfine sugar, and rum in a medium saucepan over medium heat and heat until it reaches the boiling point. Decrease the heat, add the vanilla pods, and gently simmer for 5 minutes.

2. Pour the water into a small cup, sprinkle the gelatin over the water, and leave to soak for 5 minutes.

3. Remove the cream from the heat and stir in the gelatin mixture. Strain the mixture through a fine-mesh sieve into a pitcher (jug) and set aside for 10 minutes to cool. Pour the cream into six ¾-cup (180-ml) plastic molds and refrigerate overnight, or until set.

4. To prepare the caramelized oranges, remove the zest in long strips, using a zester, and set aside. Cut the remaining skin from the oranges using a small sharp knife, ensuring all the pith has been removed and only the orange flesh remains. Slice the oranges crosswise into five rounds each and set aside.

5. Heat the superfine sugar and water together in a large frying pan over low heat without stirring until it turns golden. Stir in the brandy. Add the orange zest and orange rounds and simmer on low heat for 30 minutes, or until caramelized.

6. To serve, dip the molds into hot water and invert onto serving plates. Arrange some caramelized orange and zest to the side.

Chocolate Panna Cotta

Serves: 6 • Prep: 20 min. + 12 hr. chilling • Cooking: 10 min. • Level: 2

- 4 cups (1 liter) heavy (double) cream
- ½ cup (100 g) superfine (caster) sugar
- 1 vanilla pod, halved lengthwise and seeds scraped
- 3 ounces (90 g) dark (70% cacao) chocolate
- 1 tablespoon unflavored gelatin powder
- 2 tablespoons milk
- ¾ cup (180 g) fresh raspberries
- 6 sprigs mint

1. Heat the cream, superfine sugar, and vanilla pod and seeds together in a small saucepan over medium heat. Bring to a boil. Remove from the heat and stir in the chocolate, using a wooden spoon, until fully incorporated.

2. Soak the gelatin in the milk in a small bowl for 3 to 5 minutes, or until softened. Pour into the cream mixture, stirring to combine. Strain the chocolate cream through a fine-mesh sieve into a pitcher (jug) and set aside for 10 minutes, to cool a little.

3. Pour the cream into six ¾-cup (180-ml) plastic molds and refrigerate overnight, or until set.

4. To serve, loosen the panna cotta away from the molds using your fingers and gently invert onto serving plates. Garnish each with raspberries and a sprig of mint.

Vanilla Panna Cotta with Caramelized Oranges ▷

Raspberry Syllabub

This recipe is egg-free.

Serves: 6 · Prep: 15 min. + 30 min. chilling · Level: 1

1	pound (500 g) fresh raspberries or frozen raspberries, thawed and drained
2–3	tablespoons confectioners' (icing) sugar
1/8	teaspoon rose water
1 1/4	cups (300 ml) heavy (double) cream
1/3	cup (90 ml) sweet white wine or sherry
2	teaspoons freshly squeezed lemon juice

1. Reserve 2 tablespoons of the raspberries for decoration. Combine the remaining berries in a blender with 1 tablespoon of the confectioners' sugar and the rose water. Blend until smooth. Set the raspberry purée aside.

2. Whip the cream until it forms soft peaks. Gradually add the wine, lemon juice, and a scant tablespoon of the remaining confectioners' sugar, beating well. Lightly fold in the purée, so the cream is streaked and marbled with pink. Taste for sweetness and add more confectioners' sugar, if needed.

3. Spoon into serving glasses and sprinkle the reserved raspberries on top. Chill for at least 30 minutes before serving.

Syllabub

This dish was very popular in Britain from the 16th to the 19th century. Syllabub was originally a drink containing white wine or cider with a foamy head, which was the main element. Tradition has it that the foam was created by milking the cow straight into the drink!

Serves: 4 · Prep: 10 min. + 30 min. chilling · Level: 1

8	macaroons
1	small glass (about 1/3 cup/90 ml) sweet white wine, sherry, or Madeira
2	teaspoons finely grated lemon zest
6	tablespoons freshly squeezed lemon juice
1/2	cup (100 g) superfine (caster) sugar
1 2/3	cups (400 ml) heavy (double) cream

TOPPING

1	cup (250 g) fresh strawberries, hulled
1	tablespoon confectioners' (icing) sugar

1. Crumble two of the macaroons into each of four wine glasses.

2. Combine the wine, lemon zest, lemon juice, and superfine sugar in a large chilled bowl and stir until the sugar dissolves. Pour in the cream and beat with an electric beater or hand whisk until the mixture forms soft peaks.

3. Spoon the cream over the crumbled macaroons and refrigerate for at least 30 minutes before serving.

4. To prepare the topping, combine the strawberries and confectioners' sugar in a blender and purée until smooth. Chill until needed.

5. Drizzle the syllabub with the strawberry topping just before serving.

◁ **Syllabub**

Chocolate Pots de Crème
with Meringues

Serves: 8–10 • Prep: 45 min. + 2–3 hr. to chilling • Cooking: 70–90 min. Level: 2

1¼	cups (300 ml) light (single) cream
1	vanilla pod, split lengthwise
2	ounces (60 g) dark chocolate, broken into pieces
2	ounces (60 g) white chocolate, broken into pieces
4	large egg yolks
1	tablespoon superfine (caster) sugar
2	small pinches salt
1	tablespoon dark brown sugar

MERINGUES

4	large egg whites
¼	teaspoon freshly squeezed lemon juice
1	cup (200 g) vanilla sugar or 1 cup superfine (caster) sugar + 1 teaspoon vanilla extract (essence)

1. Heat the cream with the vanilla pod in a heavy-bottomed saucepan over low heat and bring to the simmering point, but do not allow the cream to boil. Remove the pan from the heat and leave to infuse for 20 minutes.

2. Melt the chocolates separately in heatproof bowls suspended over saucepans of barely simmering water. Set aside to cool slightly, but keep the saucepans of water for later.

3. Whisk 2 egg yolks into each bowl of melted chocolate (it should still be warm to the touch), until the mixtures are smooth. Stir the superfine sugar and a small pinch of salt into the white chocolate. Stir the dark brown sugar with a small pinch of salt into the dark chocolate mixture. Stir until all the sugar has completely dissolved.

4. Remove the vanilla pod from the cream and slowly pour half of the cream into each chocolate mixture, stirring until blended.

5. Suspend the bowls again over saucepans of simmering water, and cook until each mixture thickens and coats the back of a spoon, stirring all the time.

6. Pour the dark chocolate mixture into small liqueur glasses and the white chocolate mixture into egg cups. Chill for 2–3 hours.

7. To prepare the meringues, preheat the oven to its lowest setting, probably 250°F (130°C/gas ½). Line two large cookie sheets with parchment paper.

8. Beat the egg whites with the lemon juice with an electric mixer fitted with a whisk until stiff and silky. Add the vanilla sugar, 2 tablespoons at a time, and quickly whisk in after each addition until you have incorporated all of it. If you are using extract, whisk it in with the last spoonful of sugar. Stop whisking once the mixture is glossy and stands in peaks when pulled up by the whisk.

9. Spoon into a large pastry bag, fitted with a ⅔-inch (1.5-cm) star tip. Pipe about 30 small whirls, 1½ inches (4 cm) in diameter, on the prepared cookie sheets, spacing them 1 inch (3 cm) apart.

10. Bake for 70–90 minutes on a low oven rack, until dry to the touch. If the meringues are coloring, prop the oven door ajar with the handle of a wooden spoon to lower the oven temperature. Turn off the oven and leave them to cool with the door ajar for 30 minutes, to cook the insides further.

11. Lift the meringues off the paper and cool on wire racks. Serve with the little chocolate pots.

◁ **Chocolate Pots de Crème with Meringues**

Trifle

Trifle is a traditional English dessert made of sponge cake, custard, fruit, and whipped cream, all layered in a glass dish. The first recipe appeared in The Good Housewife's Jewel, dated 1596. Any leftover sponge cake can be used. Or use store-bought trifle or strawberry shortcake sponges, a loaf of Madeira or pound cake, or your own home-baked sponge cake.

Serves: 6 • Prep: 35 min. + 1 hr. to macerate + 4 hr. chilling • Cooking: 15 min. • Level: 2

1	pound (500 g) fresh raspberries, + extra, to decorate
2	tablespoons superfine (caster) sugar
½	teaspoon finely grated lemon zest
2	tablespoons freshly squeezed lemon juice
8	strawberry shortcake or trifle sponges or 8 ounces (250 g) homemade or store-bought sponge cake or 8 ounces (250 g) ladyfingers
⅓	cup (100 g) raspberry preserves (jam)
⅓–⅔	cup (100–150 ml) sherry or apple juice

CUSTARD
1	cup (250 ml) heavy (double) cream or half-and-half
1	cup (250 ml) milk
	Seeds from 1 vanilla pod
4	large egg yolks
½	cup (100 g) superfine (caster) sugar

DECORATION
1	cup (250 ml) heavy (double) cream
2	teaspoons confectioners' (icing) sugar
2	tablespoons flaked almonds, toasted

1. Combine the raspberries, superfine sugar, lemon zest, and lemon juice in a bowl. Stir and leave to macerate for about 1 hour.

2. To prepare the custard, heat the cream, milk, and vanilla seeds in a heavy pan over low heat until just below boiling point. Whisk the egg yolks and superfine sugar in a medium heatproof bowl. Whisk one-third of the warm cream and milk into the yolks. Whisk in the rest. Place the bowl over a saucepan of barely simmering water. Cook, stirring constantly, until the custard coats the back of a wooden spoon. Strain into a bowl, cover with plastic wrap (cling film), and refrigerate.

3. Spread the sponge cake with raspberry preserves. Fill the bottom third of a large glass bowl with a layer of sponge cake. Drizzle with the sherry. Top with the raspberries and juices. Pour the custard over the top, cover, and refrigerate for at least 4 hours.

4. Whip the cream with the confectioners' sugar. Spread over the custard. Sprinkle with almonds and top with the extra raspberries.

Cappuccino Cups

Serves: 4 • Prep: 15 min. + 3 hr. chilling • Cooking: 10 min. • Level: 1

2	cup (360 g) dark chocolate chips
¼	cup (60 ml) very strong brewed coffee
¼	cup (60 ml) coffee liqueur
2	large egg yolks
1½	cups (375 ml) heavy (double) cream
2	tablespoons sugar
1	cup (250 g) crème fraîche or sour cream
¼	cup (60 ml) light (single) cream
	Grated chocolate, for garnish
4	chocolate-coated or whole coffee beans, for garnish (optional)

1. Melt the chocolate in a medium saucepan over low heat. Add the coffee and liqueur and stir using a wooden spoon until incorporated. Add the egg yolks, stirring until combined. Heat to 170°F (85°C) then set aside.

2. Beat the heavy cream with an electric mixer fitted with a whisk on high speed until it begins to thicken. Add the sugar and continue whisking until soft peaks form.

3. Stir one-quarter of the cream into the chocolate mixture and then gently fold in the remainder. Pour the coffee mousse into four glass cups and refrigerate for 3 hours, or until firm.

4. Whisk the crème fraîche and light cream together in a medium bowl until combined. Place a large dollop of crème fraîche on top of each cup of mousse and, using the back of a spoon, or a knife, smooth it over to look like foam on a cappuccino.

5. To serve, garnish with grated chocolate and place cups on individual serving plates.

Cappuccino Cups ▷

Fruity Tiramisù

This tiramisù (the name translates from the Italian as "pick me up,") is a wholesome twist on the original. It'll pick you up with extra vitamin C.

Serves: 4–6 • Prep: 40 min. + 4 hr. chilling • Level: 2

4	ounces (125 g) dark (70% cacao) chocolate, coarsely grated + extra shavings to decorate
4	ripe passion fruits or granadillas, cut in half
2	ripe nectarines or peaches
1¼	cups (300 ml) brewed strong coffee
2	tablespoons vanilla sugar
½	cup (125 ml) Marsala wine or medium-dry sherry
2	cups (500 g) mascarpone cheese
2	tablespoons superfine (caster) sugar
2	teaspoons vanilla extract (essence)
2	tablespoons freshly squeezed orange juice, strained
8	ounces (250 g) almond cookies or biscotti
2	tablespoons unsweetened cocoa powder
	Zest of 1 orange, cut into thin strips, for decoration

1. Set out a deep glass bowl, about 8–10 inches (20-25 cm) in diameter.

2. Scoop out the passion fruit seeds and pulp and push through a fine metal sieve. Reserve the passion fruit purée. Immerse the nectarines or peaches in boiling water, leave for 2–3 minutes. Drain, cut in half, pit (stone), and peel. Finely chop the flesh and add to the purée.

3. Sweeten the coffee with the vanilla sugar and 2 tablespoons of Marsala. Pour into a shallow dish.

4. In a separate bowl, whisk the mascarpone with the superfine sugar and vanilla. Whisk in the remaining 6 tablespoons Marsala and orange juice and zest.

5. Dip half the cookies into the coffee mixture and use them to line the bottom of the glass bowl. Spread with half the mascarpone mixture and sprinkle with grated chocolate. Spoon the fruit over the chocolate, reserving 2 tablespoons. Place the remaining cookies in the dish to soak up the coffee mixture, and arrange on top of the fruit. Sprinkle with 1 tablespoon of cocoa. Spread the remaining mascarpone over the cookies, dust with the remaining 1 tablespoon cocoa powder, and sprinkle with the chocolate shavings.

6. Refrigerate for at least 4 hours. Serve with reserved fruit purée.

◀ **Fruity Tiramisù**

Raspberry Mousse

Serves: 8 • Prep: 20 min. + 2 hr. chilling • Cooking: 10 min. • Level: 1

2½	cups (625 g) fresh raspberries
	Finely grated zest and juice of 1 orange
1	tablespoon unflavored gelatin powder
2	tablespoons cold water
2	large egg yolks
½	cup (100 g) sugar
2	tablespoons brandy
2¾	cups (680 ml) heavy (double) cream
8	sprigs mint, for garnish

1. Reserve ½ cup (100 g) raspberries for a garnish.

2. Heat the remaining 2 cups raspberries with the orange zest and juice in a medium saucepan over medium-low temperature. Bring to a boil and remove from the heat.

3. Soak the gelatin and water in a small bowl for 5 minutes, or until softened. Stir the gelatin into berries and set aside to cool.

4. Whisk the egg yolks and sugar together in a small heatproof bowl with an electric mixer on high speed until thick and pale.

5. Place the bowl on top of a saucepan of barely simmering water and stir in the brandy using a wooden spoon. Simmer, stirring constantly, until the mixture heats and thickens slightly. Remove from the heat and allow to cool. Combine the raspberry and egg mixtures, stirring until incorporated.

7. Whisk the 2 cups (500 ml) of cream in a medium bowl using an electric mixer on high speed until soft peaks form. Fold the cream into raspberry mixture. Pour the mousse into eight serving cups and refrigerate for 2 hours, or until set.

8. To serve, whisk the remaining ¾ cup (180 ml) cream until soft peaks form. Place a dollop of cream on top of each mousse and garnish with the reserved raspberries and a sprig of mint.

STEAMED PUDDINGS AND SOUFFLÉS

Steamed puddings are wholesome, hearty dishes that are perfect for winter desserts and celebrations. They are traditionally served as dessert on Christmas Day in England. *Soufflé* is a French word that means "puffed up," which is exactly what these light and airy dishes should be! There are just two basic rules for success with soufflés—never open the oven door while they are baking and never let them sit around after they come out of the oven; serve them at once.

◁ **Steamed Orange Pudding with Syrup (see page 197)**

🍃 Cardamom Rice Pudding with Caramelized Peaches

This dessert does not contain eggs and is gluten-free.

Serves: 4 · Prep: 15 min. · Cooking: 75 min. · Level: 2

1½	cups (625 ml) milk
½	cup (100 g) granulated sugar
4	cardamom pods, bruised
½	vanilla pod, halved lengthwise and seeds scraped out
¼	cup (50 g) short-grain or pudding rice
½	cup (125 ml) heavy (double) cream
4	large canned peach halves
4	tablespoons confectioners' (icing) sugar

1. Combine the milk, granulated sugar, cardamom pods, and vanilla pod and seeds in a medium saucepan over medium-low heat. Bring to a boil. Add the rice, decrease the heat to low, and gently simmer for 1 hour, or until the rice is cooked and the mixture is thick. Stir occasionally with a wooden spoon.

2. Transfer into a bowl. Let the rice cool a little, then cover with plastic wrap (cling film), and refrigerate until chilled.

Whisk the cream in a small bowl until soft peaks form. Fold into the rice mixture. Remove the vanilla and cardamom pods and discard.

3. Line a small baking sheet with parchment paper. Place a 2½-inch (6-cm) ring mold 2 inches (5 cm) tall onto the prepared sheet and spoon the rice pudding into the mold, leveling it off the top. Repeat the process another three times.

4. Preheat a broiler (grill) to high.

5. Make five parallel partial slices into each peach half, ensuring that you do not cut all the way through and that the peach half stays intact. Fan the peach halves on top of the molded puddings and dust each one with 1 tablespoon confectioners' sugar.

6. Broil for 3 to 5 minutes, until the sugar caramelizes, turning a golden brown color. Serve hot.

🍃 Old-Fashioned Rice Pudding with Cherry Sauce

This is a very rich rice pudding. For a less creamy version, replace the cream with milk. Any stewed fruit can replace the Cherry Sauce. This dessert does not contain eggs and is gluten-free.

Serves: 4–6 · Prep: 10 min. + 20 min. cooling · Cooking: 2 hr. 10 min.–2 hr. 30 min. · Level: 1

½	cup (110 g) short-grain pudding rice or arborio rice
2½	cups (600 ml) milk, + more, as needed
2	cups (500 ml) heavy (double) cream
¼	cup (50 g) firmly packed light brown sugar
	Pinch of salt
2	strips lemon zest (about ⅛-inch/3 mm wide by 1 inch/2.5 cm long)
	Large pinch freshly grated nutmeg
3	tablespoons salted butter

Cherry Sauce
10	ounces (300 g) fresh morello cherries, pitted (stoned)
¼	cup (50 g) firmly packed light brown sugar + extra, to taste
3	tablespoons freshly squeezed orange juice or cranberry juice

1. Preheat the oven to 300°F (150°C/gas 2). Butter a 1½-quart (1.5-liter) deep ovenproof dish.

2. Rinse the rice in cold water and drain well. Combine the rice, 2½ cups (600 ml) milk, cream, brown sugar, salt, and lemon zest in the dish. Stir well and sprinkle half the nutmeg over the top. Dot the top with 1½ tablespoons of butter.

3. Bake for 50 minutes on a low oven rack.

4. Remove the pudding from the oven and stir in the remaining 1½ tablespoons of butter. Return to the oven for another 50–60 minutes. Remove, stir again, and add a few more tablespoons of milk if the rice looks dry. Sprinkle a little more nutmeg over and return the dish to the oven. Bake for another 30–40 minutes. The rice should have absorbed the liquid and be softly creamy, with a lovely golden crust on top. Let cool for about 20 minutes.

5. To prepare the cherry sauce, put the cherries in a saucepan with the juice and half the sugar. Bring to a simmer over low heat. Simmer for 5–7 minutes, until the cherries are just soft. Add more sugar to taste.

6. Serve the rice pudding with the cherry sauce.

Cardamom Rice Pudding with Caramelized Peaches ▷

Hot Berry Soufflés
with Mixed Berry Coulis

A coulis is a purée made from raw or cooked fruit that is served as an accompaniment to hot and cold desserts.

Serves: 6 • Prep: 40 min. • Cooking: 12–15 min. • Level: 2

COATING FOR THE DISHES
3	tablespoons unsalted butter, melted
3–4	tablespoons superfine (caster) sugar

SOUFFLÉ
½	cup (150 g) frozen mixed berries
1	teaspoon cornstarch (cornflour)
4	tablespoons superfine (caster) sugar
1½	tablespoons (25 g) unsalted butter
1½	tablespoons all-purpose (plain) flour
⅔	cup (150 ml) milk, heated
2	large egg yolks
3	large egg whites
1–2	tablespoons confectioners' (icing) sugar, for dusting

COULIS
1¼	cups (300 g) frozen mixed berries, thawed and drained
3	tablespoons granulated sugar
1	tablespoon Amaretto or Cointreau

1. Brush the insides of six 5-ounce (150-ml) ramekins or soufflé dishes with a generous coating of butter. Pour in the superfine sugar and rotate until the sides and bottom are evenly coated.

2. To prepare the soufflés, spread out the frozen berries on a plate. Mix the cornstarch with 1 tablespoon of the superfine sugar and sprinkle over the berries. As they thaw and soften, mash the berries with a fork. Leave to macerate for 30 minutes.

3. Meanwhile, make the soufflé base. Melt the butter in a saucepan over medium heat. Stir in the flour and cook, stirring, without browning, for 1 minute. Gradually add the milk, stirring with a wooden spoon, until the sauce is thick and smooth. Simmer for 1–2 minutes, or until bubbles appear on the surface, stirring all the time. Remove from the heat and let cool slightly.

4. Beat the egg yolks with 1 tablespoon of the superfine sugar and stir into the milk and flour mixture.

5. Press the macerated berries through a sieve into a mixing bowl, rubbing the purée through with the back of a spoon, and add to the milk mixture. Discard the seeds (pips) left in the sieve. (The soufflé can be prepared ahead of time up to this point and chilled).

6. Meanwhile, to prepare the coulis, combine the berries and granulated sugar in a saucepan over medium heat. Cook for 4–5 minutes, stirring, until the fruit is soft. Place a fine sieve over a bowl and pass the fruit through, to remove the seeds. Stir in the liqueur and set the coulis aside.

7. Preheat the oven to 375°F (190°C/gas 5).

8. Beat the egg whites in a medium bowl with an electric mixer fitted with a whisk at high speed until soft peaks form. Gradually add the remaining 2 tablespoons superfine sugar and whisk until stiff and glossy. Fold one-third of the egg whites into the berry mixture with a metal spoon, to loosen it. Fold in the remaining egg whites. Take care to keep as much air in the mix as possible.

9. Set the soufflé dishes on a baking sheet and spoon the mixture into them, filling to 1/2 inch (1 cm) from the rim. Level off the tops with the back of a spoon.

10. Bake for 12–15 minutes on a high oven rack, until risen and golden brown. Dust the tops with confectioners' sugar. Spoon the coulis into the center of each hot soufflé and serve immediately.

Hot Berry Soufflés with Mixed Berry Coulis ▷

Mocha Pudding with Vanilla Ice Cream

Part of the espresso coffee stays in the bottom of the pudding mold, creating a delicious coffee sauce.

Serves: 6 · Prep: 15 min. · Cooking: 40 min. · Level: 1

- 1½ cups (225 g) all-purpose (plain) flour
- 1½ teaspoons baking powder
- ⅓ cup (50 g) unsweetened cocoa powder
- 1 cup (200 g) granulated sugar
- ¼ cup (60 g) salted butter, melted
- 1 large egg, lightly beaten
- ¾ cup (180 ml) milk
- 3 ounces (90 g) bittersweet or dark chocolate (70 % cacao), coarsely chopped
- 2 cups (500 ml) hot brewed espresso coffee
  Confectioners' (icing) sugar, for dusting
  Vanilla ice cream, to serve

1. Preheat the oven to 350°F (180°C/gas 4). Lightly grease a 2½-quart (2.5-liter) baking dish.

2. Combine the flour, baking powder, and cocoa in a medium bowl. Stir in the granulated sugar, melted butter, egg, and milk until smooth and well combined. Stir in the chocolate. Pour the batter into the prepared dish. Pour the hot espresso over the top of the pudding.

3. Bake for 40 minutes, or until the pudding has risen and is springy to the touch.

4. Spoon the pudding into six serving bowls, dust with confectioners' sugar, and place a scoop of ice cream to the side.

🌿 Molten Cherry and Chocolate Puddings

This recipe is gluten-free. Be sure to buy good-quality chocolate from a reputable manufacturer that markets its product as gluten-free.

Serves: 6 · Prep: 15 min. + 3 min. resting · Cooking: 12 min. · Level: 2

- 10 ounces (300 g) bittersweet or dark chocolate chips
- ¼ cup (60 g) salted butter
- 4 tablespoons granulated sugar
- 4 large eggs, separated
- ½ teaspoon ground cinnamon
- ½ cup (125 g) dark sweet cherries, pitted and coarsely chopped, + 12 dark sweet cherries, left whole
- 1 cup (250 ml) heavy (double) cream, whipped

1. Preheat the oven to 400°F (200°C/gas 6). Line six 6-ounce (150-ml) ramekins or cups with parchment paper.

2. Combine the the chocolate and butter in the top of a double boiler over barely simmering water and melt, stirring until combined. Remove from the heat and whisk in 2 tablespoons of the granulated sugar, the egg yolks, and cinnamon. Stir in the cherries.

3. Beat the egg whites with an electric mixer fitted with a whisk on high speed until they become foamy. Add the remaining 2 tablespoons of granulated sugar and beat until stiff peaks form. Stir one-third of the egg whites into the chocolate mixture; gently fold in the remaining whites.

4. Pour the soufflé mixture into the prepared ramekins. Tap them on a work surface to knock out any air bubbles and smooth the top with the back of a knife or a spatula. Clean around the rim of the ramekins by running your fingers around the edge. Place on a baking sheet.

5. Bake for 12 minutes, or until slightly cooked in the center. Remove from the oven and let rest for 3 minutes.

6. Invert the soufflés onto individual serving plates and remove any parchment paper. Serve with a dollop of cream and cherries to garnish.

◁ **Molten Cherry and Chocolate Puddings**

Orange and Poppy Seed Syrup Puddings

Serve these little puddings hot at a family dinner or celebration.

Serves: 12 • Prep: 25 min. • Cooking: 50 min. • Level: 1

1	large orange, peeled
¾	cup (180 g) salted butter, softened
1	cup (200 g) sugar
3	large eggs
½	cup (50 g) finely ground almonds
2	tablespoons poppy seeds
1½	cups (225 g) all-purpose (plain) flour
1	teaspoon baking powder
¼	cup (60 ml) milk

ORANGE SYRUP

2	teaspoons finely grated orange zest
1	cup (250 ml) freshly squeezed orange juice
1	cup (250 ml) water
1	cup (200 g) sugar
5	cardamom pods, bruised
1½	cups (375 ml) vanilla yogurt, to serve
½	cup (50 g) flaked almonds, toasted

1. To prepare the puddings, put the orange in a small saucepan, cover with water, and bring to a boil over medium heat. Decrease the heat to medium-low and simmer for 20 minutes. Remove from the heat, drain, and set aside, allowing it to cool to room temperature.

2. Preheat the oven to 350°F (180°C/gas 4). Grease a 12-cup muffin pan with a little oil or cooking spray.

3. Break the orange into pieces and remove any seeds. Purée the orange flesh in a food processor.

4. Combine the butter and sugar in a medium bowl and beat with an electric mixer fitted with a whisk on medium speed until pale in color. Add the eggs, one at a time, beating between each addition to completely incorporate. Fold in the orange purée, ground almonds, and poppy seeds using a wooden spoon.

5. Sift the flour and baking powder over the mixture. Add the milk and stir with a wooden spoon until combined. Spoon the mixture into the prepared muffin pan.

6. Bake for 20 minutes, or until when a skewer inserted into a pudding comes out clean.

7. To prepare the orange syrup, combine the orange zest, orange juice, water, sugar, and cardamom pods in a medium saucepan over medium heat. Bring to a boil. Decrease the heat to medium-low and simmer for 10 minutes. Pour the syrup over the puddings and allow the puddings to absorb it.

8. Place the puddings in a pan and drizzle with the syrup. Transfer the warm puddings onto individual serving plates, drizzle with any remaining syrup in the dish that has not been absorbed, place a dollop of the vanilla yogurt to the side and sprinkle with toasted almonds.

Orange and Poppy Seed Syrup Puddings ▷

Rum and Raisin Pudding with Crème Anglaise

Serves: 6 • Prep: 25 min. • Cooking: 1 hr. • Level: 1

PUDDING
- ¼ cup (45 g) raisins
- ¼ cup (60 ml) rum
- ½ cup (125 g) unsalted butter, softened
- ⅓ cup (75 g) sugar
- 2 large eggs
- 2 cups (300 g) all-purpose (plain) flour
- 2 teaspoons baking powder
- ¼ teaspoon salt
- 1 teaspoon baking soda (bicarbonate of soda)
- 1 cup (250 ml) milk

- 1 recipe Vanilla Crème Anglaise (see page 279)

1. Lightly butter a 4-cup (1-liter) pudding basin or deep ceramic bowl.

2. To prepare the pudding, combine the raisins and rum in a small bowl and set aside to plump.

3. Combine the butter and sugar in a medium bowl. Beat with an electric mixer fitted with a whisk on high speed until pale and creamy. With the mixer on medium speed, add the eggs one at a time. With the mixer on low speed, add the flour, baking powder, and salt, beating to combine.

4. Dissolve the baking soda in the milk and stir into the mixture along with the plumped raisins and rum.

5. Spoon the mixture into the prepared basin and cover with aluminum foil. Place the basin in a large saucepan and add enough water to come three-quarters of the way up the side of the basin. Cover with a lid and steam over medium-low heat for 1 hour, or until the pudding is firm to the touch.

6. Prepare the Vanilla Crème Anglaise. Strain through a fine-mesh sieve into a small pitcher (jug) for serving.

7. To serve, divide the pudding into six portions, put in serving bowls, and pour some warm Crème Anglaise over the top.

Queen of Puddings

Queen of Puddings is a traditional British pudding made with a bread crumb-thickened egg custard, topped with fruit preserves and meringue.

Serves: 4–6 • Prep: 30 min. + 20 min. resting and cooling • Cooking: 40–45 min. • Level: 2

- 1½ cups (375 ml) milk
- 2 tablespoons (30 g) unsalted butter
- 2 teaspoons finely grated lemon zest
- 3 large egg yolks
- 2 tablespoons vanilla sugar or superfine (caster) sugar
- 1½ cups (85 g) fresh white bread crumbs
- 2 tablespoons raspberry preserves (jam)

MERINGUE
- 3 large egg whites
- ⅓ cup (75 g) superfine (caster) sugar

1. Preheat the oven to 325°F (170°C/gas 3). Butter a 5-cup (1.2-liter) round baking dish.

2. Warm the milk over low heat and add the butter and lemon zest. Remove from the heat.

3. Lightly whisk the yolks with the vanilla sugar and stir into the milk. Mix in the bread crumbs and pour into the pie dish. Let stand for 15 minutes.

4. Bake for 25–30 minutes, or until lightly set. Remove from the oven and let cool for 5 minutes. Increase the oven temperature to 350°F (180°C/gas 4). Warm the preserves in a small pan and spread over the top of the pudding.

5. To prepare the meringue, whisk the egg whites until soft peaks form. Add half the superfine sugar and continue whisking until glossy, stiff peaks form. Fold in the rest of the superfine sugar. Pile the meringue on top of the pudding.

6. Return the pudding to the oven and bake for 15 more minutes, or until the meringue topping is light brown. Serve warm.

Rum and Raisin Pudding with Crème Anglaise ▷

Steamed Orange Pudding with Sliced Oranges

Steamed pudding is a traditional British dish that has acquired a bad reputation. Most people think of it as an old-fashioned dessert that takes ages to make. But this classic, so rarely served today, will come as a light-textured surprise. It is quickly prepared, and all you need is 2 hours' steaming time. Serve with Vanilla Crème Anglaise (see page 279) or whipped cream.

Serves: 6–8 · Prep: 20 min. · Cooking: 2 hr. · Level: 2

PUDDING

3/4	cup (175 g) unsalted butter, softened
1	cup (200 g) firmly packed light brown sugar
1¼	cups (175 g) self-rising flour
	Pinch of salt
4	medium eggs, beaten
	Finely grated zest of 2 oranges
2	tablespoons freshly squeezed orange juice
2–3	tablespoons milk
1	tablespoon orange marmalade

ORANGE SYRUP

1½	cups (350 ml) freshly squeezed orange juice
3/4	cup (200 ml) cold water
2½	cups (500 g) superfine (caster) sugar
1	orange, thinly sliced

1. Butter a 1½-quart (1.5-liter) pudding basin or deep ceramic bowl. Fill a large pan (with a lid) two-thirds full with water and bring to a boil.

2. Beat the butter and brown sugar in a large bowl with an electric mixer on high speed until pale and creamy. Fold in the flour and salt. Stir in the eggs, orange zest, orange juice, and 2 tablespoons of the milk. Whisk for 1–2 minutes. Whisk in a little more milk if the mixture is too thick—it should have the consistency of a thick batter.

3. Spoon the marmalade into the bottom of the pudding basin or bowl and pour the pudding batter on top. Butter the lid generously, or a piece of aluminum foil if using a bowl , and put it on.

4. Place the basin in the saucepan of boiling water. The water should come about halfway up the sides of the basin. If not, add more water. If you are using a steamer, pour the boiling water into the base. Place over medium heat, cover with a lid and return to a boil. Reduce to a low heat and simmer for about 2 hours. Check every 30 minutes to make sure the pan doesn't boil dry. Add more boiling water when necessary.

5. Meanwhile, prepare the orange syrup, which needs to cook for about 40 minutes. Combine the orange juice, water, and superfine sugar in a heavy-bottomed pan. Bring to a simmer over a low heat, stirring until the sugar has dissolved. Add the orange slices and simmer for 30–40 minutes, until the liquid has thickened to a syrup consistency. Check every now and then to make sure it doesn't bubble over!

6. When the pudding is firm and a toothpick inserted into the center comes out clean, carefully lift the basin out of the pan. Let the pudding rest for 3 minutes, loosen the edges with a round-bladed knife, and turn out onto a large serving plate.

7. Spoon the warm syrup over the pudding. Serve hot.

◁ **Steamed Orange Pudding with Sliced Oranges**

Black Sticky Rice Pudding with Coconut Sauce

If you can't find the jaggery (palm sugar) substitute with the same amount of dark brown sugar. Black rice is also known as "forbidden rice," because it was so rare in China that only the emperor was allowed to eat it; for everyone else it was forbidden. Black rice can be purchased in health food stores or from online food stores. This dessert is gluten-free.

Serves: 4 · Prep: 25 min. + 1 hr. cooling · Cooking: 45 min. · Level: 1

RICE PUDDING
1½	cups (300 g) black glutinous rice, rinsed and soaked overnight in cold water
2¼	cups (560 ml) water
	Pinch of salt
1	cup (200 g) grated jaggery (palm sugar)
1	medium, ripe papaya

COCONUT SAUCE
1	cup (250 ml) cream of coconut
½	cup (125 ml) water
½	cup (100 g) grated jaggery (palm sugar)
1	teaspoon finely grated lime zest
2	tablespoons (30 ml) freshly squeezed lime juice

1. To prepare the rice pudding, combine the rice, water, and salt in a small saucepan over medium heat. Bring to a boil. Cover, decrease the heat to low, and simmer for 45 minutes. Remove from the heat, stir in the jaggery, and set aside until you are ready to serve.

2. Remove the skin from the papaya and cut in half lengthwise. Scrape out the seeds and cut crosswise into 1-inch (2.5-cm) thick slices.

3. To prepare the coconut sauce, combine the coconut cream, water, jaggery, lime juice, and lime zest in a small saucepan over medium-low heat. Bring to a boil. Decrease the heat to low and simmer for 10 minutes, or until the sauce has thickened. Let cool to room temperature.

4. Divide the sticky rice among four serving plates or bowls. Place papaya slices to the side and drizzle with the coconut sauce.

Bread and Butter Pudding

A classic for using up stale bread. This pudding can be made with almost any bread, from a white sandwich loaf to brioche, panettone, or stollen. No crumb is wasted!

Serves: 4-6 · Prep: 25 min. + 25 min. standing · Cooking: 35-40 min. · Level: 1

¼	cup (50 g) unsalted butter, softened
6	slices white day-old bread, cut 1/2-inch (1-cm) thick
⅔	cup (120 g) golden raisins (sultanas) or dark raisins
⅓	cup (60 g) ready-to-eat dried apricots, cut into small pieces
	Finely grated zest of 1 lemon
3	large eggs
¼	cup (35 g) superfine (caster) sugar
2	cups (500 ml) milk (or half milk and half cream)
1	teaspoon vanilla extract (essence)
1	tablespoon Demerara sugar, for sprinkling

1. Preheat the oven to 350°F (180°C/gas 4). Butter a small baking pan measuring about 8 inches (20 cm) square and 2 inches (5 cm) deep, or a similar ovenproof dish.

2. Spread the butter generously on the bread. Cut each slice into quarters. Layer the pieces alternating with the raisins, apricots, and lemon zest. Finish with a layer of bread, buttered side up.

3. Beat the eggs with the superfine sugar and ¼ cup (60 ml) of the milk in a medium bowl. Slowly heat the remaining 1¾ cups milk until hot but not boiling. Gradually pour into the egg mixture. Add the vanilla and stir well. Pour over the bread and let stand for 15 minutes, to let the bread soak up the custard. Sprinkle with Demerara sugar.

4. Place the baking dish in a roasting pan. Add enough hot water to the roasting pan to come halfway up the sides of the dish.

5. Bake for 35-40 minutes, until the custard is set and the top is golden and crisp. Allow to rest for 10 minutes before serving.

Black Sticky Rice Pudding with Coconut Sauce ▷

Chocolate Soufflés

These delicious little soufflés are quick and fairly easy to make. If liked, serve them with sliced fresh berry fruit on the side. This dessert is gluten-free.

Serves: 4 • Prep: 15 min. • Cooking: 15–20 min. • Level: 2

- 5 ounces (150 g) bittersweet or dark chocolate
- 1½ tablespoons (25 ml) cognac
- 6 tablespoons superfine (caster) sugar + extra, to sprinkle
- 4 large egg yolks, at room temperature, lightly beaten
- 6 large egg whites, at room temperature
  Heavy (double) cream, whipped

1. Preheat the oven to 375°F (190C/gas 5). Butter four 1-cup (250-ml) ovenproof ramekins and coat with superfine sugar, tapping out any excess.

2. Combine the chocolate, cognac, and 3 tablespoons of the superfine sugar in a heatproof bowl. Place over a saucepan of just simmering water and heat until melted, stirring to combine. Remove from the heat and stir in the egg yolks using a wooden spoon.

3. Beat the egg whites with an electric mixer fitted with a whisk on high speed until they become foamy. Add the remaining 3 tablespoons superfine sugar and beat until stiff peaks form. Stir one-third of the egg whites into the chocolate mixture; gently fold in the remaining whites.

4. Pour the soufflé mixture into the prepared ramekins. Tap them on a work surface to knock out any air bubbles and smooth the top with the back of a knife or a spatula. Clean around the rim of the ramekins by running your fingers around the edges. Place on a baking sheet.

5. Bake for 10–15 minutes, or until well risen. Place the soufflés onto individual serving plates with a dollop of cream to the side. Serve immediately.

Pain au Chocolat Pudding

Serves: 4 • Prep: 15 min. + 10 min. standing • Cooking: 30–35 min. Level: 1

- 3 stale pains au chocolat or chocolate croissants
- ½ cup (90 g) dark chocolate chips
- ½ cup (90 g) dried cherries or cranberries (optional)
- 1¼ cups (300 ml) milk
- 1¼ cups (300 ml) light (single) cream
- 3 large eggs, beaten
- 5 tablespoons superfine (caster) sugar
- ¼ cup (60 g) butter, melted
- ½ teaspoon vanilla extract (essence)

1. Preheat the oven to 350°F (180°C/gas 4). Butter a 1 quart (1-liter) shallow ovenproof dish.

2. Slice the pains au chocolat across the chocolate filling about ½-inch (1-cm) thick. Arrange the slices in the dish overlapping them to fit. Sprinkle with the chocolate chips and dried cherries, if using.

3. Combine the milk and cream in a small saucepan and warm over medium heat. Bring near to the boiling point.

4. Whisk the eggs and superfine sugar in a medium bowl. Slowly add the milk mixture and melted butter, whisking continuously until smooth. Add the vanilla and pour over the pain au chocolat. Let soak for 10 minutes.

5. Bake for 30–35 minutes, or until the pudding is set and the top is golden. Serve hot or warm.

Chocolate Volcano

Molten chocolate erupts like lava from the center of this steamed pudding when you cut into it. If you don't have a plastic pudding basin with a tight-fitting lid, cover the pan with aluminum foil. Serve with vanilla ice cream or whipped cream.

Serves: 6 • Prep: 25–30 min. + 30 min. freezing + 15 min. standing
Cooking: 65 min. • Level: 2

FILLING
- 5 ounces (150 g) bittersweet or dark chocolate (70% cacao solids), coarsely chopped
- 1 tablespoon unsalted butter
- ¼ cup (60 ml) heavy (double) cream
- 2 tablespoons superfine (caster) sugar

PUDDING
- 8 ounces (250 g) dark chocolate, coarsely chopped
- ⅓ cup (90 g) unsalted butter, softened
- ½ cup (100 g) firmly packed light brown sugar
- 6 large eggs, separated
- ⅔ cup (100 g) all-purpose (plain) flour
- 3 tablespoons cornstarch (cornflour)
- 1½ teaspoons baking powder

1. To prepare the filling, combine the chocolate, butter, cream, and superfine sugar in a medium saucepan over very low heat. Stir until the chocolate is melted and the mixture is smooth. Pour into a bowl of the same diameter as your pudding basin, cover, and place in the freezer for about 30 minutes, or until firm.

2. Butter a 1½-quart (1.5-liter) pudding basin or deep ceramic bowl and dust with flour.

3. Melt the chocolate in a double boiler over barely simmering water. Let cool for a few minutes.

4. Beat the butter and brown sugar in a large bowl with an electric mixer on high speed until pale and creamy. With the mixer on medium speed, beat in the egg yolks, one at a time. Stir in the flour, cornstarch, and baking powder.

5. Whisk the egg whites in a clean bowl until soft peaks start to form. Fold the melted chocolate and 2 tablespoons of the egg whites into the pudding mixture to loosen it. Fold in the remaining egg whites.

6. Fill the pudding basin with one-third of the pudding mixture. Take the filling out of the freezer and plop it into the basin. Cover with the remaining pudding mixture and level the top. Butter the basin lid and put it on. (If your basin does not have a lid, or if you are using a bowl, make a double foil square, about 9 inches (23 cm) square, and butter one side. Make a 1½-inch (4-cm pleat) across the middle and place the foil over the basin, buttered side downwards. Fold in the edges to seal.)

7. Place the pudding basin in a large saucepan. Fill the saucepan with enough cold water to reach halfway up the side of the pudding basin. Cover the pan with a lid and bring to a boil. Simmer over very low heat for 1 hour, or until the pudding is firm and risen. Be careful not to let the pan boil dry and add more water as necessary. Alternatively, cook the pudding in a steamer.

8. Carefully remove the basin from the saucepan and let stand for 5 minutes. Remove the lid or foil, loosen the edges with a knife, and turn the pudding out onto a serving plate. Let rest for 10 minutes before cutting into the chocolate volcano.

FRUIT DESSERTS

The simplest fruit dessert is a bowl of fresh, in-season, fruit chosen with care at a local organic farm or farmers' market. Fresh fruit salads are another healthy option—try our Pineapple Surprise with its freshly baked meringue topping (see page 205) or Balsamic Strawberries with Ice Cream (see page 205).

In wintertime, try some of our baked fruit dishes, such as the Sugar-Roasted Pears (see page 214) or the Baked Amaretti Apples (see page 210).

◁ Baked Summer Fruit (see page 208)

Pineapple Surprise

Vary the fruits in this simple dessert according to what you have on hand. If using melon, serve the dessert in the melon shells instead of the pineapple shells. This dessert is low in fat.

Serves: 6–8 • Prep: 30 min. • Cooking: 5–8 min. • Level: 1

- 1 large fresh pineapple, with leaves
- 1 orange, peeled
- 1 banana, peeled and sliced
- 1 kiwifruit, peeled and sliced
- 1 large peach or 2 apricots, peeled, pitted (stoned), and thinly sliced
- 1 mango, peeled, pitted, and chopped into small pieces
- ½ cup (125 g) fresh strawberries, hulled
- 1 small bunch of seedless grapes (about 5 ounces/150 g), halved
- 1 tablespoon freshly squeezed lime juice
- 2 tablespoons Kirsch or white rum
- 1 teaspoon vanilla sugar

TOPPING
- 3 large egg whites
- ¾ cup (150 g) superfine (caster) sugar

1. Cut the pineapple in half vertically. Scoop out the flesh, reserving the juice. Remove the hard core and chop up the flesh into bite-sized pieces. Place in a bowl with the juice. Segment the orange, and add the fruit and juice to the bowl.

2. Add all the remaining fruit to the bowl. Mix in the lime juice, Kirsch, and vanilla sugar. Spoon the fruit salad into the pineapple shells, piling it up in the middle.

3. Preheat the oven to 425°F (220°C/gas 7). To make the topping, whisk the egg whites with an electric mixer in a large, clean bowl until stiff. Reserve 2 teaspoons of superfine sugar for later and gradually whisk in the remaining sugar, 1 tablespoon at a time, until the meringue is glossy and stands in stiff peaks.

4. Spoon the meringue over the fruit salad, making sure the edges are sealed. Sprinkle with the remaining 2 teaspoons superfine sugar. Place both pineapple halves on a baking sheet and bake for 5–8 minutes, until the meringue is golden.

◁ **Pineapple Surprise**

Balsamic Strawberries with Ice Cream

The secret of this simple dessert lies in the freshness and quality of the ingredients. Make it in early summer when strawberries are at their best and be sure to use only the highest quality balsamic vinegar imported from Italy.

Serves: 4–6 • Prep: 10 min. + 1 hr. infusing • Level 1

- 1½ cups (250 g) superfine (caster) sugar
- 1 cup (250 ml) Cointreau or other orange-flavored liqueur
- ⅔ cup (150 ml) good-quality balsamic vinegar
- 2 pounds (1 kg) strawberries, hulled and halved
- 1 pint (500 g) store-bought vanilla ice cream, or homemade Rich Egg-Cream Ice Cream (see page 224)

1. Combine the superfine sugar, Cointreau, and vinegar in a large bowl. Add the strawberries, mix gently, then cover and set aside for 1 hour; this will allow the flavors to infuse.

2. Divide the strawberries among four to six serving plates or bowls and spoon the balsamic syrup over the top. Top each portion with 1–2 scoops of vanilla ice cream.

Instant Berry Buzz

The sweet mascarpone cream goes well with many different types of fruit. Replace the berries in this recipe with a mixture of peeled, chopped peaches, apricots, plums, and bananas.

Serves: 6–8 • Prep: 10 min. • Cooking: 12–16 min. • Level: 1

	About 2 pounds (1 kg) mixed summer fruits (raspberries, blackberries, strawberries, blueberries, red currants, and white currants)
1	tablespoon confectioners' (icing) sugar
1	cup (250 ml) heavy (double) cream
8	ounces (250 g) mascarpone
⅓–½	cup (70–100 g) firmly packed light brown sugar
⅓–½	cup (70–100 g) firmly packed dark brown sugar

1. Preheat the broiler (grill) to medium-high.

2. Hull and halve the strawberries and remove stems from the red currants and white currants. Mix all the fruits in a 1-quart (1-liter) ovenproof dish or a 9-inch (23-cm) pie pan. Sprinkle with the confectioners' sugar and place in the oven for 4–6 minutes, until the fruit is warmed through. Remove.

3. Meanwhile, whip the cream until it starts to thicken. Whisk in the mascarpone and spread the mixture over the fruit. Sprinkle a thick layer of the brown sugars over the cream.

4. Place under the broiler (grill) and broil for 8–10 minutes, until all the sugar has melted. Serve hot or chilled.

Melon Salad with Mint and Ginger Syrup

The combination of mint and ginger brings an intriguing touch of coolness and heat to the melon. This dessert is low in fat.

Serves: 6–8 • Prep: 15 min. • Cooking: 5–10 min. • Level: 1

1	cup (250 ml) water
½	cup (100 g) sugar
2	tablespoons candied (glacé) ginger, finely chopped
½	cup mint leaves, finely chopped
¼	small watermelon
1	small cantaloupe (rock) melon, peeled, halved, and seeded
1	small honeydew melon, peeled, halved, and seeded

1. Heat the water, sugar, and ginger in a small saucepan over medium heat and bring to a boil. Decrease the temperature to medium-low and simmer for 5 minutes, or until liquid has reduced to make a thin syrup. Remove from the heat, add the mint, and set aside to cool.

2. Slice the watermelon into ¼-inch (5-mm) wedges. Slice the cantaloupe and honeydew melons into ¼-inch (5-mm) strips.

3. Arrange the melons on a large serving dish or individual serving plates and drizzle with the mint and ginger syrup.

Instant Berry Buzz ▷

Saffron Poached Pears with Cardamom Ice Cream

Serves: 6 · Prep: 15 min. + 15 min. cooling · Cooking: 40–45 min. · Level: 1

4   cups (1 liter) white wine
2   cups (400 g) sugar
2   teaspoons saffron threads
1   vanilla pod, split lengthwise
     Zest and juice of 2 oranges
6   pears, peeled
     Cardamom Ice Cream, to serve (see page 228)

1. Heat the wine, sugar, saffron, vanilla pod, and orange zest and juice together in a large saucepan over medium-high heat until it reaches the boiling point. Decrease the heat to low and simmer for 15 minutes.

2. Add the pears and cook just below the simmering point for 20–25 minutes, until the pears are tender. Remove from the heat and let the pears cool in the syrup for 15 minutes.

3. To serve, place the still-warm pears on serving plates with 1–2 scoops of cardamom ice cream.

Baked Summer Fruit

Very ripe fruit will bake more quickly than less mature fruit. There should be plenty of juice in the pan; don't bake too long or the juices will dry out.

Serves: 4–6 · Prep: 15 min. + 1 hr. chilling · Cooking: 30 min. · Level: 1

4   peaches or nectarines, pitted (stoned) and quartered
6   apricots, halved and pitted (stoned)
1   inch (2.5-cm) piece ginger, peeled and grated
7   tablespoons light brown sugar, + more as needed
3   large red plums, pitted (stoned) and quartered
3   large yellow plums or 6 greengage plums, halved and pitted (stoned)
1   cup (250 g) fresh blueberries
3/4   cup (200 g) fresh raspberries or loganberries
     Crème fraîche, ice cream, or vanilla pudding, to serve

1. Preheat the oven to 350°F (180°C/gas 4). Set out a shallow baking dish, about 12 inches (30 cm) in diameter.

2. Arrange the peaches and apricots cut side up with the ginger in the dish. Sprinkle with 2 tablespoons of the brown sugar. Add the red and yellow plums and stir in the blueberries. Sprinkle the remaining 5 tablespoons (70 g) brown sugar over the fruit.

3. Bake for 20–30 minutes, until the fruit is tender and the juices have run. Remove the dish from the oven and stir in the raspberries. Mix gently into the hot juices. Taste for sweetness and stir in more brown sugar if needed.

4. Serve chilled or at room temperature with crème fraîche, ice cream, or vanilla pudding.

Saffron Poached Pears with Cardamom Ice Cream ▷

Baked Apples

Test to see if the apples are done by piercing with the tip of a sharp knife. They should be soft and caramelized but hold their shape. The baking time will depend on the variety of apples.

Serves: 4 · Prep: 30 min. · Cooking: 30–40 min. · Level: 1

4	large tart apples (such as Cox, Granny Smith, Greening, or Braeburn)

FILLING
2	tablespoons light brown sugar
2	tablespoons seedless raisins or currants
2	tablespoons golden raisins (sultanas)
1	tablespoon finely grated orange zest
2	tablespoons freshly squeezed orange juice
1	tablespoon orange marmalade
½	teaspoon ground ginger
1	vanilla pod, split open and scraped

FOR BAKING
16	whole cloves, for studding
4	tablespoons apple juice or apple brandy (Calvados), for the pan
2	tablespoons salted butter, diced
1	tablespoon raw sugar
	Freshly squeezed juice of 1 lemon
2	tablespoons honey
	Vanilla Crème Anglaise (see page 279), ice cream, or crème fraîche, to serve

1. Remove the core from each apple. Insert the apple corer two or three times, to make a wider hole. Score around the middle of each apple with a sharp knife, so the apples keep their shape.

2. Preheat the oven to 350°F (180°C/gas 4). Butter a shallow baking dish, small enough for the apples to fit in snugly and not topple.

3. Mix all the filling ingredients in a bowl. Divide the filling among the apples, spooning it into each cavity and piling any excess on top. Stud each apple with 4 cloves, and place in the pan. Pour in the apple juice. Top each apple with a pat of butter. Sprinkle with the raw sugar.

4. Bake, uncovered, for 20–30 minutes, basting the apples once or twice. Combine the lemon juice and honey in a small saucepan and heat gently. Drizzle the apples with the warmed honey and return to the oven for 10 minutes, until puffed up and starting to split open. Allow to cool for 10 minutes, spooning all the juices from the pan over the top. Serve warm with custard, ice cream, or crème fraîche.

Baked Amaretti Apples

Serves: 4 · Prep: 10 min. Cooking: 50 min. · Level: 1

4	tart apples, such as Granny Smith
4	teaspoons light brown sugar
4	teaspoons unsalted butter, softened
6	amaretti cookies, crushed
2	tablespoons flaked almonds
½	teaspoon ground cloves
1	cup (250 ml) apple juice
2	tablespoons honey
½	cup (125 ml) crème fraîche or whipped heavy (double) cream

1. Preheat the oven to 350°F (180°C/gas 4). Remove the cores from the apples using an apple corer. Score the skin around the circumference, so that it splits neatly when it cooks.

2. Combine the brown sugar, butter, amaretti cookies, almonds, and cloves in a small bowl, using your fingers to mix together. Stuff the apples with the amaretti filling and place in a small baking pan into which they will fit snugly.

3. Heat the apple juice and honey together in a small saucepan over medium heat for 3 minutes, or until the honey has melted. Pour the apple juice mixture over and around the apples.

4. Bake for 50 minutes, or until the apples are soft and cooked through.

5. To serve, place the apples on individual serving plates, drizzle over a little of the syrup, and place a dollop of crème fraîche on the side.

Baked Amaretti Apples ▷

Sugar-Roasted Pears

These pears look very attractive served on perfectly white or black plates. Serve them with a scoop of Cardamom Ice Cream (see page 228) for a cool accompaniment.

Serves: 6 • Prep: 35 min. + 2 hr. cooling • Cooking: 25–35 min. • Level: 1

6	large, firm pears
	Zest and juice of 1 lemon
½	cup (100 g) firmly packed light brown sugar
⅓	cup (90 g) unsalted butter, softened
	Zest and juice of 1 orange
1	tablespoon pear brandy (poire eau-de-vie)
3	star anise
1	vanilla pod, slit lengthwise

1. Peel the pears with a potato peeler, leaving them whole with the stems attached. Remove the cores from the bottom with a sharp knife, and cut off a thin slice so they can stand upright. (You can leave the cores intact for a neater finish.) Brush them lightly with lemon juice.

2. Preheat the oven to 375°F (190°C/gas 5). Place the brown sugar on a small plate or shallow saucer.

3. Using a brush, cover the pears with a good layer of butter. Roll in the brown sugar so that they are well coated. Stand the sugar-coated pears in a shallow baking pan. Roast for 15 minutes.

4. Mix the lemon zest, orange zest and juice, remaining lemon juice, and remaining brown sugar with the brandy in a small bowl. Spoon over the pears and add the star anise and vanilla pod to the pan.

5. Bake for 10–20 minutes, until the pears are tender but retain their shape (how long will depend on the ripeness of the fruit). Baste the pears two or three times with the juices during roasting.

6. Transfer to a serving dish and spoon over the aromatic juice from the pan. Spoon more over while they are cooling. Serve at room temperature.

Baked Plums with Blueberries and Mascarpone

Serves: 4 • Prep: 10 min. • Cooking: 20 min. • Level: 1

12	ripe plums or small nectarines, halved and pitted (stoned)
2	tablespoons dark brown sugar
2	tablespoons (25 g) salted butter
¼	cup (60 ml) red wine or black currant juice
⅔	cup (150 g) fresh blueberries
8	ounces (250 g) mascarpone
1–2	teaspoons vanilla sugar

1. Preheat the oven to 400°F (200°C/gas 6).

2. Place the plums in a shallow baking dish, cut side up. Sprinkle with the brown sugar, dot with the butter, and drizzle with the wine. Bake on the highest oven rack for 15 minutes

3. Sprinkle with the blueberries and bake for 5 more minutes, until the plums are softened and have released their juices. Leave in the dish or divide among four bowls.

4. Pour 2–3 tablespoons of the juices into a bowl, add the mascarpone and vanilla sugar to taste, and beat lightly. Serve the plums and juice hot or cold, topped with the flavored mascarpone.

Sugar-Roasted Pears ▷

Russian Kissel

The Russian word kissel means sour. For this fruit dessert—which is a kind of thick fruit soup—any tart-tasting fruit can be used. It was traditionally made with wild, sour cherries or berries (cranberries, blackberries, red currants, or blueberries) and thickened with potato flour or arrowroot.

Serves: 4–6 • Prep: 15 min. • Cooking: 30 min. + 2 hr. cooling • Level: 2

1¼	pounds (600 g) sour red cherries, pitted
2½	cups (600 ml) water or 1¾ cups (400 ml) water and ¾ cup (200 ml) rosé wine, plus more as needed
¼	cup (60 ml) freshly squeezed lemon juice, strained
½	cup (100 g) firmly packed light brown sugar
2	tablespoons all-purpose (plain) flour or potato flour
¾	cup (200 ml) sour cream
1–2	tablespoons granulated sugar, to sprinkle

1. Combine the cherries and water in a medium saucepan, adding more water if needed to cover the fruit. Bring to a boil, partially cover, and simmer over low heat for 15–20 minutes, stirring occasionally, until the cherries are soft.

2. Purée the mixture in a blender. Reserve 2 tablespoons for later and return the remaining puréed cherries to the pan. Add the lemon juice and brown sugar. Bring back to a gentle simmer.

3. Mix the flour and half the sour cream in a bowl until smooth. Whisk in 3 tablespoons of the hot cherry mix. Gradually stir this mixture into the simmering cherries. Continue to simmer for 5–8 minutes, stirring all the time, until the kissel thickens.

4. Remove from the heat and let cool to room temperature.

5. Ladle into bowls and serve garnished with the reserved cherries, a swirl of the remaining sour cream, and a sprinkling of sugar.

Turkish Stuffed Figs

This dessert is low in fat.

Serves: 4 • Prep: 20 min. + 6 hr. plumping figs • Cooking: 20 min. • Level: 1

STUFFED FIGS

1	teaspoon tea leaves
1½	cups (375 ml) boiling water
8	ounces (250 g) dried figs
2	tablespoons coarsely chopped walnuts
2	tablespoons coarsely chopped almonds
1	teaspoon finely grated orange zest

SYRUP

¼	cup (60 ml) rose water
3	tablespoons honey
1	teaspoon finely grated lemon zest
3	bay leaves

¾	cup (180 ml) strained plain yogurt

1. To prepare the figs, steep the tea leaves in the boiling water for 2–3 minutes, allowing the flavor to infuse. Strain the tea into a medium bowl and add the figs. Set aside to plump for 6 hours.

2. Drain the figs, reserving the liquid for later use.

3. Combine the walnuts, almonds, and orange zest in a small bowl. Make a small incision in the bottom of each fig using a sharp knife and stuff with the nut mixture. Place the figs, stems facing upwards, in an ovenproof dish.

4. Preheat the oven to 350°F (180°C/gas 4).

5. To prepare the syrup, combine the reserved tea, rose water, honey, lemon zest, and bay leaves in a small saucepan over medium-high heat and bring to a boil. Decrease the heat to low and simmer for 10 minutes. Pour the hot syrup over the figs. Bake for 20 minutes.

5. Divide the figs evenly among four serving plates or bowls and top with a dollop of yogurt.

Russian Kissel ▷

Swedish Glögg Jelly

In Sweden, this mulled red wine jelly is served to visitors at Christmastime.

Serves: 6 • Prep: 10 min. + 12 hr. macerating + 2 hr. setting • Cooking: 5 min. • Level: 1

- 6 cardamom pods, crushed
- 7 cinnamon sticks
- 2 whole cloves
  Finely grated zest of 1 orange
- ¼ cup (60 ml) vodka
- 3 heaped tablespoons golden raisins (sultanas)
- ¾ cup (180 ml) port
- 8 sheets leaf gelatin or 2 tablespoons unflavored gelatin powder
- 4 tablespoons cold water (optional)
- 1 bottle (3 cups/750 ml) fruity red wine
- ¾ cup (150 g) sugar
- ¾ cup (100 g) almonds, toasted, for decoration

1. Combine the cardamom, 1 cinnamon stick, the cloves, zest, and vodka in an airtight container and leave to macerate overnight. Combine the golden raisins and port in another container and leave to macerate overnight.

2. The next morning, soak the gelatin sheets, if using, in a bowl of cold water for about 5 minutes, until floppy. If using gelatin powder, sprinkle over the cold water in a bowl and leave to soften for 5 minutes.

3. Meanwhile, pour the red wine into a medium-sized saucepan, and add the sugar and the vodka mixture. Strain the port into the pan, reserving the raisins for later. Cook the wine mixture over medium heat, stirring occasionally, until the sugar has dissolved. When it reaches the simmering point, remove the pan from the heat.

4. If using leaf gelatin, remove the gelatin from the cold water, squeeze out any excess water with your fingers, and slip into a large pitcher (jug). If using powdered gelatin, pour the gelatin mixture into a large pitcher.

5. Strain the hot wine mixture through a fine-mesh sieve onto the gelatin, stirring all the time, until it has dissolved completely. Let cool.

6. Pour into six wine glasses or glass bowls. Refrigerate for at least 2 hours, until set. Top with reserved raisins and almonds. Decorate with cinnamon sticks and serve.

Blueberry Jelly with Mascarpone Cream

Serves: 4 • Prep: 20 min. + 12 hr. chilling • Cooking: 10 min. • Level: 1

BLUEBERRY JELLY
- 2 cups (500 g) fresh blueberries
- 3 tablespoons freshly squeezed lemon juice
- 1 cup (250 ml) water, plus 3 tablespoons
- 1 cup (200 g) superfine (caster) sugar
- 1 tablespoon unflavored gelatin powder

MASCARPONE CREAM
- ⅓ cup (80 ml) heavy (double) cream
- 3 tablespoons confectioners' (icing) sugar
- ½ teaspoon vanilla extract (essence)
- ¾ cup (180 g) mascarpone cheese

1. To prepare the blueberry jelly, combine the blueberries, lemon juice, 1 cup water, and superfine sugar in a medium saucepan over medium heat and bring to a boil. Decrease the heat to medium-low and simmer for 5 minutes.

2. Sprinkle the gelatin over the remaining 3 tablespoons water and let soak for 5 minutes, or until softened. Stir into the berries until dissolved. Remove from the heat and strain through a muslin or cloth-lined sieve into a pitcher (jug). Pour the liquid into six ½-cup (125-ml) cups or serving glasses and refrigerate overnight, or until set.

3. To prepare the mascarpone cream, whisk together the cream, confectioners' sugar, and vanilla until soft peaks form. Fold into the mascarpone and refrigerate until needed.

4. Serve the jellies with a dollop of mascarpone cream.

Blueberry Jelly with Mascarpone Cream ▷

Peaches in White Wine with Zabaglione

Peaches, wine, and cinnamon are a classic combination. The addition of Zabaglione gives the dish an extra elegant touch. Zabalione is an Italian dessert cream traditionally made with egg yolks, sugar, and Sicilian Marsala wine.

Serves: 6 • Prep: 20 min. + 1 hr, chilling • Cooking: 30 min. • Level: 2

- 2 cups (500 ml) dry white wine
- ½ cup (125 g) sugar
- 1 stick cinnamon
- ½ cup (125 ml) cold water
- 6 peaches, peeled
- 2 cups (500 ml) Zabaglione (see page 239)

1. Combine the wine, sugar, cinnamon stick, and water in a large saucepan and bring to a boil. Simmer for 5 minutes, or until the sugar has dissolved.

2. Immerse the peaches in this liquid and simmer until tender but still firm, 5 to 10 minutes. Remove from the saucepan and leave to cool.

3. Meanwhile, reduce the cooking juices over high heat until they turn to syrup. Remove from the heat and let cool. Discard the cinnamon stick.

4. Arrange the peaches in six martini glasses and pour the syrup over the top. Chill in the refrigerator for at least 1 hour.

5. Prepare the zabaglione and spoon over the peaches.

Spiced Fruit Compote

Serves: 6 • Prep: 15 min. + 2 hr. cooling • Cooking: 20–25 min. • Level: 1

- 1½ cups (375 ml) water
- 1½ cups (375 ml) red wine
- ¾ cup (180 ml) honey
- 1 cinnamon stick
- 1 whole star anise
- 1 teaspoon finely grated orange zest
- ¼ cup (60 ml) freshly squeezed orange juice
- ¾ cup (135 g) dried apricots
- ¾ cup (135 g) dried figs
- ¾ cup (135 g) prunes
- 4 tart apples, such as Granny Smiths, peeled, cored, and cut into wedges
- 4 pears, peeled, cored, and cut into wedges
- ⅓ cup (60 g) raisins
- 1 cup (250 ml) crème fraîche or heavy (double) cream
- 2 tablespoons confectioners' (icing) sugar
- 1 cup (150 g) flaked almonds, toasted

1. Heat the water, wine, honey, cinnamon stick, star anise, orange zest, and orange juice in a large saucepan over medium-high heat until it reaches the boiling point.

2. Decrease the heat to low and add the dried and fresh fruit to the spiced liquid. Cook for 15–20 minutes, until the fruits are soft. Remove from the heat, set aside, and allow to cool to room temperature.

3. Whisk the crème fraîche and confectioners' sugar together in a small bowl until combined and slightly thickened. (If using heavy cream, beat until soft peaks form).

4. To serve, place a large scoop of fruit compote into each serving bowl. Top with a dollop of crème fraîche. Sprinkle with toasted almonds.

◁ **Peaches in White Wine with Zabaglione**

Minted Mango Fool

Serves: 6 · Prep: 15 min. · Level 1

5	large ripe mangoes
4	tablespoons confectioners' (icing) sugar
2	teaspoons freshly squeezed lime juice
1	cup (250 ml) heavy (double) cream
1	cup (250 ml) plain yogurt
¼	cup finely chopped mint leaves
6	sprigs mint, for garnish

1. Place six wine goblets in the refrigerator to chill.

2. Peel the mangoes and cut the flesh away from the pit (stone), reserving three mango cheeks for later use. Combine the remaining mango in a food processor with half the confectioners' sugar and the lime juice and blend until smooth. Transfer the purée into a small bowl and set aside.

3. Whisk the cream and the remaining confectioners' sugar until thickened. Fold in the yogurt, chopped mint, and half the mango purée.

4. To assemble, remove the serving glasses from the refrigerator and slice the reserved mango cheeks into thin strips. Divide one-third of the remaining mango purée among the glasses and top with half the cream mixture. Arrange half the mango strips on top followed by another third of the purée. Repeat this process until the glasses are full. Garnish each with a sprig of mint.

Gooseberry Fool

The name "fool" probably comes from the French fouler (to mash) and has been used since the 17th century for desserts made with puréed fruit folded into cream.

Serves: 4–6 · Prep: 15 min. + 1–2 hr. chilling · Cooking: 5–10 min. · Level: 1

14	ounces (400 g) gooseberries, topped and tailed
⅓	cup (70 g) sugar, + more as required
1	tablespoon water
1	cup (250 ml) light (single) cream
¾	cup (200 ml) Vanilla Crème Anglaise, homemade (see page 279) or store-bought
	Vanilla cookies, to serve (optional)

1. Place the gooseberries in a medium saucepan and add ⅓ cup (70 g) of the sugar and the water. Stew over low heat for 5–10 minutes, until the gooseberries burst their skins and are soft. Leave to cool.

2. Transfer to a food processor—reserving a few gooseberries for decoration—and process until smooth. Taste the purée and add more sugar if needed.

3. Whip the cream until soft peaks form, then fold it into the custard. Lightly fold in the gooseberry purée so that the fool is marbled.

4. Spoon the mixture into small glasses and chill in the refrigerator for 1–2 hours.

5. Garnish each serving with a few reserved gooseberries. Serve with vanilla cookies, if liked.

Minted Mango Fool ▷

ICE CREAM AND FROZEN DESSERTS

The ultimate dessert for summer! Invest in an ice-cream

machine—if you don't already own one—and create

healthy desserts that you know are not loaded with

sugar and additives. In this chapter we have included

eight basic ice cream recipes, three sorbets, two

granitas, and two semifreddos, as well as the super

scrumptious Ice Cream Meringue Torte shown here.

◁ **Ice Cream Meringue Torte (see page 230)**

Chocolate Fudge Amaretti Sundaes

The ice cream in this recipe is a rich, egg-cream mixture based on an Italian gelato recipe. It is perfect here, but is also good on its own, with fruit coulis, or served with any of our hot crisps, cobblers, and tart recipes (see Index).

Serves: 4–6 • Prep: 15 min. + 30 min. chilling + churning time • Cooking: 20 min. • Level: 1

RICH EGG-CREAM ICE CREAM
- 2   cups (500 ml) milk
- 2   cups (500 ml) heavy (double) cream
-     Zest of ½ lemon
- 1½   cups (300 g) sugar
- 8   large egg yolks

CHOCOLATE SAUCE AND CRUNCHY LAYERS
- ⅓   cup (90 g) unsalted butter
- ½   cup (100 g) firmly packed light brown sugar
- ½   cup (125 ml) heavy (double) cream
- 2   tablespoons unsweetened cocoa powder
- 3   ounces (90 g) amaretti cookies (biscuits), coarsely crushed
- 3   ounces (90 g) chocolate-coated peanuts, coarsely chopped

1. To prepare the ice cream, place a large bowl in the freezer to chill. Combine the milk, cream, lemon zest, and ¾ cup (150 g) sugar in a heavy-bottomed saucepan over medium-low heat and bring almost to a boil. Remove from the heat and discard the lemon zest.

2. Beat the egg yolks and remaining ¾ cup (150 g) sugar in a medium bowl with an electric mixer on high speed until pale and creamy. Pour one-third of the hot milk mixture over the egg mixture, beating constantly. Beat in the remaining hot cream. Return the mixture to the saucepan. Simmer over very low heat, stirring constantly, until it just coats the back of the spoon. Do not let the mixture boil. Remove from the heat and pour into the chilled bowl. Let cool completely, stirring often. Refrigerate for 30 minutes.

3. Transfer the mixture to an ice-cream maker and churn according to the manufacturer's instructions. Transfer to a freezer container, cover with parchment paper, and freeze until you are ready to serve.

4. To prepare the sauce, melt the butter in a saucepan over medium heat. Add the brown sugar, cream, and cocoa powder. Stir until smooth. Simmer for 5 minutes. Set aside to cool a little, 10–15 minutes.

5. Layer the amaretti cookies, chocolate-coated peanuts, ice cream, and chocolate sauce in four to six serving glasses and serve.

Rum and Raisin Ice Cream

Serve this classic ice cream with the Banana Fritters on page 254. If liked, replace the rum with the same amount of sweet dessert wine for an equally delicious, fruity ice cream.

Serves: 4 • Prep: 15 min. + overnight to soak + 30 min. cooling + churning time • Cooking: 10 min. • Level: 1

- ½   cup (90 g) raisins
- 6   tablespoons (90 ml) dark rum
- 1¼   cups (300 ml) light (single) cream
- 4   large egg yolks
- ½   cup (100 g) firmly packed light brown sugar
- ¾   cup (180 ml) heavy (double) cream

1. Plump the raisins in 4 tablespoons (60 ml) of the rum in a small bowl overnight.

2. Heat the light cream in a small saucepan over medium heat until almost boiling. Remove from the heat and set aside.

3. Whisk the egg yolks and brown sugar in a medium heatproof bowl until thick and pale. Slowly pour one-third of the hot light cream into the egg mixture, whisking to combine. Pour in the remaining half-and-half. Place the bowl over a saucepan of simmering water. Cook the custard mixture, stirring continuously with a wooden spoon, until it is thick enough to coat the back of the spoon. Remove from the heat and refrigerate until cool, about 30 minutes.

4. Stir in the heavy cream and remaining 2 tablespoons (30 ml) rum. Pour the mixture into an ice-cream machine and churn according to the manufacturer's instructions until almost completely frozen. Add the raisins and churn for another 2 minutes, or until combined.

5. Transfer the ice cream to a freezer container, cover with parchment paper, and freeze until you are ready to serve.

Chocolate Fudge Amaretti Sundaes ▷

Rocky Road Ice Cream

This is an Australian "rocky road," where the classic ingredients are marshmallow, chocolate, shredded (desiccated) coconut, and peanuts.

Serves: 4–6 • Prep: 20 min. + 30 min. cooling + churning time
Cooking: 15 min. • Level: 1

- 2 cups (500 ml) heavy (double) cream
- 2 cups (500 ml) milk
- 8 ounces (250 g) bittersweet or dark (70% cacao) chocolate, coarsely chopped
- 4 large egg yolks
- ½ cup (100 g) superfine (caster) sugar
- ¼ cup (30 g) unsweetened cocoa powder
- ¼ cup (40 g) roasted peanuts
- ¼ cup (45 g) candied (glacé) cherries
- ¼ cup mini marshmallows
- 2 tablespoons shredded coconut

1. Heat the milk and cream in a medium saucepan over medium heat. Bring almost to a boil, then remove from the heat. Put the chocolate in a heatproof bowl and pour in half the hot cream, stirring until it is melted and combined.

2. Beat the egg yolks, superfine sugar, and cocoa in a medium bowl with an electric mixer fitted with a whisk until pale and creamy. Gradually pour in the remaining hot cream and the chocolate mixture, whisking to combine.

3. Return the custard to the saucepan and simmer over medium-low heat, stirring constantly, until it coats the back of the spoon. Remove from the heat and let cool, about 30 minutes.

4. Pour the custard mixture into an ice-cream maker and churn according to the manufacturer's instructions until almost frozen. Add the peanuts, candied cherries, marshmallows, and coconut and churn for 3 minutes, or until incorporated. Transfer the ice cream to a freezer container, cover with parchment paper, and freeze until you are ready to serve.

Peanut Butter Ice Cream

Serve this smooth, nutty ice cream with the Warm Chocolate Brownie on page 34.

Serves: 4–6 • Prep: 20 min. + 30 min. cooling + churning time
Cooking: 15 min. • Level: 1

- 1½ cups (375 ml) milk
- 1½ cups (375 ml) heavy (double) cream
- 6 large egg yolks
- ½ cup (100 g) firmly packed light brown sugar
- 1¼ cups (300 g) smooth peanut butter

1. Combine the milk and cream in a medium saucepan over medium heat and bring almost to a boil. Remove from the heat.

2. Beat the egg yolks and brown sugar in a medium bowl with an electric mixer on high speed until pale and creamy. Gradually pour in one-third of the hot milk mixture, whisking to combine. Whisk in the remaining milk mixture. Return the custard to the saucepan and simmer over medium-low heat, stirring continuously, until it thickens enough to coat the back of the spoon. Remove from the heat and let cool.

3. Stir the peanut butter into the cooled custard and refrigerate until chilled.

4. Pour the custard mixture into an ice-cream machine and churn according to the manufacturer's instructions. Transfer the ice cream to a freezer container, cover with parchment paper, and freeze until you are ready to serve.

Rocky Road Ice Cream ▷

Coconut Ice Cream with Black Sesame Tuile

Serves: 4 · Prep: 45 min. + churning time + 1 hr. resting batter Cooking: 15 min. · Level: 3

COCONUT ICE CREAM
- ½   cup (100 g) granulated sugar
- ½   cup (100 g) grated jaggery (palm sugar)
- ¾   cup (180 ml) water
- 1⅓ cups (400 ml) coconut milk
- 1   cup (250 ml) heavy (double) cream
- Shredded (desiccated) coconut or coconut curls, for garnish

BLACK SESAME TUILE
- 1   large egg white, lightly beaten with a fork
- 3   tablespoons (45 g) superfine (caster) sugar
- 1½ teaspoons all-purpose (plain) flour
- 3   tablespoons black sesame seeds
- 2   teaspoons cold-pressed light sesame oil

1. To prepare the ice cream, combine the sugar, jaggery, and water in a medium saucepan over medium-low and bring to a boil. Remove from the heat and stir in the coconut milk and cream. Refrigerate until cool, about 30 minutes. Pour into an ice-cream maker and churn according to the manufacturer's instructions. Transfer to a freezer container, cover with plastic wrap, and freeze until you are ready to serve.

2. To prepare the tuiles, put the egg white in a small bowl. Add the sugar, flour, sesame seeds, and sesame oil and whisk until combined. Cover with plastic wrap and leave at room temperature for 1 hour.

4. Preheat the oven to 425°F (220°C/gas 7). Line two cookie sheets with parchment paper. Make a template by cutting a 2½-inch (6-cm) circle out of a thin piece of plastic. Trace onto the parchment paper with a pencil. Place ¾ teaspoon of the tuile mixture in the traced circle and spread with a palette knife. Repeat, leaving ½ inch (1 cm) between each tuile until all the mixture is used up. You will have about 20 tuiles.

5. Have two rolling pins handy for shaping the cookies. Bake, one sheet at a time, for 5 minutes, or until tuiles are golden. Working quickly, lay the tuiles over the rolling pins, and leave to cool and harden into shape. Serve with the ice cream.

Cardamom Ice Cream

Serve this elegant ice cream on its own or try it with the Apple Pie on page 91 or Melktart on page 102.

Serves: 4 · Prep: 30 min. + churning time · Cooking: 10–15 min. · Level: 1

- ¾   cup (180 ml) milk
- ½   vanilla pod, split lengthwise
- 6   cardamom pods, bruised
- 4   large egg yolks
- ½   cup (100 g) sugar
- 1⅔ cups (400 ml) heavy (double) cream

1. Combine the milk, vanilla pod, and cardamom pods in a small saucepan over medium-low heat. Cook until it reaches the boiling point. Remove from the heat and set aside for 10 minutes, allowing the vanilla to infuse.

2. Whisk the egg yolks and sugar in a medium heatproof bowl until thick and pale. Scrape the seeds from the vanilla bean into the milk and discard the bean. Slowly pour the milk into the egg mixture, stirring to combine. Strain through a fine mesh sieve.

3. Place the bowl over a saucepan of barely simmering water. Cook, stirring constantly with a wooden spoon, until the custard coats the back of the spoon. Remove the bowl from the heat and cover the custard with parchment paper, to prevent a skin from forming. Refrigerate until cool.

4. Stir in the cream and pour the mixture into an ice-cream maker. Churn according to the manufacturer's instructions. Transfer the ice cream into a freezer container, cover with parchment paper, and freeze until you are ready to serve.

Coconut Ice Cream with Black Sesame Tuile ▷

Creamy Rice Ice Cream with Chocolate Sauce

Serves: 4 • Prep: 15 min. + 30 min. cooling + churning time • Cooking: 25 min. • Level: 1

ICE CREAM
- 2 cups (500 ml) milk
- 3/4 cup (150 g) short-grain or pudding rice
- 1 vanilla pod, slit open lengthwise
- Generous 1/4 cup (50 g) golden raisins (sultanas)
- 1/8 teaspoon salt
- Finely grated zest of 1 orange
- Finely grated zest and juice of 1 lemon
- 2 tablespoons honey or brown rice syrup

SAUCE
- 8 ounces (250 g) bittersweet or dark chocolate, grated
- 1 1/2 cups (375 ml) milk
- 2 scant teaspoons cornstarch (cornflour)
- 1/2 cup (50 g) superfine (caster) sugar

1. To prepare the ice cream, combine the milk, rice, vanilla pod, and golden raisins in a heavy-bottomed saucepan over medium heat. Bring to a boil, then lower the heat. Stir in the salt. Simmer, stirring constantly, until the rice is tender and has absorbed almost all the milk, about 15 minutes. Remove from the heat and discard the vanilla pod. Let cool completely, stirring from time to time.

2. Stir in the orange zest, lemon zest, lemon juice, and honey. Transfer the mixture to an ice-cream maker and churn according to the manufacturer's instructions.

3. To prepare the sauce, combine the chocolate and 3/4 cup milk in a saucepan over medium heat and bring to a boil. Dissolve the cornstarch in the remaining 3/4 cup milk and mix into the chocolate along with the superfine sugar. Stir constantly over low heat until thickened. Remove from the heat and whisk until smooth.

4. When the ice cream is frozen, spoon it into serving dishes and drizzle with the chocolate sauce.

Ice Cream and Meringue Torte

This frozen meringue cake makes an impressive finish to any meal. It can also be prepared with 1 quart (1 liter) each of two commercially made ice creams; choose your favorite flavors to combine.

Serves: 8 • Prep: 45 min. + churning time + 2 hours freezing
Cooking: 90 min. • Level: 2

- 1 recipe Dacquoise (see page 142)
- 1 recipe Bitter Chocolate Sorbet (see page 243)

NOUGAT ICE CREAM
- 1 cup (250 ml) milk
- 1 cup (250 ml) heavy (double) cream
- 3/4 cup (150 g) sugar
- 1 tablespoon cognac
- 4 tablespoons finely chopped firm nougat

- 2 cups (500 ml) heavy (double) cream
- Dark chocolate, grated, to decorate

1. Prepare the dacquoise and chocolate sorbet.

2. To prepare the nougat ice cream, combine the milk, cream, and sugar in a heavy saucepan over medium heat and stir constantly until the sugar has dissolved. Remove from the heat and let cool. Add the cognac and mix well. Transfer to an ice-cream maker and churn according to the manufacturer's instructions. When the ice cream is almost frozen, add the chopped nougat and finish churning. Spoon the ice cream into a container, cover with parchment paper, and place in the freezer.

3. Line a 9 1/2-inch (24-cm) springform pan with parchment paper. Let both types of ice cream stand at room temperature for 10 minutes to soften. Place one of the meringue disks in the prepared pan. Spread with a 1/2-inch (1-cm) layer of the nougat ice cream. Add another of the meringue disks. Spread with a 1/2-inch (1-cm) layer of the chocolate sorbet. Add the remaining meringue disk. Freeze for 2 hours.

4. Beat the cream in a large bowl with an electric mixer on high speed until thick. Remove the torte from the freezer, unmold, and place on a serving dish. Cover the top and sides with most of the cream. Spoon the remaining whipped cream into a piping bag fitted with a star-shaped nozzle. Decorate the top with piped cream. Sprinkle with grated chocolate and serve.

Creamy Rice Ice Cream with Chocolate Sauce ▷

🌿 Green Apple Sorbet with Calvados

Calvados is an apple brandy made in Normandy, in northern France. This recipe is low in fat, dairy-free, gluten-free, and does not contain eggs.

Serves: 4 • Prep: 15 min. + churning time • Cooking: 10 min. • Level: 1

- ³⁄₄ cup (150 g) sugar
- 1 cup (250 ml) water
- 2 tablespoons (30 g) glucose or light corn (golden) syrup
- 2–3 drops green food coloring, optional
- 2 Granny Smith apples
- Freshly squeezed juice of 1 lemon
- Calvados, at room temperature

1. Combine the sugar, ³⁄₄ cup (200 ml) of the water, glucose, and food coloring, if using, in a saucepan over medium heat and bring to a boil. Remove from the heat and let cool.

2. Peel and core the apples, then slice thinly. Put in a bowl of cold water with the lemon juice.

3. Drain the apples and chop in a food processor until smooth. Measure 1 cup (250 g) of the apple purée and stir it into the cooled sugar syrup. Stir in the remaining ¼ cup (50 ml) water.

4. Transfer to an ice-cream maker and churn according to the manufacturer's instructions.

5. Serve the sorbet in 4–6 small glasses filled not quite to the brim. Top up with Calvados.

🌿 Sage Sorbet

This unusual sorbet makes a refreshing dessert after a hearty meal. This recipe is low in fat, dairy-free, gluten-free, and does not contain eggs.

Serves: 4 • Prep: 10 min. + 1 hr. 30 min. infusing and freezing + churning time • Cooking: 5 min. • Level: 1

- ³⁄₄ cup (150 g) sugar
- 1¹⁄₃ cups (350 ml) water
- 2 tablespoons (30 g) glucose or light corn (golden) syrup
- 10 fresh sage leaves + a few extra, to garnish

1. Combine the sugar and 1 cup (250 ml) of water in a large saucepan over medium heat and bring to a boil. Simmer until the sugar has completely dissolved, 2–3 minutes. Remove from the heat and add the glucose and 10 sage leaves. Set aside to infuse for 30 minutes.

2. Discard the sage leaves and add the remaining ¹⁄₃ cup (90 ml) water. Freeze for 1 hour.

3. Transfer to an ice-cream maker and churn according to the manufacturer's instructions.

4. Spoon the frozen sorbet into four serving glasses or bowls and garnish each one with 1–2 fresh sage leaves.

◁ **Green Apple Sorbet with Calvados**

🌿 Lemon Granita

For a special touch, moisten the rims of four to six martini glasses with lemon juice and dip them in superfine (caster) sugar to frost. Scoop the granita into the glasses and serve at once. This recipe is low in fat, dairy-free, gluten-free, and does not contain eggs.

Serves: 4 • Prep: 10 min. + 1 hr. freezing + churning time • Cooking: 5 min. • Level: 1

2	cups (500 ml) water
¾	cup (150 g) sugar
½	cup (125 ml) freshly squeezed lemon juice

1. Combine the water and sugar in a heavy-bottomed saucepan over low heat and stir until the sugar is dissolved. Remove from the heat and let cool to room temperature.

2. Stir in the lemon juice, then pour the syrup into a plastic or stainless steel container about 10 inches (25 cm) square. Cover tightly with plastic wrap (cling film).

3. Freeze for 1 hour. Use a fork or hand blender to break the granita up into large crystals. If using an ice-cream maker, transfer to the machine at this point and follow the manufacturer's instructions. To continue by hand, replace the container in the freezer for 30 minutes, then break up again with a fork. Repeat three or four times, until the crystals are completely frozen.

4. Scoop into glass serving bowls and serve.

🌿 Citrus Tea Granita

This recipe is low in fat, dairy-free, gluten-free, and does not contain eggs.

Serves: 4 • Prep: 25 min. + 1 hr. freezing + churning time • Cooking: 5 min. • Level: 1

2	cups (500 ml) water
1	teaspoon loose tea leaves
	Generous ½ cup (125 g) sugar
	Finely grated zest and juice of 1 orange
	Finely grated zest and juice of 1 lime + peel, to garnish
¼	cup (60 ml) dark rum
½	teaspoon vanilla extract (essence)

1. Bring 1 cup (250 ml) of the water to a boil in a small saucepan over high heat. Put the tea into a teapot and cover with the just-boiled water. Let brew for 10 minutes. Strain the tea using a tea strainer. Let cool completely.

2. Combine the remaining water in the same saucepan with the sugar and orange and lime zests. Bring to a boil over medium-low heat, stirring constantly until the sugar has dissolved, 2–3 minutes. Remove from the heat and let cool to room temperature.

3. Stir in the rum, tea, orange juice, lime juice, and vanilla, mixing well. Pour the mixture into a plastic or stainless steel container about 10 inches (25 cm) square.

4. Freeze for 1 hour. Use a fork or hand blender to break the granita up into large crystals. If using an ice-cream maker, transfer to the machine at this point and follow the manufacturer's instructions. To continue by hand, replace the container in the freezer for 30 minutes, then break up again with a fork. Repeat three or four times, until the crystals are completely frozen.

5. Scoop into four chilled glasses. Garnish with the lime peel and serve with long-handled dessert spoons.

Lemon Granita ▷

Mini Bombe Alaska

These eyecatching little desserts will please everyone. They can be served at children's birthday parties or adult dinner parties with equal success.

Serves: 6 · Prep: 45 min. + 30 min. cooling + churning time · Cooking: 15 min. · Level: 2

STRAWBERRY ICE CREAM
- 2   cups (500 ml) heavy (double) cream
- ½   vanilla bean, split lengthwise and seeds scraped
- 5   large egg yolks
- ½   cup (100 g) superfine (caster) sugar
- 2   cups (500 g) fresh strawberries, hulled
- 1   tablespoon (15 ml) strawberry liqueur

MERINGUE TOPPING AND BASE
- 3   large egg whites
- ½   cup (100 g) superfine (caster) sugar
- ¼   cup (80 g) raspberry preserves (jam)
- 12   small ladyfingers (sponge fingers)

1. To prepare the strawberry ice cream, combine the cream and vanilla bean and seeds in a medium saucepan over medium-low heat and bring to a boil. Remove from the heat and set aside.

2. Beat the egg yolks and superfine sugar in a medium heatproof bowl with an electric mixer fitted with a whisk on high speed until pale and creamy. Slowly pour one-third of the hot cream into the egg mixture, stirring until combined. Stir in the rest.

3. Place the bowl over a saucepan of barely simmering water and cook, stirring constantly with a wooden spoon, until the custard coats the back of the spoon. Remove from the heat, discard the vanilla bean, and cover custard with parchment paper, to prevent a skin from forming.

4. Purée the strawberries and liqueur in a blender and strain through a fine-mesh sieve to remove the seeds. Stir the strawberry purée into the custard and refrigerate until cooled, about 30 minutes.

5. Pour the mixture into an ice-cream maker and churn according to the manufacturer's instructions. Transfer the ice cream to a freezer container, cover with parchment paper, and freeze until you are ready to serve.

6. Preheat the oven to 425°F (220°C/gas 7). Line a baking sheet with parchment paper.

7. To prepare the meringue topping, beat the egg whites in a medium bowl with an electric mixer fitted with a whisk on high speed until soft peaks form. Gradually add the superfine sugar and beat until the mixture is glossy and forms stiff peaks.

8. Melt the preserves in a small saucepan over medium-low heat. Brush generously on one side of the ladyfingers. Sandwich two fingers together using a little meringue mixture as glue, and place side by side on the prepared sheet. Continue this process until you have six sponge finger bases. Place a scoop of the strawberry ice cream on top of each base. Cover completely with a large dollop of the meringue. Create decorative peaks using a spatula or the back of a spoon.

9. Immediately bake for 4 minutes, or until the meringue is golden.

10. Transfer to individual serving plates using a palette knife and serve immediately.

Mini Bombe Alaska ▷

Zabaglione Semifreddo

Follow steps 1 and 2 in this recipe to make a classic Zabaglione which can be served as is, spooned over fresh fruit, piped into cream puffs, and many other ways too.

Serves: 6–8 · Prep: 25 min. + 5 hr. freezing · Cooking: 10–15 min. · Level: 1

- 8 large egg yolks
- 1 cup (200 g) superfine (caster) sugar
- 1 cup (250 ml) Marsala wine
- 2 cups (500 ml) heavy (double) cream
  Langue de chat cookies, ice cream wafers, or thin butter cookies, to serve

1. To make the zabaglione, beat the egg yolks and superfine sugar in a large heatproof bowl with an electric mixer fitted with a whisk on high speed until very pale and creamy. Gradually beat in the Marsala, 1 tablespoon at a time.

2. Place the bowl over barely simmering water and beat until thick and creamy, 10–15 minutes. Remove from the heat and let cool.

3. Beat the cream in a large bowl with an electric mixer on high speed until thick.

4. Set aside ¼ cup (60 ml) of the zabaglione. Fold the whipped cream into the remaining zabaglione.

5. Oil six to eight ¾ cup (180 ml) ramekins with almond oil. Spoon the semifreddo into the ramekins. Freeze for at least 5 hours.

6. Just before serving, turn the semifreddo desserts out onto serving dishes and spoon the reserved zabaglione over the top.

Jaffa Semifreddo

Serves: 6–8 · Prep: 30 min. + 1 hr. 45 min. infusing and chilling + 12 hr. freezing · Cooking: 10 min. · Level: 1

- 4 tablespoons candied orange peel
- 1 cup (250 ml) milk
- 5 large egg yolks
- ½ cup (100 g) sugar
- ¼ cup orange-flavored liqueur, such as Grand Marnier
- 3 ounces (90 g) dark chocolate, melted
- 2 cups (500 ml) heavy (double) cream
- 2 tablespoons candied orange peel, finely sliced, to decorate
- 2 ounces (60 g) dark chocolate, shaved with a vegetable peeler

1. Line a 9 x 5-inch (13 x 23-cm) loaf pan with parchment paper.

2. Combine the 4 tablespoons candied orange peel and milk in a small saucepan over medium heat and heat until it almost reaches the boiling point. Remove from the heat and set aside for 1 hour to allow the flavors to infuse.

3. Strain the infused milk through a fine-mesh sieve into a medium heatproof bowl, discarding the orange peel. Beat in the egg yolks, sugar, and liqueur with an electric mixer until pale and creamy. Place the bowl over a saucepan of barely simmering water. Cook the custard mixture, stirring constantly with a wooden spoon, until it is thick enough to coat the back of the spoon. Remove from the heat and whisk in the melted chocolate. Refrigerate for 45 minutes.

4. Whisk 1 cup (250 ml) of the cream until stiff. Fold the whipped cream into the cooled custard mixture. Pour the mixture into the prepared pan, cover with parchment paper, and freeze overnight.

5. Whip the remaining 1 cup (250 ml) cream until stiff.

6. Dip the bottom of the loaf pan into warm water for 20 seconds and invert the semifreddo onto a cutting board. Remove the parchment paper and, using a hot knife, slice into six to eight portions, placing them on individual serving plates. Place a dollop of whipped cream to the side and garnish with a few strips of candied orange peel and chocolate shavings.

◁ **Jaffa Semifreddo**

Raspberry Ripple Sundae

Children will love this dessert and they will also enjoy helping you assemble it in the glasses.

Serves: 4 · Prep: 30 min. + 1 hr. chilling + churning time · Cooking: 10 min. · Level: 1

ICE CREAM
- ³/₄   cup (180 ml) milk
- 1   vanilla bean, split lengthwise
- 4   large egg yolks
- ½   cup (100 g) granulated sugar
- 1²/₃   cups (400 ml) heavy (double) cream

RIPPLE
- 2   cups (500 g) fresh or frozen raspberries, defrosted and drained, if frozen
- ¼   cup (60 ml) light corn syrup
- ½   teaspoon ground cinnamon

CHOCOLATE SAUCE
- 4   ounces (120 g) semisweet (dark) chocolate, coarsely chopped
- 1   tablespoon (15 ml) water
- 2   tablespoons (30 g) unsalted butter
- 4   tablespoons (60 g) superfine (caster) sugar

TO SERVE
- 1   cup (250 g) fresh raspberries

1. To prepare the ice cream, heat the milk and vanilla pod in a small saucepan over medium-low heat until it reaches the boiling point. Remove from the heat and set aside for 10 minutes, allowing the vanilla to infuse.

2. Whisk the egg yolks and granulated sugar in a medium heatproof bowl until thick and pale. Scrape the seeds from the vanilla bean into the milk and discard the bean. Slowly pour the milk into the egg mixture, stirring to combine. Place the bowl over a saucepan of barely simmering water. Simmer, stirring constantly, until the custard coats the back of the spoon. Remove the bowl from the heat and cover the custard with plastic wrap (cling film), to prevent a skin from forming. Let cool, then refrigerate for at least 1 hour.

3. To prepare the ripple, combine the raspberries, corn syrup, and cinnamon in a blender and process until smooth. Strain the raspberry purée through a fine-mesh sieve. Cover with plastic wrap. Refrigerate until you are ready to use it.

4. Stir the cream into the cooled custard mixture and pour into an ice-cream maker. Churn according to the manufacturer's instructions, until the ice cream is almost completely frozen. Add the raspberry purée and continue to churn for 1 minute, or until the purée is swirled but not completely blended through. Transfer the ice cream to a freezer container, cover with plastic wrap, and freeze until you are ready to serve.

5. To prepare the chocolate sauce, melt the chocolate in the water in a small saucepan over low heat. Stir in the butter and superfine sugar until combined and thickened.

6. To serve, place two scoops of ice cream into each of four glass serving dishes or dessert cups. Sprinkle with fresh raspberries and drizzle with chocolate sauce.

Bitter Chocolate Sorbet

Be sure to use a top quality bittersweet or dark chocolate for this sorbet—everything depends on the taste of the chocolate.

Serves: 4 · Prep: 15 min. + 2 hr. chilling + churning time · Cooking: 5 min. Level: 1

2½	cups (625 ml) water
1¼	cups (250 g) sugar
2½	teaspoons instant coffee granules
⅓	cup (50 g) unsweetened cocoa powder, sifted
3½	ounces (100 g) good-quality bittersweet or dark (at least 70% cacao) chocolate

1. Combine the water, sugar, coffee, cocoa powder, and chocolate in a medium saucepan over medium-low heat and bring to a boil. Simmer for 5 minutes.

2. Remove from the heat and strain through a fine-mesh sieve into a bowl. Refrigerate for 2 hours, or until cool.

3. Pour the mixture into an ice-cream maker and churn according to the manufacturer's instructions.

4. Transfer the sorbet into a freezer container, cover with parchment paper, and freeze until you are ready to serve.

◁ **White Chocolate and Macadamia Praline Parfait**

White Chocolate and Macadamia Praline Parfait

Serves: 6 · Prep: 45 min. + 12 hr. freezing · Cooking: 20 min. · Level:

MACADAMIA PRALINE

1¼	cups (190 g) macadamia nuts
1	cup (200 g) superfine (caster) sugar

WHITE CHOCOLATE MOUSSE

1¼	cups (300 ml) heavy (double) cream
1	vanilla bean, split lengthwise
3	large egg yolks
8	ounces (250 g) white chocolate, coarsely chopped, plus extra to garnish
1¼	cups (300 ml) heavy (double) cream, whipped

1. To prepare the praline, line a 15½ x 11½-inch (39 x 29-cm) baking sheet with parchment paper and grease lightly with oil or cooking spray. Toast the macadamia nuts in a large frying pan over medium heat for 3 to 5 minutes, or until light brown. Place in a small bowl.

2. Melt the superfine sugar in a small saucepan over medium heat until it is an even golden color. Remove from the heat and stir in the macadamia nuts. Pour the caramel nut mixture onto the prepared baking sheet and let cool. Chop roughly in a food processor.

3. To prepare the mousse, heat the cream and vanilla bean in a small saucepan over medium heat until it reaches boiling point. Remove from the heat. Whisk the egg yolks in a medium heatproof bowl. Gradually pour one-third of the hot cream into the egg yolks, whisking all the time. Then whisk in the rest. Add the chocolate and place the bowl over a saucepan of barely simmering water. Stir with a wooden spoon until the mixture coats the back of the spoon. Let cool to room temperature. Fold in the whipped cream and praline.

4. Line six 1-cup (250-ml) metal dariole or baba molds with two long strips of parchment paper, leaving the ends to hang over the edge. These will be used to help remove the parfait when frozen. Pour the white chocolate mixture evenly into the molds, tapping the bottoms on the work surface to remove any air bubbles. Cover with aluminum foil or plastic wrap and freeze overnight.

FRITTERS, WAFFLES, AND CREPES

Fried foods need not be unhealthy. As an occasional treat they really are unbeatable. There are two ways of frying food—pan-frying and deep-frying. Most desserts are deep-fried so you will need at least 4 cups (1 liter) of clean, good-quality frying oil on hand. We recommend you use olive oil—not the expensive extra-virgin olive oil, but rather a good-quality plain olive oil. Make sure the oil is hot when you add the food.

◁ Cannoli (see page 248)

Churros with Chocolate Sauce

Serves: 6 · Prep: 40 min. · Cooking: 20 min. · Level 2

CHOCOLATE SAUCE
½	cup (125 ml) water
¼	cup (50 g) sugar
1¼	cups (225 g) dark chocolate chips
1	tablespoon cocoa powder
¼	cup (60 ml) milk

CHURROS
3	tablespoons sugar
2	cups (500 ml) water
3	tablespoons butter
2½	cups (375 g) all-purpose (plain) flour
	Pinch of salt
2	large eggs, lightly beaten
6	cups (1.5 liters) vegetable oil, for deep-frying

1. To prepare the chocolate sauce, heat the water and sugar over medium heat until the sugar dissolves. Decrease the heat to low and add the chocolate, cocoa powder, and milk. Cook, stirring continuously, until the chocolate melts to form a smooth sauce. Set aside, keeping warm.

2. To prepare the churros, combine the sugar, water, and butter in a large saucepan over medium heat and bring to a boil. Stir in the flour and salt with a wooden spoon and cook for 2 minutes, until the dough comes away from the sides of the pan. Remove from the heat and beat in the eggs, stirring continuously until incorporated.

3. Heat the oil in a deep-fryer or deep saucepan to 365°F (190°C). If you don't have a frying thermometer, test the oil temperature by dropping a small piece of bread into the hot oil. If the bread immediately bubbles to the surface and begins to turn golden, the oil is ready.

4. Spoon the dough into a pastry bag fitted with a ½-inch (1-cm) star tip nozzle. Pipe 4-inch (10-cm) lengths into the hot oil and fry until golden. Remove from the oil with tongs or a slotted spoon and drain on paper towels. Continue until all the dough is used.

5. Pour the sauce into six espresso cups and place on individual serving plates with the churros to the side.

FRYING FOOD STEP-BY-STEP

Fried food need not be soggy and difficult to digest. Follow a few easy rules and you can serve crisp, light churros and other fritters. The most important rule is to make sure the oil is hot enough; the outside of the churro or fritter should "seal" on contact with the oil, so that the oil stays outside and the inside remains light.

1 Heat the oil over medium heat to 365°F (190°C). If you don't have a frying thermometer, drop a small piece of bread into the hot oil. If the bread immediately bubbles to the surface and begins to turn golden, the oil is ready.

2 For churros, pipe the dough directly into the oil. If not using a piping bag, lower pieces of dough carefully into the oil using a spatula or slotted spoon. Turn the churros carefully during frying to ensure even browning.

3 Remove the churros from the hot oil using tongs or a slotted spoon. Drain on plenty of paper towels.

Cannoli

Cannoli are filled with fresh ricotta cheese sweetened with candied fruits and chocolate. They are a traditional dessert in Sicily. You will need cannoli molds to prepare them.

Serves: 4–6 • Prep: 15 min. + 1 hr. resting • Cooking: 30 min. • Level: 2

CANNOLI

- 1⅓ cups (200 g) all-purpose (plain) flour
- 1 tablespoon unsweetened cocoa powder
- 2 tablespoons granulated sugar
- Generous 1 tablespoon (20 g) lard, softened
- 2 large eggs, lightly beaten
- 2 tablespoons Marsala wine
- 4 cups (1 liter) vegetable oil, for deep-frying
- Confectioners' (icing) sugar, to dust

FILLING

- 2 cups (500 g) ricotta cheese
- 1½ cups (300 g) granulated sugar
- 1 teaspoon vanilla extract (essence)
- 4 ounces (125 g) dark chocolate, chopped
- ½ cup (100 g) chopped candied fruit or peel

1. To prepare the cannoli, mix the flour and cocoa in a medium bowl. Stir in the granulated sugar, lard, eggs, and Marsala to make a smooth dough. Shape into a ball, wrap in plastic wrap (cling film), and set aside for 1 hour to rest. Roll out the dough on a lightly floured surface to ¼ inch (3 mm) thick. Cut into twelve 4-inch (10-cm) rounds.

2. Heat the oil in a deep-fryer or deep saucepan to 365°F (190°C). If you don't have a frying thermometer, test the oil by dropping a small piece of bread into the hot oil. If the bread immediately bubbles to the surface and begins to turn golden, the oil is ready.

3. Wrap a pastry disk around each of the cannoli molds, pressing the overlapping edges together to seal. Fry the cannoli, still on the mold, in small batches, for about 5 minutes, or until bubbly and golden brown. Remove with a slotted spoon and drain on paper towels. Let cool slightly before carefully removing the mold.

4. To prepare the filling, beat the ricotta with the granulated sugar and vanilla with a wooden spoon in a large bowl. Add the chocolate and candied fruit. Just before serving, pipe the filling into the pastry tubes and arrange on a serving dish. Dust with the confectioners' sugar and serve.

Apple Fritters with Ice Cream

Serve these fritters with Rich Egg-Cream Ice (see page 224) or Creamy Rice Ice Cream (see page 230). If pushed for time, serve with good-quality store-bought vanilla ice cream.

Serves: 6 • Prep: 15 min. + 1 hr. resting • Cooking: 30 min. • Level: 2

- 1 cup (150 g) all-purpose (plain) flour
- 1 teaspoon ground cinnamon
- 1 large egg, lightly beaten
- ⅓ cup (90 ml) sweet champagne
- 2 large egg whites
- 4 sweet apples, such as Golden Delicious or Gala
- 1 lemon, juiced and strained
- 6 cups (1.5 liters) vegetable oil, for deep-frying
- Confectioners' (icing) sugar, for dusting
- Ice cream, to serve

1. Combine the flour and cinnamon in a medium bowl. Make a well in the center and pour in the whole egg and half the champagne. Whisk together, ensuring there are no lumps, and gradually add the remaining champagne. Cover the bowl with plastic wrap (cling film) and rest in the refrigerator for 1 hour.

2. Whisk the egg whites together in a small bowl until stiff, fold into the batter, and set aside.

3. Peel and core the apples and cut each one crosswise into three thick rings. Lay the rings on a tray and drizzle with lemon juice to prevent browning.

4. Heat the oil in a deep-fryer or deep saucepan to 365°F (190°C). If you don't have a frying thermometer, test the oil temperature by dropping a small piece of bread into the hot oil. If the bread immediately bubbles to the surface and begins to turn golden, the oil is ready.

5. Dip the apple rings in the batter to coat. Fry, in small batches, for 4 minutes on each side, or until golden. Remove the apples from the oil using a slotted spoon or tongs and drain on paper towels.

6. Dust the fritters with confectioners' sugar and serve hot with a scoop of ice cream.

Apple Fritters with Ice Cream ▷

Coconut Pineapple Fritters

Serves: 6 · Prep: 30 min. + 1 hr. resting · Cooking: 30 min. · Level: 2

²⁄₃ cup (100 g) glutinous rice flour
½ cup (60 g) shredded (dessicated) coconut
¼ cup (50 g) sugar
1 tablespoon black sesame seeds
¼ cup (60 ml) coconut milk
¼ cup (60 ml) water
6 cups (1.5 liters) vegetable oil, for deep-frying
6 pineapple rings
  Vanilla ice cream, to serve

1. To prepare the batter, whisk the rice flour, coconut, sugar, sesame seeds, coconut milk, and water in a medium bowl until combined. Cover the bowl with plastic wrap (cling film) and rest in the refrigerator for 1 hour.

2. Heat the oil in a deep-fryer or deep saucepan to 365°F (190°C). If you don't have a frying thermometer, test the oil temperature by dropping a small piece of bread into the hot oil. If the bread immediately bubbles to the surface and begins to turn golden, the oil is ready.

3. Dry the pineapple rings on paper towels and dip into the prepared batter until evenly coated. Fry two at a time, for 3 minutes on each side, or until an even golden color. Remove the pineapple rings from the oil using a slotted spoon or tongs and drain on paper towels.

4. Serve the pineapple rings hot, with a scoop of vanilla ice cream.

Fruit and Nut Fritters

Prepare these nutritious fritters in the fall and winter with the new season's nuts and dried fruits.

Serves: 6–8 · Prep: 25 min. + 1 hr. resting · Cooking: 25–30 min. · Level: 2

1²⁄₃ cups (250 g) all-purpose (plain) flour
¾ cup (180 ml) milk
⅓ cup (70 g) granulated sugar
3 tablespoons unsalted butter, melted
3 large egg yolks
1 teaspoon baking powder
1 tablespoon dry Marsala wine
1 teaspoon ground cinnamon
⅛ teaspoon salt
1²⁄₃ cups (300 g) mixed dried fruit and nuts, such as prunes, pineapple, papaya, pear, apricots, peanuts, hazelnuts, pecans, walnuts, or figs
4 cups (1 liter) vegetable oil, for frying
½ cup (75 g) confectioners' (icing) sugar, for dusting

1. Combine the flour, milk, granulated sugar, melted butter, egg yolks, baking powder, Marsala, cinnamon, and salt in a large bowl. Beat with an electric mixer at medium speed until smooth. Cover with a clean cloth and let stand in a warm place for 1 hour.

2. Chop the dried fruit and nuts in a food processor or until very finely chopped. Shape the fruit and nut mixture into balls the size of walnuts. Dip the balls into the batter, turning to coat well.

3. Heat the oil in a deep-fryer or deep saucepan to 365°F (190°C). If you don't have a frying thermometer, test the oil temperature by dropping a small piece of bread into the hot oil. If the bread immediately bubbles to the surface and begins to turn golden, the oil is ready.

4. Fry the fritters in batches, turning often, until crisp and golden brown all over. Drain well on paper towels. Dust with the confectioners' sugar and serve hot.

Coconut Pineapple Fritters ▷

Orange Fritters

Make a lemon-flavored version of these fritters by substituting the Cointreau with Limoncello (sweet lemon liqueur) and flavoring with freshly grated lemon zest instead of orange zest.

Serves: 6 · Prep: 20 min. + 1 hr. rising · Cooking: 30–35 min. · Level: 2

- 1 ounce (30 g) fresh compressed yeast or 2 (¼-ounce/7-g) packages active dry yeast
- 1 cup (250 ml) milk, lukewarm (110°F)
- 3⅓ cups (500 g) all-purpose (plain) flour
  Pinch of salt
- ¾ cup (150 g) sugar
- 2 tablespoons Cointreau
- ¼ cup (60 g) unsalted butter, melted
- 2 large eggs
  Finely grated zest of 2 oranges
- 4 cups (1 liter) vegetable oil, for frying

1. Combine the yeast and ¼ cup (60 ml) of the milk in a small bowl and stir until the yeast dissolves. Set aside until foamy, about 10 minutes.

2. Sift the flour and salt into a large bowl. Stir in half the sugar, the Cointreau, and butter. Add the eggs, one at a time, and mix well. Add the yeast mixture, orange zest, and remaining ¾ cup (180 ml) milk. Mix well with a wooden spoon until a soft dough forms. Cover and let rise in a warm place for 1 hour.

3. Heat the oil in a deep-fryer or deep saucepan to 365°F (190°C). If you don't have a frying thermometer, test the oil temperature by dropping a small piece of bread into the hot oil. If the bread immediately bubbles to the surface and begins to turn golden, the oil is ready.

4. Drop spoonfuls of the batter into the oil and fry, turning often, until golden brown all over. Remove with a slotted spoon and drain on paper towels. Sprinkle with the remaining sugar and serve hot.

◁ **Date and Orange Wantons**

Date and Orange Wontons

Serves: 4 · Prep: 30 min. · Cooking: 20 min. · Level: 2

- 1¼ cups (250 g) sugar
- ½ cup (125 ml) water
  Finely grated zest and juice of 2 oranges
- 3 tablespoons rose water
- 1 cup (180 g) dates, pitted
- ¼ cup (30 g) walnuts
- 12 wonton wrappers
- 6 cups (1.5 liters) vegetable oil, for deep-frying
  Crème fraîche or sour cream, to serve

1. Combine the sugar, water, and orange juice in a small saucepan over medium-low heat and cook until the sugar has dissolved. Increase the heat to medium-high and simmer for 5 minutes, or until syrupy. Remove from the heat, add 2 tablespoons of the rose water, and set aside.

2. Combine the orange zest, dates, walnuts, and remaining 1 tablespoon rose water in a food processor and process until a smooth paste forms.

3. Lay out the wonton wrappers and place a teaspoon of the date mixture at the center of each. Brush the edges of the wrapper with water and draw them up over the filling into a pouch shape, pinching them together at the top to seal.

4. Heat the oil in a deep-fryer or deep saucepan to 365°F (190°C). If you don't have a frying thermometer, test the oil temperature by dropping a small piece of bread into the hot oil. If the bread immediately bubbles to the surface and begins to turn golden, the oil is ready.

5. Fry the wantons in batches, turning often, until golden brown all over. Remove using tongs or a slotted spoon and drain on paper towels.

6. To serve, reheat the syrup, dip the wontons in the syrup, and place three onto each serving plate. Drizzle with a little more syrup and place a dollop of crème fraîche to the side.

Jelly Doughnuts

These luscious jelly doughnuts (or jam doughnuts if you are not North American), can also be made with strawberry or other flavored preserves.

Serves: 10 · Prep: 25 min. + 1 hr. rising · Cooking: 45 min · Level: 2

- ½ cup (125 ml) milk, plus extra for brushing
- ½ ounce (15 g) fresh compressed yeast or 1 (¼-ounce/7-g) package active dry yeast
- 1 tablespoon superfine (caster) sugar, + extra for rolling
- 1⅓ cups (200 g) all-purpose (plain) flour
- ¼ cup (60 g) unsalted butter, melted
- 2 large egg yolks, lightly beaten
- 1 cup (325 g) raspberry preserves (jam)
- 6 cups (1.5 liters) vegetable oil, for deep-frying

1. To prepare the doughnuts, gently heat ½ cup (125 ml) milk to lukewarm (110°F/43°C). Combine with the yeast and and 1 tablespoon superfine sugar in a small bowl and leave in a warm place for 10 minutes, or until it begins to foam.

2. Sift the flour onto a clean surface and make a well in the middle with your hand. Pour in the yeast mixture, melted butter, and egg yolks and knead until a smooth dough forms. Place the dough in a large clean bowl, cover with a clean cloth, and leave in a warm place to rise for 1 hour.

3. Roll the dough out on a lightly floured surface to ¼ inch (5 mm) thick. Using a plain cookie cutter, cut out forty 2-inch (5-cm) rounds. Place a tablespoon of raspberry preserves in the center of half the rounds. Brush the edges with a little milk and place the remaining rounds on top, pressing the edges together with your fingers to seal. Leave the rounds in a warm place to rise for 30 minutes.

4. Heat the oil in a deep-fryer or deep saucepan to 365°F (190°C). If you don't have a frying thermometer, test the oil temperature by dropping a small piece of bread into the hot oil. If the bread immediately bubbles to the surface and begins to turn golden, the oil is ready.

5. Fry the doughnuts a few at a time, turning, until the doughnuts are an even golden color. Remove the doughnuts from the oil using a slotted spoon or tongs and drain on paper towels. Roll the hot doughnuts in superfine sugar. The doughnuts can be served warm or at room temperature.

Banana Fritters with Rum and Raisin Ice Cream

Serves: 4 · Prep: 15 min. + 1 hr. resting · Cooking: 20 min. · Level: 2

- 1 cup (150 g) all-purpose (plain) flour
- 1 teaspoon ground cinnamon
- 1 large egg, lightly beaten
- ⅓ cup (90 ml) sweet champagne or ginger ale
- 2 large egg whites
- 4 small sweet bananas, such as ladyfinger bananas
- 6 cups (1.5 liters) vegetable oil, for deep-frying
  Confectioners' sugar, for dusting
  Rum and Raisin Ice Cream (see page 224)

1. Sift the flour and cinnamon into a medium bowl. Make a well in the center and pour in the whole egg and half the champagne. Whisk together, ensuring there are no lumps and gradually add the remaining champagne. Cover the bowl with plastic wrap (cling film) and rest in a cool place for 1 hour.

2. Whisk the egg whites together in a small bowl until stiff, fold into the batter, and set aside.

3. Heat the oil in a deep-fryer or deep saucepan to 365°F (190°C). If you don't have a frying thermometer, test the oil temperature by dropping a small piece of bread into the hot oil. If the bread immediately bubbles to the surface and begins to turn golden, the oil is ready.

4. Peel the bananas and dip in the batter to coat. Fry, two at a time, turning every 2 minutes, until the fritters turn an even golden color. Remove the fritters from the oil using a slotted spoon or tongs and drain on paper towels.

5. Dust the bananas with confectioners' sugar and serve hot with a scoop of rum and raisin ice cream.

Banana Fritters with Rum and Raisin Ice Cream ▷

Deep-Fried Ice Cream with Honey Syrup

Deep-frying ice cream may sound like a recipe for disaster but, if you work quickly with plenty of very hot oil, the cake on the outside will seal in the cold ice cream so that it doesn't melt.

Serves: 4 • Prep: 30 min. + overnight freezing • Cooking: 20 min. Level: 3

HONEY SYRUP
- ½ cup (125 ml) honey
- ½ cup (125 ml) water
- 4 tablespoons sugar
- 2 tablespoons unsalted butter
- 2 cloves

DEEP-FRIED ICE CREAM
- 8 scoops good-quality vanilla ice cream, store-bought or homemade Rich Egg-Cream Ice Cream (see page 230)
- 1 large egg, lightly beaten
- 10 ounces (300 g) plain sponge cake, cut into eight ¼-inch (5 mm) thick slices
- 6 cups (1.5 liters) vegetable oil, for deep-frying

1. To prepare the honey syrup, combine all the syrup ingredients in a small saucepan over medium-high heat and bring to a boil. Immediately decrease the heat and simmer for 3–5 minutes, or until the mixture becomes syrupy. Remove the cloves and set aside.

2. To prepare the deep-fried ice cream, line a small baking sheet with parchment paper and put the scoops of ice cream on top. Freeze for 2 hours, or until the ice cream is hard.

3. Lay the slices of sponge cake on a clean surface and brush one side with the beaten egg. Place the scoops of ice cream on top and wrap the sponge tightly around, shaping with your hands form a round ball evenly covered with cake. Return to the baking sheet and freeze overnight.

4. Heat the oil in a deep-fryer or deep saucepan to 365°F (190°C). If you don't have a frying thermometer, test the oil temperature by dropping a small piece of sponge cake into the hot oil. If the cake immediately bubbles to the surface and begins to turn golden, the oil is ready.

5. Cook the ice cream balls two at a time, until golden brown, and drain on kitchen towels. Serve hot, drizzled with the honey syrup.

Rice Fritters with Amaretti Cookies

Serves: 6–8 • Prep: 15 min. • Cooking: 1 hr. 15 min. • Level: 2

- 2 cups (500 ml) milk
- ½ teaspoon vanilla extract (essence)
- ¼ teaspoon salt
- 2 tablespoons all-purpose (plain) flour
- ½ cup (100 g) short-grain rice (pudding rice or sticky rice)
- 2 tablespoons unsalted butter
- ⅓ cup (70 g) sugar
- 2 large eggs
- ½ cup (60 g) crushed amaretti cookies (biscuits)
- ½ cup (75 g) fine dry bread crumbs
- 4 cups (1 liter) sunflower oil, for deep-frying

1. Combine the milk, vanilla, and salt in a large saucepan. Add the flour and rice and mix well. Bring to a boil over medium heat. Lower the heat and simmer, stirring from time to time, until the mixture is thick and creamy and the rice is tender, about 45 minutes. Remove from the heat.

2. Stir in the butter, half the sugar, 1 egg, and the amaretti cookies. Turn the mixture out onto a greased surface sprinkled with bread crumbs. Spread the mixture out until it is ½ inch (1 cm) thick. Let cool.

3. Cut the mixture into disks using a 3-inch (8-cm) cookie cutter. Beat the remaining egg in a small bowl. Put the remaining bread crumbs on a plate. Dip the fritters in the beaten egg and then in the bread crumbs, making sure they are well coated.

4. Heat the oil in a deep-fryer or deep saucepan to 365°F (190°C). If you don't have a frying thermometer, test the oil temperature by dropping a small piece of bread into the hot oil. If the bread immediately bubbles to the surface and begins to turn golden, the oil is ready.

5. Fry the fritters in small batches until golden brown all over, about 5 minutes per batch. Remove with a slotted spoon and drain on paper towels. Sprinkle with the remaining sugar and serve hot.

Deep-Fried Ice Cream with Honey Syrup ▷

Caramel Dumplings

Serve these dumplings straight from the pan. They should be nice and hot so that the ice cream melts on contact.

Serves: 4 • Prep: 15 min. • Cooking: 25 min. • Level: 2

DUMPLINGS
1¼	cups (180 g) all-purpose (plain) flour
1	teaspoon baking powder
⅛	teaspoon salt
2	tablespoons (30 g) unsalted butter, softened
⅓	cup (70 g) granulated sugar
⅓	cup (90 ml) milk
1	teaspoon vanilla extract (essence)

CARAMEL SAUCE
2	tablespoons (30 g) unsalted butter
1½	cups (300 g) firmly packed light brown sugar
1	cup (250 ml) water
½	cup (125 ml) heavy (double) cream

Confectioners' (icing) sugar, for dusting
Vanilla ice cream, to serve

1. To prepare the dumplings, mix the flour, baking powder, and salt in a medium bowl. Rub in the butter with your fingertips. Stir in the granulated sugar. Combine the milk and vanilla and pour into the dry mixture, stirring with a wooden spoon to combine, and set aside.

2. To prepare the sauce, combine the butter, brown sugar, water, and cream in a medium saucepan over medium-high heat. Bring to a boil, then decrease the heat to a simmer. Drop tablespoons of dumpling dough into the sauce, until the dough is finished. Cover the saucepan and simmer over low for 20 minutes, until the dumplings are swollen and cooked through. Gently shake the pan from time to time during cooking to distribute the sauce evenly.

3. Divide the dumplings among four serving bowls, dust with confectioners' sugar, and top each serving with a scoop of vanilla ice cream.

Crepes with Raspberries and Pastry Cream

Serves: 4 • Prep: 15 min. + 1 hr. resting • Cooking: 30 min. • Level: 1

CREPES
½	cup (75 g) all-purpose (plain) flour
	Pinch of salt
4	large eggs
1	cup (250 ml) milk
3–4	tablespoons butter

12	ounces (350 g) fresh raspberries + extra, to garnish
3	tablespoons Cointreau
¼	cup (30 g) confectioners' (icing) sugar
	Finely grated zest of 1 orange

PASTRY CREAM
1¼	cups (300 ml) milk
2	tablespoons cornstarch (cornflour)
¼	cup (50 g) granulated sugar
2	large egg yolks
2	tablespoons (30 ml) Cointreau
½	cup (50 g) finely chopped toasted hazelnuts, + extra, to garnish

1. Prepare the crepes following the instructions on page 261.

2. Combine the raspberries with the Cointreau, 1 tablespoon of the confectioners' sugar, and the orange zest in a large bowl. Set aside.

3. To prepare the pastry cream, bring the milk to a boil in a large saucepan over low heat. Beat the cornstarch, sugar, and egg yolks in a medium bowl. Stir in the Cointreau. Slowly add one-third of the hot milk, beating constantly. Add the remaining milk. Return the mixture to the saucepan. Simmer over low heat, stirring constantly, until thickened, about 5 minutes. Stir in the hazelnuts and remove from the heat.

4. Spread each crepe with some pastry cream and cover with raspberries. Roll up the crepes and dust with the remaining 3 tablespoons confectioners' sugar. Garnish with raspberries and hazelnuts and serve hot.

Caramel Dumplings ▷

Crepes with Rum and Berryfruit Filling

Replace the preserves with fresh sliced strawberries and the rum with the same amount of freshly squeezed lemon juice. Dust with confectioners' sugar to serve.

Serves: 4 · Prep: 15 min. + 1 hr. to rest · Cooking: 20 min. · Level: 1

CREPES

½	cup (75 g) all-purpose (plain) flour
	Pinch of salt
4	large eggs
1	cup (250 ml) milk
3-4	tablespoons unsalted butter

FILLING

1½	cups (375 g) red currant (or other berry) preserves (jam)
1	tablespoon rum
½	cup (125 ml) heavy (double) cream
	Fresh berries, to garnish

1. To prepare the crepes, mix the flour and salt in a medium bowl. Beat in the eggs, one at a time. Gradually add the milk, beating until smooth. Set the batter aside to rest for 1 hour.

2. Melt 1 teaspoon butter in a crepe pan or frying pan over medium heat. Pour in 2-3 tablespoons of batter and swirl the pan so the batter forms a large, thin crepe. Cook for 2 minutes on each side, or until golden brown. Remove from the pan and stack on a plate. Continue making crepes until all the batter is used, adding additional butter to grease the pan as needed. Stack the cooked crepes and keep warm in a warm oven.

3. Melt the preserves in a small saucepan over low heat. Stir in the rum. Remove from the heat.

4. Beat the cream in a large bowl until stiff.

5. Spread each crepe with a layer of preserves. Fold in half and then in half again to form triangles. Arrange on four serving dishes. Decorate with whipped cream and the fresh berries. Serve at once.

Crepes with Cherry–Grand Marnier Sauce

Serves: 4 · Prep: 15 min. + 1 hr. to rest the batter · Cooking: 30 min. Level: 1

CREPES

½	cup (75 g) all-purpose (plain) flour
	Pinch of salt
4	large eggs
1	cup (250 ml) milk
3-4	tablespoons unsalted butter

FILLING

12	ounces (350 g) cherries, pitted
1	cup (250 ml) water
½	cup (100 g) granulated sugar
¼	cup (60 ml) Grand Marnier
2-4	tablespoons confectioners' (icing) sugar, to dust 1.

1. To prepare the crepes, mix the flour and salt in a medium bowl. Beat in the eggs, one at a time. Gradually add the milk, beating until smooth. Set the batter aside to rest for 1 hour.

2. Melt 1 teaspoon butter in a crepe pan or frying pan over medium heat. Pour in 2-3 tablespoons of batter and swirl the pan so the batter forms a large, thin crepe. Cook for 2 minutes on each side, or until golden brown. Remove from the pan and stack on a plate. Continue making crepes until all the batter is used, adding additional butter to grease the pan as needed. Stack the cooked crepes and keep warm in a warm oven.

3. To prepare the filling, combine the cherries, water, and sugar in a medium saucepan over medium heat. Bring to a boil. Lower the heat and simmer until the sauce has thickened to make a syrup, about 10 minutes. Remove from the heat and let cool. Stir in the Grand Marnier.

4. Spread each crepe with some of the cherry sauce. Fold the filled crepes in half and then in half again to form triangles. Dust with confectioners' sugar and serve.

◁ **Crepes with Cherry–Grand Marnier Sauce**

Banana and Butterscotch Waffles

Our English word "waffle" comes from the Dutch wafel. Waffles have been a popular dessert or snack in the Netherlands and Belgium for centuries.

Serves: 4 · Prep: 25 min. + 30 min. chilling · Cooking: 40 min. · Level: 2

WAFFLES
- 2   large eggs, separated
- 2   teaspoons granulated sugar
- ³⁄₄   cup (180 ml) milk
- ¹⁄₂   cup (125 ml) water
- 1   teaspoon vanilla extract (essence)
- 2   cups (300 g) all-purpose (plain) flour
- 1   teaspoon baking powder
- 2   tablespoons cornstarch (cornflour)
-     Pinch of salt
- ¹⁄₂   cup (125 g) unsalted butter, melted
- 4   small sweet bananas, such as ladyfinger

BUTTERSCOTCH SAUCE
- ³⁄₄   cup (150 g) superfine (caster) sugar
- ¹⁄₄   cup (60 ml) water
- ²⁄₃   cup (160 ml) heavy (double) cream
- 5   tablespoons (75 g) unsalted butter, cubed

1. To prepare the waffles, whisk the egg yolks and sugar in a small bowl. Pour in the milk, water, and vanilla, whisking to combine. Mix the flour, baking powder, cornstarch, and salt in a medium bowl. Gradually add the milk mixture and melted butter, stirring with a wooden spoon to form a batter.

2. Whisk the egg whites together in a small bowl until stiff peaks form. Gently fold the whites into the batter. Cover the bowl with plastic wrap (cling film) and refrigerate for 30 minutes.

3. To prepare the butterscotch sauce, heat the sugar and water in a small saucepan over medium heat and bring to a boil. Simmer until the syrup is a dark caramel color. Slowly pour in the cream, stirring continuously to incorporate. Bring back to a boil, then remove from the heat. Whisk in the butter cubes one at a time. Set aside to cool.

4. Heat the waffle iron and lightly grease. Pour in ¹⁄₂ cup (125 ml) of batter and cook for 5 minutes, until golden brown and crisp. Repeat with the remaining batter until you have eight waffles. Keep warm in a warm oven. Place two hot waffles on each serving plate, slice a banana over the top, and top with butterscotch sauce.

Waffles with Baked Plums

For a simpler dessert, prepare the waffles and then serve with whipped cream or maple syrup.

Serves: 4 · Prep: 25 min. + 30 min. chilling · Cooking: 40 min. · Level: 2

WAFFLES
- 2   large eggs, separated
- 2   teaspoons granulated sugar
- ³⁄₄   cup (180 ml) milk
- ¹⁄₂   cup (125 ml) water
- 1   teaspoon vanilla extract (essence)
- 2   cups (300 g) all-purpose (plain) flour
- 1   teaspoon baking powder
- 2   tablespoons cornstarch (cornflour)
-     Pinch of salt
- ¹⁄₂   cup (125 g) unsalted butter, melted

BAKED PLUMS
- 4–8   purple (blood) plums, halved and pitted (stoned)
- ¹⁄₂   cup (125 ml) pure maple syrup
- 4–8   scoops good-quality vanilla ice-cream
- 2   tablespoons confectioners' (icing) sugar

1. To prepare the waffles, whisk the egg yolks and sugar in a small bowl. Pour in the milk, water, and vanilla, whisking to combine. Mix the flour, baking powder, cornstarch, and salt in a medium bowl. Gradually add the milk mixture and melted butter, stirring with a wooden spoon to form a batter.

2. Whisk the egg whites together in a small bowl until stiff peaks form. Gently fold the whites into the batter. Cover the bowl with plastic wrap (cling film) and refrigerate for 30 minutes.

3. Preheat oven to 350°F (180°C/gas 4). To prepare the plums, place the plums cut side down on a small baking sheet. Bake for 10 minutes, turn over, and bake for 5 more minutes. Remove from the oven and keep warm.

4. Heat the waffle iron and lightly grease. Pour in ¹⁄₂ cup (125 ml) of batter and cook for 5 minutes, until golden brown and crisp. Repeat until you have eight waffles. Keep warm in a warm oven.

5. Place two hot waffles on each serving plate, arrange two plum halves and a scoop of ice cream on top. Drizzle with maple syrup.

Banana and Butterscotch Waffles ▷

CANDY

A platter of homemade candy makes a wonderful finish

to any dinner. You can serve any of these candies

instead of dessert, or bring them out later, accompanied

by little cups of strong black coffee.

◁ **Chocolate Truffles (see page 266)**

Chocolate Hokey Pokey

This candy comes from New Zealand where "hokey pokey"—a kind of honeycomb toffee—is also a top-selling type of ice cream. Try making this recipe without the chocolate coating and stirring the broken pieces into a basic homemade ice cream (see Rich Egg-Cream Ice Cream, page 230).

Makes: about 20 pieces • Prep: 10 min. + 35 min. cooling • Cooking: 10 min. • Level: 2

5	tablespoons (60 g) sugar
2	tablespoons corn (golden) syrup
1	teaspoon baking soda (bicarbonate of soda)
8	ounces (250 g) bittersweet or dark chocolate

1. Butter a 9-inch (23-cm) square baking pan.

2. Combine the sugar and corn syrup in a medium-large saucepan over low heat. Stirring constantly, bring to a gentle boil. Simmer gently for 4 minutes, stirring often.

3. Remove from the heat and stir in the baking soda. The mixture will bubble up, quickly doubling or tripling in volume. Working rapidly, pour into the prepared pan. Let cool to room temperature.

4. Melt the chocolate in a double boiler over barely simmering water. Let cool for 5 minutes. Remove the toffee from the pan and break or cut into bite-size pieces. Using tongs, dip the pieces into the chocolate, swirling to coat well. Place on a baking sheet.

5. Let set for at least 30 minutes before serving.

Chocolate Truffles

Serve these truffles in brightly colored mini paper cups or pile them into martini glasses and place on the table at the end of a meal.

Makes: about 30 pieces • Prep: 30 min. + 2 hr. chilling • Level: 1

3½	tablespoons unsalted butter, softened
⅓	cup (50 g) confectioners' (icing) sugar
⅓	cup (90 ml) heavy (double) cream
2	tablespoons vanilla sugar
12	ounces (350 g) dark chocolate, grated
4	tablespoons unsweetened cocoa powder

1. Beat the butter and confectioners' sugar in a medium bowl until pale and creamy.

2. Bring the cream to a boil in a small saucepan over medium heat. Add the vanilla sugar and stir to dissolve. Pour the hot cream into the butter mixture and stir in the chocolate. Chill for at least 2 hours.

3. Form the mixture into balls just slightly larger than hazelnuts and roll in the cocoa. Store in the refrigerator until you are ready to serve.

Chocolate Hokey Pokey ▷

Chocolate Walnut Fudge

This fudge is as good to eat as it is easy to make. You can speed things up considerably by placing the buttered pan in the freezer while the fudge cooks and by placing the pan with the cooked fudge in a larger pan or bowl of ice cold water as you beat it to thicken. Be careful it doesn't set in the pan! Pour into the chilled pan and let it set in the refrigerator. If preferred, leave the walnuts out.

Makes: about 25 pieces • Prep: 10 min. + 1–2 hr. chilling • Cooking: 8–10 min. • Level: 1

2	cups (400 g) sugar
½	cup (125 ml) milk
⅓	cup (90 g) salted butter, cut up
⅓	cup (50 g) unsweetened cocoa powder
1	teaspoon vanilla extract (essence)
1	cup (125 g) coarsely chopped walnuts

1. Butter an 8-inch (20-cm) square baking pan.

2. Combine the sugar, milk, butter, and cocoa powder in a medium saucepan over medium-low heat. Stir slowly and continuously as it comes to a boil. Make sure that the sugar has dissolved completely before it reaches a boil. Simmer gently for 3–4 minutes, or until it reaches the soft ball stage, 238°F (116°C) on a candy thermometer. At this temperature, if you drop a spoonful of the mixture into ice water, it will make a limp, sticky ball that flattens when you remove it from the water. Remove from the heat and let cool for 5 minutes.

3. Add the vanilla and walnuts and beat with a wooden spoon until thick and almost set, about 5 minutes. Pour into the prepared pan.

4. Chill in the refrigerator until firm, 1–2 hours. Cut into 1½-inch (4-cm) squares.

White Chocolate and Macadamia Fudge

Makes about 30 pieces • Prep: 30 min. + 1–2 hr. chilling • Cooking: 4 min. • Level: 1

1	cup (250 g) unsalted butter
1½	cups (375 ml) milk
2½	cups (500 g) sugar
1	teaspoon vanilla extract (essence)
4	ounces (125 g) white chocolate, finely chopped
1	cup (120 g) macadamias, chopped

1. Oil an 8 x 10-inch (20 x 25-cm) baking pan.

2. Combine the butter, milk, and sugar in a saucepan over medium heat. Bring to a boil and stir until the sugar begins to dissolve. Simmer the mixture until it reaches the soft ball stage, 238°F (116°C) on a candy thermometer. At this temperature, if you drop a spoonful of the mixture into ice water, it will make a limp, sticky ball that flattens when you remove it from the water.

3. Remove from the heat and beat until the mixture starts to thicken, about 5 minutes. Add the vanilla and chocolate and stir until the chocolate has melted. Fold in the macadamias. Pour the mixture into the prepared pan.

4. Let cool to room temperature. Chill in the refrigerator until firm, 1–2 hours. Cut into 1½-inch (4-cm) squares.

Chocolate Walnut Fudge ▷

Caramels

These creamy homemade caramels look really pretty when wrapped individually in plastic wrap. Gather the tops of the wrap and tie with colored ribbon.

Makes: about 35 pieces • Prep: 20 min. + 1 hr. cooling • Cooking: 10 min. Level 1

1½	cups (300 g) sugar
½	cup (125 ml) light corn (golden) syrup
1	cup (250 ml) heavy (double) cream
⅓	cup (90 g) unsalted butter
1½	teaspoons vanilla extract (essence)

1. Butter a 9 x 13-inch (33 x 23-cm) baking pan.

2. Combine the sugar, corn syrup, and cream in a medium saucepan over low heat, stirring until the sugar dissolves. Increase the heat to medium and simmer until the mixture turns pale gold and reaches the soft ball stage, 238°F (116°C) on a candy thermometer. At this temperature, if you drop a spoonful of the mixture into ice water, it will make a limp, sticky ball that flattens when you remove it from the water.

3. Remove from the heat and stir in the butter and vanilla. Beat well until thickened and almost set. Pour into the prepared pan. Let cool to room temperature, at least 1 hour. Cut into squares.

Peanut Brittle

Makes: about 40 pieces • Prep: 20 min. + 1 hr. cooling • Cooking: 10 min. • Level 1

2	cups (400 g) sugar
1	cup (250 ml) light corn (golden) syrup
¾	cup (180 ml) water
2	cups (300 g) raw peanuts, halved
3	tablespoons unsalted butter

1. Butter a large baking sheet.

2. Combine the sugar, corn syrup, and water in a large saucepan over low heat, stirring until the sugar dissolves. Increase the heat to medium and simmer until the mixture turns golden brown and reaches the hard-crack stage, 300°F (150°C) on a candy thermometer. At this temperature, if you drop a spoonful of the mixture into ice water, it will form stiff threads that break easily when you remove them from the water.

3. Remove from the heat and stir in the peanuts and butter. Beat well until thickened and almost set. Pour onto the prepared sheet, spreading quickly with a spatula to about ½ inch (1 cm) thick.

4. Let cool to room temperature, at least 1 hour. Break into bite-size pieces.

◁ **Peanut Brittle**

Coconut Ice

Serves 8–10 • Prep: 10 min. + 1–2 hr. chilling • Cooking: 3–4 min. • Level: 1

3	cups (450 g) confectioners' (icing) sugar
½	cup (125 ml) milk
¼	cup (60 g) unsalted butter, cut up
¼	teaspoon salt
1	cup (125 g) unsweetened shredded (desiccated) coconut
	Few drops red food coloring

1. Butter an 8-inch (20-cm) square baking pan.

2. Combine the confectioners' sugar, milk, butter, and salt in a medium saucepan over medium heat. Bring to a gentle boil, stirring often. Simmer gently for 3–4 minutes, or until it reaches the soft ball stage, 238° F (116°C) on a candy thermometer. At this temperature, if you drop a spoonful of the mixture into ice water, it will make a limp, sticky ball that flattens when you remove it from the water. Remove from the heat and let cool for 5 minutes. Stir in the coconut. Remove from the heat and let cool for 5 minutes.

3. Pour half the mixture into a metal bowl. Add enough food coloring to turn the mixture pink. Beat until cool and thickened. Pour into the prepared pan. Beat the remaining mixture until thickened and pour over the top.

4. Chill in the refrigerator until firm, 1–2 hours.

Chocolate Popcorn

Prepare this simple but delicious treat ahead of time and serve to family or friends after dinner as they gather round the TV or home theater screen to watch a movie.

Serves: 8–12 • Prep: 25 min. + 1 hr. cooling • Cooking: 10 min. • Level: 1

1	tablespoon sunflower oil
4	tablespoons (75 g) unpopped popcorn
14	ounces (400 g) dark chocolate
2	ounces (60 g) white chocolate

1. Line a large baking sheet with parchment paper.

2. Heat the oil in a large heavy saucepan over medium heat. When hot, add the popcorn, cover quickly with the lid, and cook until all the corn has popped, shaking the pan lightly during cooking for even popping.

3. Melt both chocolates separately in double boilers over barely simmering water. Pour the popped corn into the semisweet chocolate and stir until well coated. Spread out on the prepared baking sheet and drizzle with the white chocolate. Leave to set, about 1 hour.

Coconut Ice ▷

BASIC RECIPES

Here we have included a few basic recipes for sauces, coulis, custards, ganaches, and pastry creams that occur throughout the book.

◁ Caramel Sauce (see page 276)

Caramel Sauce

This simple sauce is delicious with ice cream, bananas, or plain cakes.

Makes: 1 cup (250 ml) · Prep: 5 min. · Cooking: 2 min. · Level: 1

¼ cup (60 g) unsalted butter
¼ cup (60 ml) light cream
½ cup (100 g) firmly packed dark brown sugar
½ teaspoon vanilla extract (essence)

1. Combine the butter, cream, brown sugar, and vanilla in a small saucepan over medium heat. Cook, stirring constantly, until the sugar dissolves. Increase the heat to high and boil for 2 minutes.

2. Remove from the heat and set aside to cool and thicken.

Lemon Curd

Replace the lemon with lime for a slightly different but equally delicious citrus cream.

Makes: 1 cup (250 ml) · Prep: 25 min. + 1 hr. cooling · Cooking: 25 min. Level: 1

⅓ cup (70 g) superfine (caster) sugar
¼ cup (60 ml) freshly squeezed lemon juice
2 teaspoons finely grated lemon zest
3 large egg yolks
¼ cup (60 g) unsalted butter, cubed

1. To prepare the lemon curd, combine the superfine sugar, lemon juice, and zest in a small saucepan over medium heat until the sugar dissolves.

2. Whisk the eggs yolks together in a heat-proof bowl and gradually add the hot lemon mixture. Strain mixture through a fine-mesh sieve. Return to the heat-proof bowl and place over a saucepan of barely simmering water. Cook, stirring continuously, until the mixture coats the back of a wooden spoon. Do not allow the mixture to boil.

3. Remove from the heat and add the butter cubes, one at a time, stirring until fully combined. Cover the mixture with parchment paper and refrigerate for 1 hour, until cooled.

Candied Orange Zest

Makes: ¹⁄₂ cup (125 g) · **Prep:** 15 min. · **Cooking:** 2 min. · **Level:** 1

3	large oranges
¼	cup (50 g) sugar
¼	cup (60 ml) water
	Superfine (caster) sugar, for tossing

1. Bring a small saucepan of water to a boil over high heat. Remove long strips of zest off the oranges using a zester. If you do not have a zester, use a small sharp knife to remove the zest in strips, making sure there is no white pith attached. Blanch the orange zest in the boiling water for 30 seconds, drain, and set aside.

2. Heat the sugar and water in a small saucepan over medium heat, stirring until the sugar dissolves. Increase the heat to high and boil for 2 minutes. Add the orange zest and decrease the heat to low, so it is just simmering. Simmer the orange zest for 10 minutes, then leave to cool in the syrup.

3. Remove the orange zest and drain thoroughly on a kitchen towel. Toss the zest in superfine sugar and set aside until needed.

Vanilla Pastry Cream

This is a basic sweet pastry cream. It is very versatile—you can use it to fill a Napoleon or sponge roll, or spoon it over a fruit dessert.

Makes: about 3 cups · **Prep:** 10 min. · **Cooking:** 10 min. · **Level:** 1

5	large egg yolks
¾	cup (150 g) sugar
⅓	cup (50 g) all-purpose (plain) flour
2	cups (500 ml) milk
¼	teaspoon salt
½	teaspoon vanilla extract (essence)

1. Beat the egg yolks and sugar until pale and thick.

2. Bring the milk to a boil with the salt and vanilla, then stir it into the egg and sugar.

3. Cook over low heat, stirring constantly with a wooden spoon, until the mixture lightly coats a metal spoon. Let cool.

VARIATIONS

Hazelnut or Almond Cream: Add 2 tablespoons ground hazelnuts or almonds to the cream while still hot.

Liqueur Cream: Add one or two tablespoons rum, cognac, or other liqueur to the cream while still hot.

Lemon Cream: Boil the finely grated zest of 1 lemon in the milk and omit the vanilla extract.

Chocolate Ganache

This makes a dark chocolate ganache. You can make milk chocolate ganache or white chocolate ganache by simply replacing the dark chocolate with milk chocolate or white chocolate.

Makes: about 2 cups (500 ml) · Prep: 5 min. · Cooking: 10 min. · Level: 1

- 8   ounces (250 g) dark chocolate, coarsely chopped
- 1   cup (250 ml) heavy (double) cream

1. Melt the chocolate in a double boiler over barely simmering water. Pour in the cream and stir until smooth and well combined.

2. Set aside to cool.

Raspberry Coulis

Replace the raspberries with the same quantity of strawberries for strawberry coulis. You can add some zip to the flavor by adding a tablespoon of freshly squeezed lemon juice

Makes: about 1 cup (250 ml) · Prep: 5 min. · Level: 1

- 2   cup (300 g) fresh raspberries
- ⅓   cup (50 g) confectioners' (icing) sugar

1. Process the raspberries and confectioners' sugar in a food processor or blender for about 30 seconds, until smooth.

2. Chill until needed.

Chocolate Pastry Cream

Makes: about 3 cups (750 ml) · Prep: 10 min. · Cooking: 10 min. · Level: 1

- 6 large egg yolks
- ³⁄₄ cup (150 g) granulated sugar
- ¹⁄₃ cup (50 g) all-purpose (plain) flour
- 2 cups (500 ml) milk
- 5 oz (150 g) bittersweet (dark) chocolate, finely chopped

1. Place the chocolate in a large bowl and set aside.

2. Beat the egg yolks and one-third of the sugar with an electric mixer on high speed until pale and creamy. With mixer on low speed, beat in the flour.

3. Combine the remaining sugar and milk in a saucepan over medium heat and bring to a boil. Pour the hot milk mixture onto the egg mixture gradually, stirring continuously. Pour the mixture back into the pan and simmer over low heat for 2 minutes.

4. Pour this egg mixture onto the chocolate. Stir until the chocolate has completely melted. Cover and let cool.

Vanilla Crème Anglaise

This classic vanilla custard can be made in no time. You will find the results better than any pre-packaged custard mixture.

Makes: about 1½ cups (375 ml) · Prep: 10 min. · Cooking: 10 min. Level: 1

- 1 cup (250 ml) milk
- ½ vanilla bean, split lengthwise
- 3 large egg yolks
- ¼ cup (50 g) sugar

1. Heat the milk and vanilla bean in a small saucepan over medium-low heat, until just simmering. Remove from the heat.

2. Whisk the yolks and granulated sugar in a medium bowl until thickened. Slowly pour in one-third of the hot milk, whisking continuously. Then pour in the rest and whisk until fully combined.

3. Pour the mixture into a clean small saucepan and cook on low heat, stirring continuously with a wooden spoon, until the mixture has thickened enough to coat the back of the spoon.

4. Strain the custard through a fine-mesh sieve into a small pitcher (jug) for serving.

Index

Throughout this book you will find some recipes marked with a green icon. This means that these recipes are suited to people with special health needs, such as egg-, dairy-, and gluten intolerances. We have also marked some low-fat recipes.